We can spend most if not all of our lives taking for granted that our mothers are merely our mothers—not bothering to acknowledge and appreciate them beyond the one-dimensional roles we've assigned to them as such. But the talented writers gathered in this collection know much better. They have taken the time to delve into their mothers' lives to discover and honor the full breadth of their womanhood, their motherhood, and the wonderful complexities of their humanity. As Anaïs Nin noted, writers taste life twice. And these writers do just that—with pen in hand they "taste" again their lives alongside their mothers' lives, feeling their mutual vulnerabilities and sorrows, joys and triumphs. What's more, they do so with immense compassion and wisdom, knowing that in giving voice to their mothers, they are giving voice to themselves as well; knowing that in exploring who their mothers were, they are also resolving who they are; knowing that their own stories began with, and are a continuation of their mothers' stories.

—RICHARD BLANCO, Presidential Inaugural Poet

A group of women met regularly to write their mothers' stories, and what resulted was huge and beautiful. I was deeply moved by this book.

—MONICA WOOD, author of *When We Were the Kennedys* and *The One-in-a-Million Boy*

This is an exceptional read. The authors have created something new and startling here, a testimony of their own hearts and an invitation to all readers and writers. This is a quiet, profound study of five mothers, the limitations they faced in their historical moment, and their complex relationships with these daughters. We come to a troubled compassion for each of them, even as we witness the legacy of their failures. These brave writers serve as our guides, exploring an unmapped path as they search for the women who happened to become their mothers. This is a remarkable anthology, and even more remarkable in its generous invitation to all writers to make this same journey.

—MEREDITH HALL, *Without a Map: A Memoir* (Beacon, 2007) Professor Emerita, UNH MFA in Writing Program

This rich collection of mother stories abounds with compassion and nostalgia and insight about all that it means to be a daughter born of a mother. Because it is no small thing, this business of daughters and mothers. The five Maine writers in this collection generously unpack their pasts, and in doing so they achieve something quietly radical: a distance with which to see their own mothers as their mothers saw themselves, long before they had the daughters who wrote this timely book. The journey here is full of humor and love and forgiveness, and we can read it to understand more about what it means to be a woman.

—SUSAN CONLEY, author of *The Foremost Good Fortune, Paris Was the Place,* and *Stop Here. This is the Place: A Year in Motherhood*

Compassionate Journey evokes emotions the authors lived through. It is honest and direct, just like the authors. What an honor to be given an opportunity to peek into the lives of these women!

—DOROTHEA JOHNSON, founder of The Protocol School of Washington. She is a coauthor with granddaughter, actress Liv Tyler, of *Modern Manners: Tools to Take You to the Top,* now translated into six languages.

This remarkable collection is a love story to women searching for a way to make peace with their mothers. Five women writers describe their individual journeys to discover a new mother story, one devoid of the wounded memories they had been carrying all their lives. By shifting their lens from their personal grievances to one of viewing their mother through her family background and the historical era she occupied, they developed new understandings and love for their mothers. *Compassionate Journey* belongs on every woman's bookshelf!

—PAT TAUB, author of *The Mother of My Invention* and founder of the blog WOW (Women's Older Wisdom)

This is a book of light and darkness, of sorrow, anger, tenderness and insight. A book of gripping images that appear like radiant falling stars and linger for the reader: scarlet lipstick and vintage earrings—a table set like an artistic masterpiece. A young woman racing from the United States to Canada to attend her dying mother, skillfully interweaving it with her mother's own journey to Canada from war-wracked Europe. A teenager ordered out into the midnight streets of a dangerous South

Boston by her mother to bring a favored drunken brother home from a bar. A mother, who despite limited resources points out the wonders of nature to her children, rejoicing in a bird singing in the turbulence of a big city. A woman who recounts one of her few precious memories— her mentally ill mother explaining how she applies makeup in a genuine moment of mother–daughter bonding. The pleasure of an unexpected tea party with a child's china set in the midst of emotional chaos. A mother who brings an encyclopedia to the table to settle disputes and acts out stories with grandchildren. How do we understand our mothers as women separate from us, shaped as much by their early experiences as we are by ours? These five women, while sharing their own unique compassionate journeys, illuminate the complex universality of mother–daughter relationships.

—MICHELLE CACHO NEGRETE, author of *Stealing: Life in America*

COMPASSIONATE JOURNEY
Honoring Our Mothers' Stories

Maggie Butler, Cheryl Gillespie,
Jenny Radsma, Martha Rice, Jane Sloven

Designed and Produced by
Maine Authors Publishing
12 High Street, Thomaston, Maine 04861
www.maineauthorspublishing.com

Printed in the United States of America

Table of Contents

Introduction

"**Y**ou're wearing *that?*"

We've all heard those words from the mouths of our mothers. Those voices echo in our ears, affecting us long after we've outgrown the need for their assessment of our choices. We may be thirty, forty, or fifty years old, and still, we react.

Mothers and daughters are bound by powerful forces in relationships that may be loving and supportive, angry and critical, or a combination of all those aspects. These relationships, close or distant, sometimes fraught, have been written about for decades. *Compassionate Journey: Honoring Our Mothers' Stories* offers a different perspective through the path of writing as a way to examine the forces that bind us to our mothers and to loosen the hold of memories and conclusions that may be encrusted with inaccurate assumptions.

The five contributors to this anthology met at a workshop in May of 2012, which was led by Pat Taub, feminist, writer, activist, blogger, and former radio host. The workshop, "Discovering Our Mothers' Stories," was sponsored by the Maine Writers & Publishers Alliance. The seeds of *Compassionate Journey: Honoring Our Mothers' Stories* were planted that day.

Pat, who authored *The Mother of My Invention,* raised provocative and powerful questions that day: Could we begin to see our mothers as they saw themselves? Could we relinquish the hold of the mother/daughter stories that had congealed in our consciousness, stories often "carved from wounds," in order to find a new and perhaps more realistic mother story? Pat's workshop offered the process of writing as a way to explore some of these questions and to make peace with our mothers and the memories we clung to.

After the workshop, based on a suggestion made by Jenny Radsma, a number of us decided to continue this exploration together. We invited a few other women writers to join us. Over time and for a variety of reasons, some women left the group. The five of us took up the challenge and remained a group, collaborating to bring this work to publication.

The questions we asked ourselves were these: Could we allow our mothers to break free from our insistence on seeing, evaluating, and judging them primarily as our mothers? Could we allow our mothers to inhabit the selves they were long before they became our mothers? Could we begin to view them as young women deeply affected by the era in which they were raised, the families that formed them, the mores and social structures of their time? Could we take into account the narrow range of choices offered to them, in a time much more constricted than the era in which we grew up? Could we see the courage and pathos in the choices they each made? Could we begin to understand that their lives, though very different from ours, were affected by circumstances out of their control, just as our lives have been affected by circumstances out of our control? Could we bring empathy and compassion to the ways in which their choices and beliefs affected us, in the ways they raised us, in the values they espoused, in the expectations they held for us and our futures?

As it turned out, delving into our mothers' histories provided enough compelling material to keep five of us together in a rich collaboration over five years. From the beginning, we identified as a writing group, first and foremost. Over time, we moved from friendly acquaintances and writing partners to colleagues committed to helping each other become better writers.

Despite our diverse histories, we discovered many commonalities in our mothers' stories. Through our shared research and writing, we gained a deeper understanding of the personal, cultural, and historical forces that shaped the lives of our mothers, women who were all born within a decade of each other. Some of our mothers were immigrants, or the daughters of immigrants, who suffered traumatic losses before and during the Second World War, when they left one country to settle in another.

When we explored the mores and norms of our mothers' era, it became more clear to us why our mothers made certain choices, and we certainly felt more keenly the limited options available to them. Their significant life choices were made prior to the women's movement (in fact, our mothers were born either before or during the suffrage movement). Aside from World War II, which presented women with a brief window of opportunity to work in jobs traditionally filled by men, our mothers experienced rigidly defined roles and significant inequality between men and women, not only in the workplace, but in life.

"Women's work" largely defined our mothers: in addition to any work outside the home, they spent countless hours cooking and cleaning, running errands, caring for children and ailing relatives, ferrying children and their friends from one function to another. Like women everywhere, their work at home and in the community was unpaid and undervalued.

Typical of their time, our mothers never thought to discuss their feelings and emotions publicly, and they didn't seem to be mentioned in private, either. So-called "normal people" didn't go to therapy to deal with their grief, anxiety, frustration, or trauma. Because therapy was neither acceptable nor available to our mothers, endless amounts of antianxiety medication, such as Valium and Librium, were prescribed to ease their "nerves," with no discussion of the significant side effects. If a woman was ill enough to need serious psychiatric help, the treatment available was primitive and negligible. The diagnosis of mental illness carried with it a harsh and undeserved stigma, not only for the patient, but for their families.

As women of a certain age, in our fifth, sixth, or seventh decade of life, we can look back at our mothers and our relationships with them through a wider perspective afforded by time and distance. We can feel a sense of compassion that, for some of us, was in much shorter supply while our mothers were alive. We appreciate psycho-analyst Donald Winnicott's notion of "good enough mothering" and acknowledge that often our mothers were "good enough." But we also know that for some of us, they weren't. As adults we will continue to take responsibility for our own healing by unpacking the burdens we still carry. For us, unlike our mothers, help is widely available without stigma.

This writing project, and the relationships we've developed, have nurtured and surprised us, always leading us to places and outcomes we would never have found alone. Our work together has allowed our mothers to inhabit the larger space of the lives they created, and allowed us to see more clearly the powerful, loving, and complicated women who mothered us. In this often tender collab-oration, we have honored our mothers in ways we never imagined possible, on the page and in our hearts.

Any group of individuals can engage in a similar venture. At the back of the book, you will find a tool kit of suggestions and prompts to encourage and cheer you on. We also include discussion questions for book groups.

We hope you enjoy our journeys. Perhaps you will consider taking one of your own.

Natasha *by Jane Sloven*

A few days before my mother's seventieth birthday, she fled New York in a state of dread. No one knew where she'd gone. Cell phones were less common in 1990, and her voicemail filled up with messages from many relatives and friends hoping to wish her a happy birthday. Eventually, we discovered she'd flown to California and checked into an elegant hotel. Later, when questioned about her sudden disappearance, my mother said she'd been driven to flee by psychological forces and the family lineage. She was desperate, terrified by the possibility someone might throw her a party.

Once she'd returned home and had time to catch up with her hundred or so close friends and relatives, I reached her by phone. "Hi, Mom," I said. "Happy belated birthday."

"Who is this?" she said.

"Jane," I said.

I was Natasha's only daughter, but by my thirties, when our conflicts had become deeply entrenched, my mother acted as if she didn't recognize my voice. If she was in a particularly hostile mood, she'd up the ante once I'd identified myself and say "Jane who?"

This time I ignored the provocation. "So what happened?" I asked. "Why did you disappear?"

"Hold on," she said. "I have to take off my earring." I heard a buzzer in the background and figured she was in her galley kitchen, wearing an apron over linen slacks and a silk blouse, walking to the oven with the phone receiver tucked in the crook of her neck. I heard a clunk and a scrape and knew she was sliding something delicious from her wall oven.

"I just made a coffee cake," she said. "A terrific new recipe from *The Times*. I left town because I didn't want a party, and you know my friends—they would have insisted." It was true of her friends. With the simmering tensions in our relationship, it was hardly likely I'd have thrown her a party.

"And what would have been the problem with a birthday party?" I asked.

She gasped. "You don't remember? Your grandfather died shortly after a big party for his seventieth birthday. Once you reach seventy, a big birthday party is *farboten*. A seventieth birthday party invites the *eyn-ore*—the evil eye."

The evil eye brought misfortune and death. Natalie, or Natasha as she preferred to be called in her later years, loved a party, but under the circumstances, even I thought she'd made a reasonable choice to fly to California. Odd superstitions emigrated from Russia with my relatives and attached themselves to my mother the way autumn leaves stick to a slick sidewalk. I'm fairly sure my mom watched her grandmother whirl a dead chicken over her head to expiate sins in preparation for Yom Kippur. I often gaped at my well-dressed great-aunts, sitting on the living room sofa, spitting over their shoulders to ward off the evil eye. My mother and her friends relinquished the tradition of spitting, exchanging it for exclamations of *pooh pooh pooh, God forbid*, and *kenahora*.

Death framed my mother's experiences. As a child, she watched her father collapse regularly from congestive heart failure. He died when she was nineteen. Her grandparents, mother, and uncles fled anti-Semitic pogroms in Russia only to be re-traumatized by the horrors of the Second World War and the murders of European relatives. This lineage of trauma burdened my mother with a ubiquitous anxiety focused on a certain set of fears: illness, death, aging, poverty, and confinement in a nursing home.

Given this lineage, my mother's relationship with God was understandably ambivalent. "As Jews, we can argue with God, complain to God, and deny God's existence," she'd say. "But we celebrate Shabbat and holidays, we go to synagogue, and we support the Jewish community. We are all that is left, and we will not let the Nazis win."

My mother took Judaism's focus on blessing and celebrating life, *L'chayim*, to heart. She nurtured family and friends, filled life with dinner parties, stories, and laughter. When I was young, she was a loving, caring, dedicated mother. As I moved into my teens, the paradoxes in her personality, the wounds of her childhood, and the stressors in her life combined to precipitate unpredictable moodiness and anger, which affected our relationship. During my twenties, she was alternately loving and hostile. By my thirties and forties, my mother was more often extremely hostile, and I was extremely reactive. By the time my mother's seventy-fifth birthday approached, thanks to therapy and my training in a spiritual healing process, I'd become less reactive and more compassionate. Though mindful of superstition, I wanted to host a party to honor her and the detente we'd finally reached.

———•———

Red and orange leaves filter light through the living room windows of my mother's apartment. She settles into my grandmother's French Provincial chair, pours tea into floral teacups, and sets the china teapot on the marble-topped coffee table.

Gesturing to the light-green tapestry on her chair, she asks, "Do you like the material I used to reupholster this? I got it in Hong Kong when I visited your brother."

"It's lovely," I say. I am sitting on the forest-green velvet sofa from our old house. It too has been reupholstered. A large gold-framed mirror on the wall reflects flourishing plants, art, a glass bowl filled with Hershey's Kisses, and my mother, slim as always in tailored black slacks, a creamy cashmere sweater, antique gold jewelry. Her silver hair is short and chic. Her makeup is perfectly applied. I sip my steaming tea before tentatively broaching the subject.

"I want to celebrate your birthday this year. And, yes—" I hold up one hand like a traffic cop, and to avoid interruption, continue without taking a breath. "I understand the superstitions. But I still want to throw you a party. I know your friends would love the opportunity to celebrate you. We can make the party any size you want. We can have a dinner, luncheon, or a brunch—whatever you want. And we can hold it any place you'd like." I stop, anticipating her refusal.

My mother crosses her ankles and stares at me for a long minute before responding. To my surprise, she says, "I'll think about it."

To this day, I have no idea why she agreed to my proposal, but after my return to my home in Maine, we entered negotiations by phone. She chose a restaurant near her apartment. We devised the guest list and the menu. I mailed invitations, and there were many because Natalie made lifelong friends in grocery stores, synagogues, and airports. She never stood in line anywhere without engaging her neighbor in conversation. For the party, I asked guests to write a story—how they met Nat, a memory they cherished, a funny anecdote, all of which would become part of a keepsake notebook. I poured over photographs to create a poster board for the party filled with images of Natasha with friends and family. We recorded the party, and when I watch the DVD, the past becomes the present.

Light floods through large multipaned windows as we enter the reserved room on Natasha's birthday, July 13th, 1995. The wallpaper, a garden of trailing vines and colorful flowers, blooms with as much cheer as the baskets of daisies decorating each table. One by one, friends and relatives stand to read their stories.

Delta Dorothy, my mother's cohort on the California adventure, says, "I met Nat on a Delta Airline flight." She pauses as everyone laughs. "Yes, Natalie gave me my nickname. We were seated next to each other. Once we started talking, we never stopped. I love her."

Others rise to share their stories: many a hilarious escapade with Nat, the perfection of the desserts emanating from her kitchen, the humor with which she meets each new disaster, the innumerable kindnesses she's shown.

Nat is dressed informally in a sweater and a pair of slacks. Her hair shines silver in the light as she rises to offer thanks. "If I'd known I was going to live this long, I would have done two things: taken better care of myself and saved my money." As the laughter dies down, she adds, "You know how important you all are in my life, and I'm sitting here thinking how wonderful this is because I'm hearing my own eulogies, and now I can take my time dying."

Three months later, I stand in a hospital corridor on Long Island, watching my mother being wheeled into surgery. During the many hours she is under the knife, my husband Joe and I sit in the large waiting room, read, and walk the halls with my brother Marc and his wife Abbe. Finally, the surgeon appears.

He stands in his scrubs, face wan, his eyes tired. "Your mother is in recovery," he says. "We spent eight hours scouring her body, removing ovarian cancer from all the places to which it migrated. But she's a fighter. We'll discuss chemotherapy once she recovers from surgery."

We tiptoe into the ICU to stand by my mother's bedside. Attached to tubes and beeping machines, she is not conscious. Her face is so pale, I wonder if she'll ever awaken.

After a few moments, I whisper to Joe. "Do you see the older man tucked behind the machines at the head of the bed?"

"No," he whispers back. "Who is it?"

"I don't know, but he looks familiar." I pause. "He just disappeared." Fortunately, these kinds of experiences have become more common for me, and I am not frightened.

That evening, I settle into the sofa in my mother's living room and page through her photo albums.

"Joe," I say, "come look. The man I saw in the hospital room is my maternal great-grandfather Moses Seidlin. Remember this photo from the birthday display? My mother adored him. When she was a child, he took care of her when she was ill."

Joe smiles. "It makes perfect sense that he'd be here with her now, don't you think?"

I stare at the photographs. Moses's dark-gray beard and mustache contrast with his white hair. His smile and light-colored eyes cast warmth through the photographs. In one, he sits on porch steps with my mother, who is just a toddler, perched in his lap.

I nod. "Of course. In case she needs to transition out of this life or to recover." I imagine my great-grandfather's presence comforting my mother. It surely comforts me.

———•———

I wondered if the party had been a mistake. Blaming was as pervasive in my family as buttering bread, so I expected my mother to blame me for tempting the evil eye. But she didn't. The party was life-changing. She took in all the love her friends offered through their presence and testimonials, and continued receiving it through next the four and a half years of her life.

———•———

My legs dangle from the wooden chair as I sit at the round oak table by the bay windows. It's gray and rainy outside, but warm and cozy in the kitchen. The floor is newly poured, red with twinkles of blue and silver. The walls are yellow. My mother and I have a very close and loving relationship in these early years. We are sipping tea and nibbling on *mandelbrodt,* a Jewish form of biscotti. This version, still warm from the oven, is studded with chocolate chips. My mother is in a storytelling mood.

"Did I ever tell you Grandma Luba wanted to be a doctor?"

I shake my head. "She really wanted to be a doctor?" At the age of ten, I am fascinated by this news.

"A lost opportunity." My mother shakes her head as if the tragedy occurred last month.

"As Jews, we never know when we'll have to leave everything we love. My mother, her two brothers, and parents had to flee from their home in Russia, and they were the lucky ones."

I bite into the crunchy mandelbrodt, feeling the rich chocolate tingle on my tongue. The stories are both enthralling and terrifying.

"My grandfather Moses owned a prosperous lumber mill in Russia. Jews weren't allowed to own such businesses there, but his partner wasn't Jewish, so they were able to pair up to run the lumber yard. The business did well. My grandparents had a nice home and enough money to send my Uncle Felix to college in the United States." She smiles, briefly. "But Felix came home full of himself and got into an argument with a Russian soldier. And that was *the end.*" Natalie raises her eyebrows for emphasis. "Russia was never safe for Jews. Drunken Cossacks rode horses through the shtetels setting everything on fire and murdering us." I shiver. My mother is satisfied with my response.

"Jews with sense never argued with Russian soldiers. Neighbors warned the family that they were in danger. They would be murdered if they stayed. So they packed what they could and fled overnight. You know the photograph of Grandma Luba with the flowered hat?"

I look through the open doorway into the dining room, where the photo hangs on the wall.

"It was taken in England, just before they got on the boat for America. In New York, they stayed with a relative who suggested they settle in the Catskills. He said it would remind them of Russia, so they moved to the Borscht Belt."

I look up quizzically, picturing my grandmother's red beet soup topped with sour cream.

My mother notices my confusion. "Russian Jews liked borscht, and many of them vacationed in the Catskills during the summer. That's how it came to be called the Borscht Belt. My grandparents bought a farm and turned it into a boarding house catering to intellectual Jewish immigrants." My mother sighs and sips her tea. "Felix, who started all the trouble, finished college, got married, and died only a few years later from a kidney disease. My grandparents never made enough money to be financially comfortable again."

"That's sad," I say.

"Yes. Although my grandfather's partner in Russia sent him money from the business for a number of years, it just wasn't enough. And it was particularly hard on my mother. She had no chance to go to medical school here. She could have become a doctor in Russia. Here, her younger brother Joseph, who was brilliant, went to college. He got a PhD in mathematics and became a professor and dean at Alfred College. Luba had to help her mother in the boardinghouse—baking, serving guests, and even killing chickens. She hated that."

I cringe, recognizing the theme. Narrow escapes, victims, villains, loss, tragedy, and the essential unfairness of life. I feel scared and suffocated. Will I suffer persecution? Will I have no choices? I don't want to listen to the stories anymore. "That's so unfair."

"Life isn't fair. Especially for women." My mother purses her lips, as if all this happened yesterday, to her, personally. I love special time with my mother, the coziness, the tea and treats, but her stories often leave me feeling powerless and claustrophobic.

I sip my tea and try to change the subject. "How did you and Daddy meet?"

"At a wedding," she smiles. "I was fixed up with someone else, but your father was so handsome. And what a dancer! We were married within a year." She pinches my cheek. "You and your brothers are the light of my life." I feel embraced by her love.

The busy lumberyard my father managed was a ten-minute walk from my parents' first house in Lynbrook, Long Island. I'm five, Larry seven, Marc two. We trail my mother into the main building. The sweet smell of newly sawn wood fills the room. Red, white, and blue *Steinbrook Lumber* pencils with pointy tips fill pencil holders and men's shirt pockets. Everyone smiles. Salesmen slip their hands into the pockets of their pants and pull out hard candies wrapped in cellophane, as if they are just waiting for us. Life seems perfect to me, but my mother is struggling with the demands of extended family. My father's older brother and mother, both suffering from clinical depression, visit every weekend.

When I was older, my mother described the strain. "My doctor gave me tranquilizers and told your father if the overnight visits didn't stop, he'd put me in a hospital for a rest."

Strong, capable, and opinionated in her own endeavors, yet deferential at home, my mother was dependent on my father financially. She worried about her lack of career skills, in case my father died and left her like her mother was left, unprepared to support herself or her family. History eerily repeated itself when my father died at fifty-six, leaving my mother without enough savings and insurance to ensure a comfortable future.

When I was six, we moved to Rockville Centre, a neighboring town, where the houses were larger, and there was a greater preponderance of Jewish families.

I drove through Rockville Centre recently, down the street where I lived for thirteen years, past the ghostly inhabitants of my childhood. The streets are wide and lined with stately old maple trees. The sidewalks are concrete, perfectly sized for hopscotch. The lawns are manicured, separated by slate walks, landscaped in red and yellow azaleas interspersed with honeysuckle, rhododendron, and arborvitae.

My house—it will always be mine in some odd function of memory and wistfulness—is fieldstone and brick, with a gray slate roof, metal casement windows, and purply red shutters, which were brown in my time.

So many happy memories fill me. So much I remember—family gatherings, dinner parties, card games, my parents' friends filling the space with stories and jokes and serious talk, too—cigarette smoke rising from lipsticked mouths, smoke rings levitating toward the ceilings, laughter punctuating the conversations, always laughter. I see people nibbling on appetizers still warm from the oven. I hear the clinking of ice in glasses, the rustling of fingers picking through bowls of peanuts, cashews, and chocolate—innumerable forms of chocolate—M&Ms, Tootsie Rolls, Thin Mints. So much to love in the remembering.

On this trip, like many of my trips to Rockville Centre, my brother, Marc, drives in from New Jersey to visit family friends with me. We park in front of the house and sit there, just looking, just looking and remembering, wishing ourselves back there for the good times, for the family gatherings, the stories, and the laughter. We see them—our father, our mother, our relatives and family friends—gathered in the living room and the dining room, inhabiting a space and time that isn't now and isn't quite then either, but remains alive somehow, still.

———•———

The move to Rockville Centre brought financial stress. The mortgage was larger, and the house needed a lot of work. The kitchen was in shambles. Rockville Centre was wealthy, and keeping up appearances was the norm. My mother didn't budget, though she shopped at discount stores. Within a year or two of our move, my father returned from work in a fury. "He wants to sell the lumberyard."

"What?" my mother said. "He couldn't have mentioned that before we bought this house?"

"I can't let someone else buy the business," my father said. "I haven't spent all these years working my way from truck driver to manager to risk losing my job security now."

After a long, stressful year, my father found two silent partners and managed to buy the business. At home, repairs slid to the back burner. For the first year, I shared a room with my brothers, until my father built a small bedroom for me by reducing the size of the large upstairs landing.

My mother was especially irritable on Saturday mornings. She still had housework to do, but my father was off golfing.

———•———

"Get up!" my mother shouts. "Get up! You don't get to sleep if I have to clean the house. And there's a lot to do. I'm not doing it myself." I hear the clanking of the vacuum cleaner as she drags it up the stairs. She walks into my room. "Get up and get ready to help. And wake up your lazy brothers." I hop out of bed, strip off my pajamas, and pull on clean clothes.

"Wash up. Then I want you to take this furniture spray and use it on all the wooden furniture upstairs and downstairs. Use this cloth. Then strip the beds and put on clean sheets." She turns to my brothers. "Marc, you're going to sweep up the kitchen, the broom is down there already. And Larry, you take out the trash and clean up the basement."

"Now?" Marc whines.

"This minute. Get moving!" She's beleaguered. When the house is clean, my mother takes a deep breath and we move into the better half of the day.

———•———

My mother's talents at decorating on a tight budget were put to use furnishing the house. Marc and I tagged along as she plucked accoutrements off the shelves of dusty antique shops and dragged out furniture she could easily transform into the stuff of home-design magazines. Old wicker chairs and a sofa came home to be painted white and covered with jaunty floral cushions. Twin beds with pine-apple posts and matching bureaus were given to us from a friend of my mother's. Those decorated the room my two brothers shared. Eventually, that room and the lovely beds became mine.

My mother could create a glamorous appearance by snagging designer dresses at bargain prices and negotiating deals on hidden gems of jewelry languishing in junk shops. She transformed into a sophisticate for the weddings, anniversaries, country club dinners, and bar mitzvahs she and my father attended, courtesy of invitations from their large extended families and an equally large circle of friends.

Though my mother didn't believe it, she was beautiful. Her eyes were lovely, deep-set and hazel—and a source of shame.

"I became cross-eyed as a child," she'd say, "after a high fever. My mother put me into a tub filled with ice. When she saw my eye turn in, she started screaming. I was so scared! For years my mother took me to a Manhattan ophthalmologist. I did my eye exercises, and eventually was no longer cross-eyed, but the sight in that eye was gone. And my brother Phil teased me mercilessly. He called me four-eyes and carrottop and skinny-minnie."

Shame tinged my mother's perceptions. She couldn't ask for what she wanted because asking precipitated shame. At times, her behavior assured an undesirable outcome. No one could meet her unexpressed needs. We all lacked the capacity to mind-read.

"Why didn't you help me unpack the groceries? Why didn't you know what I wanted? How could you not understand what was important to me?"

Our failures engendered shame in us because despite our best efforts, we would fail my mother. And those failures were never forgotten. My mother nursed resentments and clung to regrets. Hurts incurred as far back as childhood seemed as fresh when recounted as the day they occurred.

Even as a child, I felt my mother's shame. I noticed that when-ever a photographer approached, she'd say, "Take the picture from this side with my good eye."

Despite her inability to see herself clearly, it is obvious from photographs that by the time my mother married, she'd transformed into a swan. With sultry eyes, high cheekbones, a warm smile filled with beautiful teeth, a straight nose, and soft, clear skin, Natalie stood out as attractive, beautiful, or stunning, depending on the occasion. On evenings she and my father were going out, I was fascinated by her metamorphosis from mommy to sophisticate.

It's early evening. The sitter is ensconced in the kitchen downstairs, warming dinner. I perch on my parents' brass bed and intently observe my mother's preparations. Natalie peers into the triple mirror of a mahogany vanity and applies black eyeliner, gray eye shadow, and red lipstick. She twists and twirls her burnished auburn hair up and around into a circle atop her head, securing the bun in place with hair pins and topping it with tall black lacquered sticks, brass charms dangling from their tips. Pearl earrings shine in her earlobes. She slips into a dress inexpensively tailored for her in Chinatown, a shimmering weave of silver and gold on an ebony background. Mandarin-collared and formfitting, it falls slightly below her knee. She slides into jet-black high heels and is transformed into a woman worthy of a fashion shoot.

"Mommy, you look so beautiful," I say.

She scrunches up her nose to convey skepticism, never completely banishing the embarrassments of her childhood.

"Nat, are you ready yet?" My father's voice floats up the stairwell.

I traipse down the steps behind my mother to the front foyer where my father stands, prematurely gray hair curling around his head. His blue eyes sparkle. Dimples crease his cheeks as he wraps a mink stole around my mother's shoulders. She turns to smile at me, and as she links her arm through my father's, seals an image of elegance in my mind—along with a lifelong lust for red lipstick and sparkling jewelry.

Feeding people was my mother's most uncomplicated, consistent manner of expressing unconditional love. She created delicious meals for Shabbat, holidays, and the dinner parties she hosted for friends, relatives, and my father's business associates. The kitchen was her command center, a laboratory for the creation of things of beauty, objects of desire, and culinary masterpieces. An alchemist in the kitchen, she combined common constituents into wondrous culinary concoctions, creating a world mediated, modulated, and punctuated by the preparation, presentation, and consumption of food.

My mother stands at one end of our rectangular dining room table. I stand at the other.

"I'm going to pull this lever, and when I say go, we'll both pull on our ends of the table."

"Okay, Mom," I say. She gives the cue, we pull, and the table slides open.

"Now, honey, I need your help with these two leaves." I hold one end of a heavy wooden leaf, and she holds the other. We carefully maneuver each one under the chandelier and into place before pushing each end of the table closed and setting down felt-backed pads.

"Can you take out the ivory tablecloth and napkins?" she asks.

"Yes, Mom," I say, sliding the third drawer of the sideboard open and removing a freshly ironed damask tablecloth and ten matching napkins. They coordinate with the wallpaper, a soft maroon, interspersed with climbing vines inside vertical cream stripes.

"It's time for you to polish the silverware," my mother says. "I have dessert to tend to."

"Okay." I remove the good silverware from the top drawer of the sideboard and carry it to the kitchen, where I don rubber gloves, slather on smelly polish, and rub off any hints of tarnish.

When the silverware is gleaming, I set the knives, forks, and spoons in their proper places before helping my mom set out the good dishes.

In the kitchen, Natalie stands at the yellow Formica counter. She is focused on mincing onions and sliding them off the cutting board into a large bowl filled with chopped meat and white rice. She carries the bowl to the kitchen table where steamed cabbage leaves lie ready to be filled.

"Help me roll these into the cabbages, honey," she says, laying one meatball after another on a platter. I join her, filling each large cabbage leaf with a meatball, rolling it up, and securing it with a toothpick. Tomato sauce bubbles on the stove. She stirs in raisins, brown sugar, lemon juice, and crushed ginger cookies, lifting a wooden spoon to her mouth to taste the sauce after the addition of each new ingredient.

"Perfect," she says, setting a large glass baking dish onto the table. We carefully place the cabbage rolls into this baking dish, cover them with tomato sauce, and slide the casserole into the oven.

I go off to read, returning a few hours later. My mother is icing a double-layer chocolate cake with thick dark-chocolate frosting. "Do you want to lick the bowl?" she asks.

I smile, happy my brothers aren't home to compete for this pleasure. I carry the silver mixing bowl and the rubbery spatula to the kitchen table, where I demolish every drop of leftover icing. When I finish, I set the bowl into the sink and fill it with sudsy water.

My mother places the cake on the dining room sideboard next to a pie oozing sweet blueberries. She surveys the dining room. "Beautiful." She smiles, drawing me close for a hug. "I can always count on you, sweetie."

A few hours before guests arrive, my mother asks, "Are the Thin Mints out? The salted peanuts? The chocolate kisses?"

"Yes, Mom. It's all done." She plants a kiss atop my head. I bask in her glow.

"Let's get cleaned up. As the little maid tonight, you'll be earning your wages." My mother pays me to help serve dinner and to clean up.

I love carrying a silver tray around the living room. It's laden with hors d'oeuvres: cheese sticks, potato knishes, tiny kosher frankfurters in puff pastry. I hand them out with cocktail napkins and toothpicks while my father mixes drinks. When the guests settle in the dining room, I help serve entrees from silver chafing dishes before returning to the living room to collect used plates, glasses, and napkins bearing lipstick. I like listening to the conversations about books, politics, and the struggles of Israel. Laughter fills the house.

During these years, though extended family responsibilities remain demanding, my mother seems to be happy. She has many friends, a lovely house in a beautiful neighborhood, family who visit for Jewish holidays and vacations, a close synagogue community, and healthy children. During these years, I feel my mother's love. I feel cherished and I love my mother deeply.

———•———

For Natalie, cooking was not simply the transformation of meat, tomato sauce, and cabbage into an entree of multiple tastes and textures pleasing to the tongue, it included the presentation, which had to be pleasing to the eye. Occasionally, she'd take advantage of rare solitude to indulge in a chocolate dessert, a cup of coffee, and a cigarette. Despite the cooking, baking, and eating, and her disdain for exercise, Natalie rarely veered from a petite size six, courtesy of coffee, cigarettes, and a metabolic blessing, which unfortunately, did not pass on to me.

My mother did pass on her love of the kitchen and joy in entertaining. She taught me to cook fearlessly and creatively, to set a table with lovely dishes, silverware, tablecloths, and napkins. She taught me to enjoy being a hostess to friends and family, to value people, and to cherish close relationships.

———•———

Relationships were central to Natalie's vision of life. She kept far-flung relatives connected. An address book stuffed with extra papers sat in a drawer under the telephone. Our phone rang constantly. Natalie called to check on relatives if they'd been out of touch. She remembered everyone's birthday with a call, a card, and a gift. We visited relatives, they visited us, and our beds housed rotating occupants. Growing up with these loving relationships taught me to feel comfortable with affection, and to receive it and offer it easily and generously.

In order to remain connected, my father frequently drove to the city to pick up elderly relatives, usually with me in tow.

My father navigates the city streets. He finds a parking place and we walk down a street of brownstones lined with overarching trees before entering an apartment building.

My father points to a button. "Do you want to buzz them, honey?"

I nod and press. A voice comes through the speaker. "Who is there?"

"Yokie and Janie," my father says, using his childhood nickname.

"We'll be right down." We stand in the lobby and wait for Aunt Josephine and Uncle Izzy to step from the tiny elevator. She's powdered, perfumed, lipsticked, and outfitted in a dressy dress. He is wearing a suit smelling of cologne and cigars. They're short, like me, and when we hug, I feel wrapped in their warmth and scent. We settle in the car for the drive back to Long Island. My mother greets our guests with delight. The day is filled with stories, laughter, and delicious food. My mother packs up leftovers for them, and I hop in the car with my father for the return trip to the city. Before we return to our home in Rockville Centre, I'm fast asleep.

Perhaps the plentitude of food in my family was a way of honoring those who had starved in the concentration camps, a way of celebrating life, and culture, and survival. My mother's meals were the centerpiece of a well-lived American life. She was a masterful artist. Her medium was food, her galleries our dining room, her customers our family and friends. Yet Natalie was far from just "the little woman in the kitchen." She was a keen observer who bested Ann Landers with her insights and advice. As a humorist, she rivaled any comedian with her capacity to draw laughter from a recapitulation of the mundane. She was a caretaker and caregiver, a collector of lost souls, a woman of fierce determination, firm conviction, and affection.

Like many Jewish mothers, Nat felt entitled to share her opinions, certain that others would benefit from the wisdom of her counsel. Not only did she feel it was her prerogative to offer her opinions to others—in her mind, they should be happy to receive it.

"Tell your boss you're not working for peanuts anymore. If he doesn't like it, he can try to find someone else who'll work so hard, for so little, without complaining. There's no way he could replace you, darling. No way."

"That boyfriend of yours is bad news. What are you doing with him? He doesn't have the gumption or the brains to make something of himself."

When the eyes of a softhearted recipient filled with tears, Natalie would pat her shoulder. "If I don't tell you, honey, who will?"

Nat was also free with the compliments if your taste met her standards, although the compliments could also carry a sting.

"You've lost weight. Good. Now that you have a waist, you should emphasize it."

"Fabulous haircut. You look so much better than you did with that last style."

Not everyone had the pleasure of her one-on-one evaluations. When friends were over for a card game or a dinner party, my mother, remaining true to the roots of her Borscht-Belt humor, entertained them by drawing laughter from daily life.

"You should have seen the schlemiel I encountered at the post office this morning," she'd say, describing a hapless man who had crossed her path, highlighting his incompetence with a skilled application of the absurd, imitating his voice and manner, and making use of the Yiddish lexicon to convey character assassination in shorthand. "What a schlimazel! What a schlemiel!"

My mother's avid audience would double over in sustained laughter; in that way my mother was gifted. Nat could make anything funny or tragic in the telling. She overflowed with personality and never lacked for company. Her phone rang constantly, and she met friends and family for lunches, shopping excursions, and theater.

My mother was extremely close to her mother, feeling both dependent and deeply responsible for her well-being. They spoke by phone multiple times a week, and my mother eagerly awaited visits. The baking intensified when my grandmother settled in for her four-month stay. I remember my excitement when Luba took over the first-floor "Grandma bedroom."

————————

Grandma Luba's powders and toilet waters fill the downstairs bathroom. At night her teeth sit in a glass of water on the bathroom sink. During the day, our kitchen is transformed into a magical place. Donning aprons, tying their hair in kerchiefs, my mother and grandmother transform our kitchen into a bakery. Luba measures flour, sugar, and butter into the Mixmaster's silver bowl, and the ingredients morph into dough. She sets it on the flour-covered kitchen table.

"Come here, Janie, and help me roll out this dough," she says. "Press down here, see, in the middle of the ball of dough, yes, and roll it up and down. Good. Flatten it some more, yes, make it even. Good. Now, turn the glass upside down and press it into the dough. Yes, and again. Good. Try to make the circles close together so we don't waste dough. Yes!" She pats my shoulder. "Now we have the cookie tops and bottoms. Spoon the raspberry jam on every other circle like this." She demonstrates. "Your turn. Good. Now use the tiny glass to make a hole right in the center of the empty circle. Perfect! That will be the top of the cookie. You did a great job. Now take the fork and use the tines to make a design on the outside edge of the cookie like this, see?" She shows me how to do it. I try. "Perfect! Now we place them very carefully on the baking sheet."

Grandma Luba points to a bowl of cinnamon, sugar, and raisins. "Okay, honey," she says, "sprinkle this onto the strips of dough, like this, watch me." I follow her example. "Good, now roll it up like this, good, and now let's make a mound of this one, right!" We lay our *rugelach* and *mandelbrodt* on large baking sheets, and Grandma sets them in the oven.

My mother points to the measuring cup. "Pour in this much sugar," she says. "Now stir it and the vanilla into the farmer cheese and then put a big spoonful on this blintz." I carefully lay the mixture on the crepes, lined up on the kitchen table on wax paper. "Okay now, watch me fold them into blintzes." For dessert that night, she'll fry them in butter and serve them topped with jam or sour cream. Luba finishes up by laying strips of lattice across her spectacular cherry pies before sprinkling the concoctions with sugar and sliding them into the oven. I'm part of the magic. When the buzzers ring, desserts reappear—irresistible sweet pleasures.

I am sitting underneath Grandma Luba's sewing machine in the downstairs bedroom. She is sitting on the twin bed, the pincushion beside her filled with straight pins topped by colored balls. She's basting the hem of my new dress, a silver taffeta, to which she's added smocking and embroidery. We are watching Phil Silvers on television and laughing. She hangs up my dress and bends to peek under the sewing table. She extends her hand to me.

"Let's make ourselves a snack. Some hot tea with honey and cookies?"

I crawl out from my little nest, slip my hand into hers, and we walk to the kitchen to prepare our snacks. She carries a tray with our treats to her room. We sit on her bed together, watching TV and noshing.

Luba is preparing to go out to a luncheon. I am fascinated with the gold compact she is opening and the little round powder puff she uses to powder her nose. She slips into a flowered dress and does up the buttons in front. I watch as she opens the jewelry drawer and reaches overhead to do the clasp on her pearl necklace. She clips matching pearl earrings on her earlobes.

"They are so pretty," I say. "But do they hurt your ears?"

"No," she says. "Though if you prefer, when you're older, you can pierce your ears."

I squirm at the thought of making holes in my ears, but already I'm enamored of earrings.

Grandma sprays toilet water behind her ears and on the inside of her wrists before setting a hat with feathers and flowers on her head. She slips on white gloves, kisses me, and walks to the front door, where a friend will pick her up. Later in my life, I wonder if she was raised to dress so impeccably or whether all the traumas of anti-Semitism she both experienced and witnessed influenced some of her choices. Did she think that by dressing so well she could fit in and ensure her safety? There were so many ways, both conscious and unconscious, that all Jews were (and continue to be) affected by our history. Luba was a survivor, and her capacity to weather the financial strains of widowhood with grace and self-respect served as guidance to my mother later in her own life.

———•———

The summer I turn nine, my cousin Marsha comes to visit for the first time. She is twelve. Before my father leaves for the airport, we gather in the living room for a conversation. We have already had a number of these conversations. My parents want to prepare us for Marsha's arrival, to ensure we treat her with the utmost compassion. They sit beside each other on the sofa. Larry sits in my father's chair, and I sit in the French Provincial chair, both flanking the sofa. Marc sits on the green carpet.

"Now remember," my father says, "I'm picking Marsha up at the airport, and she may be shy when she walks into a houseful of strangers."

"She's been an only child," my mother adds, "so it may be a lot to deal with for her to become part of a family like ours. But I think she'll like sharing the boys' room with you, Janie. She enjoys reading, like you."

"Will she cry?" I ask, feeling nervous.

"I don't know," my mother says, patting the seat beside her on the sofa. I move over to be close to her. She puts her arm around me and draws me near. "Marsha was only four when her father died, and your father may remind her of him."

"And I'm sure she misses her mom," my father says. "It's only a few months now since she died."

I consider how awful it would be to lose my mother—to never again feel the softness of her skin, the coolness of her cheek, to lose the scent of her breath, the scent of her skin. I feel overwhelmed with grief. I wonder how Marsha is coping. "Will she stay with us forever?" I ask.

"We'd like her to," my father says, "but she may not want to leave her grandparents and friends in Los Angeles. We'll have to see."

I can't wait to have a sister. An ally to buffer my brothers, Marc, six, and Larry, eleven. Shortly after Marsha arrives, my brothers and I bring her to our finished basement where we play games and watch TV.

"Do you want to see my imitations?" I ask. "I did them in the school talent show."

"Okay," Marsha says.

I twirl a fake strand of pearls around my fingers, swing my hips, and repeat a Mae West line: "Why don't you come up and see me sometime?" Marsha laughs.

Larry and Marc tell Marsha their favorite jokes, and she soon settles into our raucous household as a fourth sibling. Though she prefers to live in California, she comes out every holiday and summer until midway through college. My parents become her surrogate parents, and during the summers, the wide, long beaches of Long Island become our playground.

———·———

"Larry, bring the cooler out now! Jane, take your nose out of that book." My mother's voice softens as she corrals my cousin. "Marsha, put away your book and get in the back seat with Jane and Larry." Smiling, she turns to Marc. "Honey, hop in the front seat."

My mother is wearing a white shirt tied around her waist, sky-blue pedal pushers, and white sandals, which show off her shiny pink toenails. Her light-brown hair is cut in a short style and streaked with blond highlights. She loads beach chairs and blankets into the back of our red station wagon.

"Come on, you slowpokes, let's get there before the sun sets!" Natalie settles into the driver's seat, dons large dark-framed sunglasses, and maneuvers out the long driveway for our daily trip to Long Beach. En route, we play Mad Libs until Natalie hands our pass to the parking guard at the beach club. She scopes out the spaces before nabbing one close to the entrance. She checks herself out in the rearview mirror, refreshes her red lipstick, and steps out of the car.

"All set," she says gaily, loading each of us up with supplies. We lug our bags across the hot black-topped lot with its smell of tar and sun, and through the cool shaded entrance. We weave, like a conga line, around the chaise lounges crowding the poolside patios and trudge down the long concrete sidewalks bordered by sand and cabanas until we reach our own. We cannot afford summer camps. We can only afford a cabana if it's shared with multiple families from my mother's vast circle of friends. But we don't care. We may not have the wealth of our Rockville Centre neighbors, half our clothes may be hand-me-downs, but we are privileged. We have an intact family, a beautiful home, plenty of food, and we are blessed to spend each day soaking up the sun and submerging ourselves in the big, warm waves of New York's Atlantic Ocean.

We unload our possessions and strip off our clothes to prance in the swimsuits beneath them, grab our beach towels, and race each other down the long wooden boardwalk and through the hot sand. We drop our towels and blankets where instructed and sprint toward the water.

"Come on, Marsha," I yell. She is rubbing Coppertone into her skin. She always burns.

Running in and out of the sea, jumping, splashing, and laughing, we take breaks to create sandcastles and moats. "Stop throwing sand at me, Marc, or I'm going to drag you into the water!" I yell. He throws more sand, and we're off running down the beach.

Natalie is lying in a chaise, reading a novel or chatting with a friend, wearing a wide-brimmed hat and applying suntan oil to herself and to us. She sports the latest in swimsuit fashions available from the discount stores on the Island. But she is also keeping an eagle eye on us. There are usually two lifeguards sitting on a high white stand with binoculars and whistles strung around their necks, and zinc oxide slathered on their noses. The surf on Long Island can host a threatening undertow, and it sometimes claims a summer swimmer.

We return to the sea to jump over waves until goose bumps colonize our arms and legs or a breeze whips up. "Come in now," my mother calls. She wraps us in beach towels. We shiver.

"Your lips are turning blue. Why can't you kids figure out when enough is enough! Okay," my mother says, "collect your things. You can warm up in the cabana shower before dinner."

As the sun begins to sink in the sky, she herds us off the beach while shushing our arguments over who gets dibs on the first shower and the chance to change in the little room at the back of the cabana. We climb over each other shouting and laughing, ready to strip off our sandy suits and rinse the grit from our bodies. We emerge clean and sunburnt, dressed in the shorts and tops she's packed. She rubs calamine lotion into our sunburned skin, musses our hair, and settles us down.

Sometimes Dad meets us there, fresh from a day of golf, his smile flashing white against the darkening sky. We stop at Nathan's or The Texas Ranger en route home, or cook dinner on the charcoal grill at the cabana, hamburgers in rolls with coleslaw, franks in buns topped with sauerkraut, relish, and mustard. Toasted marshmallows pressed between graham crackers and squares of chocolate. Donning sweatshirts to fend off the evening chill, we head home as the sky fills with stars. Our life on these summer days is idyllic: sun, water, waves, books, family, and friends, all together, laughing. In my memory, these are the happiest times in our lives.

One snowy January morning, I lie in bed, home from school because of a sore throat. Grandma Luba comes into the room, kisses my forehead, and says, "I'm taking the train to the city to see my dermatologist and to visit friends. I'll be back in time for dinner."

That afternoon, I overhear my mother's worried voice on the phone. "What? Call a doctor! And call me right back." Between Luba's appointment with her dermatologist and a visit with friends, she suffered a heart attack. Her friends, distraught and overwhelmed, phoned from their apartment. My grandmother was only seventy-four. She died on their couch.

I remember my mother's wails, my fear, the soft embraces of relatives and family friends, the tears. We sat Shiva, observing a period of mourning. Friends brought food. We recited Kaddish. Nothing mitigated the hole Luba's death left in our family.

No death in our family occurred without some degree of self-blame, or blame of others—as if death was not inevitable. "Why didn't the dermatologist recognize signs of a coronary? Why did my mother's friends waste precious time before calling a doctor? Why didn't they get an ambulance? My mother could have survived." Recriminations allowed anger to displace grief.

After Luba's death, my mother struggled with deep grief, which slid into depression and increased anxiety. She embedded herself further in the kitchen and stopped even giving a nod to kosher cooking. When disasters struck others, she baked more and mailed off care packages. Nieces and nephews slept on borrowed cots or sofa beds for days, weeks, or entire summers. Natalie attempted to mitigate others' sadness by supplying them with baked goods and offering the pleasure of eating. My cousins experienced the healing properties of hot chocolate topped with tiny marshmallows and chocolate chip cookies so fresh from the oven the chips melted on their fingertips. This aspect of my childhood created an emotionally laden relationship with food, fusing food with pleasure, comfort, and affection.

Though large family gatherings characterized holidays in my childhood, life is different now, with family spread across the country and the globe. But I'm at ease in the kitchen—throwing together a meal for ten is fun, and filling the house with friends and relatives brings me joy. I consider these talents to be gifts from my mother and grandmother.

Death framed not only my mother's life experience, it framed my own. My father's first coronary occurred only ten months after Luba's death. He was forty-eight.

I am standing in the living room next to my Aunt Sarah, one of my mother's closest friends and the wife of my mother's older brother, Herb. Sarah is a beautiful, intelligent, and wise woman. My mother adores her. Sarah has left her husband and three children in Washington, D.C. to tend to us.

"When is Daddy coming home?" I ask.

"In a few weeks," she says, tucking a tissue in her apron pocket. Her face is wan.

"But he's been in the hospital for two weeks already. Will he get better? Will he die?"

"He won't die," she says, putting her arm around my shoulder. "He's very ill, but he'll come home. Don't worry."

I look at Marc, crouched under the dining room table. "Come out, Marc. Let's play." He tosses out a string of curses shocking for an eight-year-old.

Aunt Sarah's face turns red. "Stop that! Those are terrible things to say!"

Larry has disappeared. He is off with his friends. I read books to keep my mind occupied and try to help my aunt. It's the worst year of my life. In addition to my grandmother's death and my father's heart attack, I experience a coordinated shunning from a small group of neighborhood girls. I learn hard lessons that year: people are unpredictable, life is tenuous, and loss is inevitable.

My father finally returned home, thinner and pale and weakened from a month in the hospital. His recuperation included walking. Each evening, as part of his recuperation, we strolled the leafy streets of our neighborhood. I can still feel the comfort of my small hand in his, our fingers entwined, my immense relief that he was still alive.

My relationship with my mother was negatively affected by the traumas of that year. I longed for a sense of safety, but it was in short supply. When Natalie engaged in gossip and criticism of others, I identified with those who felt the pain of her barbs. That caused me to distance from her. My mother was also terribly burdened by her own grief and fear. The death of her mother and the life-threatening illness of her husband had cracked the foundation of her sense of safety in the world. She became irritable and angry, and sometimes distant. I grew closer to my father and felt more grounded by his presence. He anchored my place in the family. After one of my mother's rages, I could talk about my feelings with my father. He didn't take sides. He'd try to explain all that my mother was coping with, and at times, he'd mediate disputes.

Finances became even more strained. Every few months, a big box arrived in the mail or was dropped off by family friends, filled with a motley assortment of hand-me-downs.

———•———

My mother pulls off the masking tape and we begin to sort through the contents.

"There's nothing here I can wear," I grouse. "It's all so ugly!" I hold up a blue taffeta dress that's years out of style.

"These are perfectly nice things," my mother says. "Don't be ungrateful. Look at this red sweater and this plaid skirt. What about this pink dress?" She holds up some wrinkled items.

"Those colors look awful on me," I complain. "And that's too big, and this is too small."

"You'd better find something you like because it's all you're going to have to wear."

I pick out a few things, black tights, black tops, and some skirts—and make do.

———•———

Natalie began college, preparing to support herself if my father had another heart attack. "Every woman must be able to earn a living," she'd say. "You're going to go to college to learn a career. You'll never have to worry about supporting yourself." Unfortunately, family responsibilities interfered, and my mother had to again defer her pursuit of the elusive college degree. Instead, she started a small business based on her love of antique jewelry.

———•———

My mother and I are standing in an antique store on Long Island. I'm peering into the glass display case watching my mother point to different pieces of jewelry. As she negotiates with the store owner, I meander the dusty aisles, where I take pleasure in exploring delicately flowered china, old wooden furniture, and white ironstone pitchers. When we arrive home, my mother lays her acquisitions on a piece of black velvet on top of the dining room table.

"That is beautiful!" I point to a pin studded with garnets.

"Look at these." My mother slips on three garnet bracelets.

"They're gorgeous." We admire their sparkle.

"How about these delicate stick pins?" She points to four of them, all decorated with tiny diamonds, rubies, pearls. "Virginia will love them. And my friends can show me the pieces they love and then send their husbands over to buy their birthday gifts!"

"I love these." I pick up gold earrings decorated with fiery opals and shimmery pearls. "Aunt Anne, right? She'll like these the best, and this." I pick up a gold Victorian locket with an etched design of birds and flowers. It's magical to see these gems sparkling in the light cast by the chandelier. My mother's taste is exquisite, but her squeamishness about earning a profit from friends and neighbors dooms this endeavor.

My mother plied other skills as co-president of the PTA with my father. I followed her example of volunteering in the community by co-chairing a scholarship-fund drive in high school and tutoring Cuban refugees in English. In college, I organized sit-ins and volunteered at a Spanish-speaking legal clinic.

In private, Natalie struggled with anxiety and irritability, like her mother did. I later understood her feelings were a consequence of trauma and grief, and side effects of the Valium and Librium her doctors generously prescribed. As a therapist, I learned that memory loss, irritability, hostility, and aggression can result from those medications. From that perspective, she struggled with emotions beyond her control.

We're playing crazy eights at the round wormwood card table in the living room. Larry is sixteen, Mark is eleven, Marsha is seventeen, and I'm fourteen. The plaster walls are painted a soft willow green and the sofa cushions are attired in their summer wardrobe, a floral crewel pattern on a beige background. The fragrance of blossoming roses wafts in the windows. My mother accompanies a friend to the front door.

"Break up with that guy," she says. "He's a schnook who'll never amount to anything."

We're quiet as she speaks, but as soon as her friend leaves we return to arguing. "You cheated!" Marc shouts.

"You should talk," Larry snarls. Marsha and I snicker behind our cards, sure one of them is right. We play until Marsha's friend walks up the front path. Natalie holds the door open. Marsha tosses down her cards and rises to retrieve her purse. Natalie takes a long look at Marsha and says, "That eyeliner makes you look like a prostitute. Wash it off."

"No, Aunt Nat," Marsha says. "This is normal for Los Angeles and I'm not washing it off."

My mother, shocked at the rebuff, turns to Marsha's friend. "With your legs, you should *not* be wearing a miniskirt."

"That was mean, Mom," I say after they've left.

Her nostrils flare at the audacity of my complaint. "What, it bothers you? You're just soooo sensitive? Too damn bad. If you don't like it, don't listen."

I seethe, but there is little I can do. I am sensitive—to my mother's words, to facial expressions, to the emotional temperature in a room. Nat swings quickly from warm and loving to rageful, directing her anger at me more and more often as I move into high school and college. I never know what to expect—her love or her anger—yet her many friends and our relatives adore her. To them, she is consistently loving, kind, and generous.

The same dynamics arise in family gatherings, where catching up on the lives of far-flung friends and family is both a delight and a test of inner strength. One can anticipate affection, fascinating stories, and laughter, but one never wants to be the first to depart. Once you leave the room, your flaws will be elaborately dissected, with the commentary led by my mother. My self-esteem is often a vicarious casualty. Just hearing "With an ass like that, she shouldn't be wearing slacks" makes me wince. In such a milieu, who can ever be good enough?

Natalie didn't seem to fear others' critiques of her. Perhaps she knew no one would dare. And she had so much charisma. She could, and did, turn just about everyone she met and liked into a friend. Everyone in the extended family and her large coterie of friends also knew she could always be counted upon to offer assistance whenever it was needed.

"You're not feeling well? I'll bring you chicken soup for dinner."

"You need something for the luncheon? I'll drop off a banana bread."

"What do you mean you have no place to go for the holidays? You'll come here!"

My mother picked up the phone whenever it wasn't ringing to check on her friends, their children, or the neighbors. She invited the lonely, elderly, widowed, or childless to dinner. As she aged, she didn't lose her compassion for those who were suffering or bereaved.

By high school, it became clearer to me that I couldn't measure up to my mother's expectations. She was an extrovert who craved social engagements. I was an introvert who loved to write, daydream, spend time with my friends, and read. I loved biographies of women, mysteries with girl sleuths, and novels.

"Come to the beauty parlor with me," my mother says. "You need to get your eyebrows tweezed, and you could do with a haircut and a manicure."

"No thanks. It's too noisy in there, and it hurts when they tweeze my eyebrows. I like my hair the way it is, and I can't stand the smell of all that nail polish. Besides, I'm in the middle of a great book."

"You need to make yourself look pretty. It doesn't just happen. You need a little help," she says. But I'm not that interested. When my cousin Lorrie, eight years my senior, visits, I feel mixed emotions, knowing she and my mother are two peas in a pod. They love shopping, gossiping, and going to beauty parlors. I understand now how much those pleasures served as a respite from ongoing sorrows.

A major source of conflict with my mother, one which intensified as I moved into my late teens, arose from my refusal to accept her worldview—people were either victims or victimizers. I understood how my family history led my mother to that conclusion, but at that time, I rejected the assertion that people were powerless over their fate. Perhaps even then, I intuitively feared becoming entrapped in the roles my mother so often assigned to people.

We are sitting at the kitchen table, nibbling on brownies from a new recipe my mother has tried. I am fifteen. My mother is telling a dramatic story of a friend's divorce. "She couldn't do anything. Not a thing. Her husband left her with no money and a house she couldn't afford."

"But Mom," I say, "Hannah chose the attorney. She could have chosen a different one. She could have changed attorneys. She's not a victim. Those are the consequences of her choices. She's responsible for the choices she made."

My mother purses her lips, infuriated. "You just don't get it. And you never will!"

I think I have gotten it. As a therapist, I became familiar with the consequences of victimization and trauma, and the ways it echoes through the generations. I have been a witness to many clients' stories of victimization. I understand how trapped people can be. I understand the shame that can haunt them. Shelters for battered women didn't exist in my mother's era as they do now. My mother lived during a time and in an era when women had neither the advantages nor the choices available to men. She was a trauma survivor who lived with ongoing traumatic stress. We were Jewish. Our family members and members of our faith who were unable to escape from Europe before or during the Second World War were mercilessly victimized and murdered. Most of them had no choice, no refuge, and no hope.

* * *

As I became more independent, my relationship with my mother grew more strained. The summer before tenth grade, a friend and I joined a group bicycle trip through New England. I loved camping, cooking over smoky campfires, pedaling, and even pushing my three-speed bike up the many hills. I cycled between thirty and sixty miles a day and returned proud and triumphant.

"You're as brown as a berry," my mom said with a laugh. "But you didn't lose any weight." I was five foot three and weighed 116 pounds, but I was still not thin enough for Natalie.

Before the trip, my mother mentioned her desire to throw me a sweet sixteen party.

"*I don't want one*," I emphasized. "I just want dinner at home with a few friends."

A few days after my return, Natalie surprised me. "Here are the invitations I sent out for your sweet sixteen. I've booked a wonderful restaurant, hired a band, and counted the RSVPs. You can look over the list now." Her handwritten invitations included a verse of instructions to attendees to dress like little girls. She handed me a dark-brown mini tent dress with huge blue polka dots, a white Peter Pan collar, and short sleeves with white cuffs. I felt trapped, mortified, enraged, and simultaneously ashamed of my ingratitude. I also felt unadulterated hatred for my mother, who had yet again completely ignored my wishes. At the time, I did not understand that my mother couldn't fathom our differences. If she wanted me to have a party, then in her mind, I had to feel the same way. And, in another sense, my mother was throwing me the party she wanted.

The confusing misfit between us intensified over the next few years. My mother found my distaste for her pleasures tedious. I found her disdain for my pleasures and my appearance painful. After taking me bra shopping, she once said with disgust, "You're so zaftig." (Plump or curvaceous). "You certainly don't take after my side of the family!" It wasn't a compliment.

———•———

One evening, my parents ask me to join them in the living room. They sit together on the sofa. I sit in my father's club chair.

"Larry talked to us about some concerns he has about you," my mother says.

"What concerns?" I ask suspiciously. Larry isn't often on my side.

"He says you're turning down dates so that you can babysit," my father says.

"I'm not interested in dating the boys who've asked me out."

"It's important for you to date, to be more outgoing, to get involved in school activities."

"I love babysitting. I like the kids. I like the money. I don't want to date Larry's friends. They tell each other everything after a date. I hear them talking in his room. It's creepy."

My parents glance at each other. "That's normal for this age," my father says.

"There's no one I want to date. And I don't want to give up babysitting."

"We're sorry," my mother says, "but from now on you're going to go on dates when you're asked, get more involved socially at school, and stop babysitting."

This feels like a forced conversion to extroversion, but I acquiesce. I run for student government office and win. I like committee meetings and organizing. I like talking to everyone in every kind of group, and to kids without a group. I enjoy finding ways for people to connect. But I still find plenty of time to spend with my two closest friends, to daydream, and to read.

In my junior year, I began a romance with a handsome, sexy guy I'd adored for years. He was in college and far more exciting than my classmates. My parents approved. I was becoming more outspoken. Influenced by both the women's movement and my mother's earlier admonitions, I was determined to have a career. Ambivalent about having children, I decided to wait until I was at least thirty before marrying. Men of that era had careers, influence, and at least superficially, more control over their lives. I wanted all the choices and power they appeared to have.

The summer after my freshman year of college provided challenges for me, my two brothers, and my parents. Until then, I'd been a compliant, respectful daughter. My first year of college, I marched in anti-war demonstrations, wore dungarees, and embroidered peasant blouses. My parents were unprepared for my growing independence and my arguments about the curfews they set. They were appalled at my crush on my best friend's college pal, a curly-haired charmer on a cross-country motorcycle trip. The noise of his motorcycle would awaken the household every night when he pulled into the driveway to drop me off. One night, in an act of rebellion and defiance, I went to a party in the city with friends and didn't call home to say I was staying out until dawn.

"Where the hell have you been all night? Have you any idea how worried we've been?" my mother yelled when I returned home at eight o'clock in the morning. I crawled into bed and stayed there until my father returned from his golf game and met me in the upstairs hall outside my bedroom.

His face was bright red as he yelled. "What were you thinking? Didn't you know we'd worry about you? We called the police and the hospitals. We had no idea where you were, or if you were alive or dead!"

I listened to him yell for a while and then interrupted. "If you want to tell me how upset you are, I'll listen. I'll apologize. But if all you want to do is scream at me, I'm going back into my bedroom and locking the door."

My father stood there, stunned. Then he reached out, wrapped his arms around me, and began to sob. I wrapped my arms around him and sobbed, too.

"We're sending you to California," my mother said, a few weeks later. "We need a break from each other, and you can spend some time with Marsha. Hopefully, she'll talk some sense into you." I was happy to fly to LA and spend two weeks with my cousin, but a sense of dread pursued me up and down the California coastline. I stopped in Chicago the Tuesday before Labor Day to visit a friend for the holiday weekend. But my dread exploded into uncontrollable anxiety, and I called home that evening. "Is everything okay there?" I asked.

"Yes, everything's fine," my mother said. "Your father is golfing tomorrow, and we're having a dinner party tomorrow night. Your cousins will be here over the weekend. Why?"

"I feel horrible anxiety. I felt dread in California, but now it's worse. I think something awful is going to happen. I have to come home. I can't stay here."

"See if you can change your flight. If you can fly in tomorrow afternoon, I'll pick you up at the airport."

I arrived in time for the dinner party. My father and I stood in the foyer between the living room and dining room, wrapped in a long embrace. "I love you, Daddy," I said. "And I'm sorry for giving you such a hard time this summer."

"I love you too, sweetie," he said. "And it's okay. I'm glad you're home."

The next day, a humid scorcher, my father played thirty-six holes of golf. His chest pain began that night, but he ignored it. Mid-morning the next day, the Friday of Labor Day weekend, he phoned home, asking my mother to pick him up. When she brought him home, he lay on the green velvet sofa in the living room, sweaty and uncomfortable. I sat on the floor beside him, petting our dog, Roxie. My mother called my father's cardiologist. There was confusion over which hospital my father should be taken to because his cardiologist didn't have privileges at Mercy Hospital, which was only a few blocks away.

Marc told our neighbor what was going on. She volunteered at Mercy and marched right over. After taking one look at my father's face, she turned to my mother and said, "You're taking him to Mercy's ER right now. You can't wait a minute longer!"

In 1970, coronary treatment was lightyears behind today's, but I am certain my father's denial and the hour on the living room couch didn't extend his life. My mother and brother helped my father into our station wagon. As my brother backed the car out of the driveway heading for the hospital, I extracted a compendium of medical conditions, the *Merck Manual*, from the bookshelf and turned the page to "coronary." I was filled with horror when I read the words on the page: "Usually followed by sudden death."

The last time I saw my father, he lay in a hospital bed in the ICU, his breathing labored, a tangle of tubes hooked into his body. As I held his hand for my allotted five-minute visit, I knew the gray pallor of his face confirmed the words in the *Merck Manual*. I knew he was going to die. Overwhelmed by shock and sadness, I was unprepared when he said, "Take care of your mother for me, Janie. Please take care of her." It was difficult for him to speak, and though I am sure I told him I loved him and he said the same, what I remember most is his request, which seemed far beyond my capacity to fulfill.

I thought my father meant to ask Larry but didn't get the chance. I was mistaken. Decades later, Larry enlightened me—my father had made the same request of him en route to the hospital.

Life would have been easier for us both if we'd known the burden was shared.

As my father struggled for his life in the ICU, my mother asked me to sleep beside her. We snuggled in search of comfort and fell into fitful sleep. She shook me awake at five that morning.

"I had a terrible nightmare," she said. "I saw a bird bite the head off a turtle."

Bird dreams were omens of death in my family. My mother and I stared anxiously at each other for a few moments before the phone rang. A doctor at Mercy Hospital said, "I'm sorry to inform you your husband just passed away."

My father was fifty-six when he died, my mother fifty-one. I was nineteen, Larry was twenty-one, and Marc was sixteen. My father's death shattered the foundation of our family and fulfilled my mother's worst fears, leaving her financially insecure and forcing her to transform her life.

The month before his death, my father had made an unfathomable decision to cancel a generous life insurance policy, and the consequences were devastating. Additionally, although he'd spent the summer in negotiations to set a buy-out price for his share of the lumberyard in the event of his death and to ensure a place for my brother, Larry, in the business, the contract was not finalized. My mother was forced to negotiate a hasty sale. Yet even as her worst fears manifested, she discovered unexpected fortitude, courage, and skill.

Just before my father's funeral, my older brother pulled me aside. "You killed him," he said. "If you hadn't given him so much grief this summer, he wouldn't have had a heart attack and died."

For years, I felt guilt-ridden, unable to fully grieve my father's death because I felt so responsible. I wondered if my mother blamed me too, but she never said so.

My older brother and I returned to college. I don't know how his senior year was paid for, but I walked into the financial aid office at American University the minute I returned to campus.

The department head ushered me into his office. "How can I help you?"

"My father just died of a heart attack," I said and began to sob. "My mother doesn't know if she can keep our house. He canceled life insurance a month before he died. I don't think there's even money for my first semester." American University ensured my continued education with generous scholarships, a few small loans, and work-study jobs for the next three years.

At home, Marc was just beginning high school. He and my mother grew closer. He brought friends to the house, included my mother in his activities, and kept her laughing. They ate dinner in front of the television, watching *The Odd Couple*. Their closeness never faltered, fed by deep affection. Marc's stories are still filled with sweetness, and he's unable to finish his own jokes without laughing. His response to my questions about family history is typical: "I don't remember any problems. Mom and Dad were like Ozzie and Harriet. The TV show reminded me of our family. Mom was a cross between Donna Reed and Hillary Clinton. Perfect."

In contrast, my mother and I became entrenched in a painful pattern. She wanted acquiescence. I wanted autonomy.

"I miss Daddy," I'd say on visits home. I wanted to sit close to my mother on the living room sofa, wanted to feel her arm around me, her hand brushing the top of my head.

But my mother wasn't grief-stricken, she was absolutely furious. "I can't believe how irresponsible he was. He betrayed me. He knew how my mother struggled financially when she was widowed. How could he have left me in the same position? How could he have been so selfish and stupid?"

"It was stupid, but I still miss him." My grief seemed to enrage my mother further, perhaps because my vulnerability reminded her of her own, or perhaps because my grief felt like another betrayal. The life insurance policies my father unfathomably canceled the month before his death had been carefully thought-out and purchased with the intention of ensuring a comfortable future for my mother should my father die prematurely. My mother had no means of supporting herself, or me and my brothers. The house was mortgaged. My father's cancellation of those policies, so hard to come by after his earlier heart attack, was an act of such irresponsibility and thought-lessness that my mother could not forgive him. With one decision, without consulting her, he ensured that her future would be the one she'd always feared—life with a lack of financial resources that mirrored her own mother's life as a widow. My mother's rage toward my father burned unabated for the remaining twenty-eight years of her life. That anger was often projected onto me, and it morphed into eviscerating character assassinations.

"You're so selfish. You never think of anything or anyone but yourself. You act as if everything is coming to you. And you think you're so smart, don't you? Your father thought every word that came out of your mouth was a pearl of wisdom. But I know better. You're not so smart, despite your grades. I could teach you a thing or two. You're an emotional cripple—so serious and sensitive. I worry about you. I do."

I felt safer keeping my distance, staying in D.C. during the summer to work. Larry, also subject to tongue-lashings, moved home after college, and Natalie interfered with his romances.

"Can you just leave Larry alone and let him date the women he wants to date?" I said during one trip home. "It's not fair for you to interfere so much."

"I'm his mother. That gives me the right to interfere. And I'm going to continue to interfere if I don't like the girls he's dating. Mind your own business."

Larry moved to California and married his first wife in a civil ceremony before my mother even met her. They moved to Hong Kong. His first and second marriages ended in divorce. He kept his distance physically but helped my mother financially for the rest of her life.

My mother wanted me to move home after graduation. Perhaps she wanted me to replicate her choices, helping to support her mother after her father's death. But I'd lost my sense of belonging. My college boyfriend and I had broken up shortly after my graduation, and I was a mess.

My mother's repeated refrain was emotionally devastating to me. "You're so fragile," she'd say with disgust. "I worry about how emotionally dependent you are."

I moved to Boston where cousins had settled and found an apartment, a job, and a therapist. My work at a law reform agency inspired me to apply to law school.

"Why do you want to go to law school?" my mother asked. "You should teach."

"I've never wanted to teach. Don't worry, I'm not asking you for money. I'm going to take night classes and keep my job. I'll be able to cover living expenses and tuition."

"Good, because I'm not paying for this. I don't have the money and even if I did, I wouldn't give it to you for law school."

"You help Larry and Marc whenever they need money."

"That's different. You're making a big mistake. Why don't you ever listen to me?"

"Maybe I have my own ideas about life."

"What do you know? Nothing. You know nothing, and you're impossible to deal with. Both you and Larry. You know, I can cut the two of you out of my life. I do that. I erase people. I don't need either of you. I have Marc. One out of three isn't bad."

My mother might have intuitively known that law was not the best career for me, but her approach was not a kind one, nor one that offered an avenue for thoughtful consideration. At the time, I loved the law reform programs I worked with and felt idealistic about how these new interventions might take hold in the legal system. I ignored my mother's advice and chose to work during the day while attending class at night. I graduated cum laude, and with only a small amount of debt.

My relationship with my mother did not improve. All too often she seemed to morph from loving to hateful, from ally to sniper in seconds, driven by forces so unconscious there was no path of escape. I know now that some of my mother's mood swings were the consequence of side effects of medications. Some of her frustration and anger was the result of untreated depression and anxiety. I could not at that time understand that while her rage was directed toward me, it was not about me. I loved my mother and I feared her. My fear began to crowd out my love. Perhaps my mother was also fearful. She certainly faced an uncertain and financially strained future herself. She was learning about the work world, taking on her first professional job as head of volunteer services in a local government agency. She was attending college at night, working diligently to graduate with a Bachelor's Degree in Social Work.

Perhaps my mother wanted my support. Possibly she wanted more affection and attention from me. Maybe my focus on my own future and my life as an independent adult widened the chasm between us. Perhaps the age-appropriate individuation and independence I was reaching for felt like another loss to my mother and caused her to increasingly lash out, which unfortunately further assured my distance.

With my mother's anger so often the overwhelming force between us, I sought support and affection from friends, select relatives, a few of my mother's friends, and therapy. Natalie was a trusted source of affection, loving friend, and a devoted family member for so many people, but she was not a safe, reliable, or consistently loving parent to me.

———•———

I fell in love with a sexy Boston Irish-Catholic man whose attraction, I suspect, stemmed not only from his charm but the likelihood that he would offend my mother.

We're in a Boston restaurant. The walls are natural wood. The ceilings soar, green plants abound. A small vase of flowers sits on each table. I watch my mother evaluate Kevin's appearance. She sits across from us. Kevin's green eyes sparkle, ready for a duel. His curly reddish hair is a bit on the long side, like his thick mustache. He's wearing jeans, a tailored shirt, a brown leather vest. My mother is in her usual tailored skirt and blazer, hair coiffed, gold jewelry shining in the candlelight. She slips a cigarette from her pack of Tareytons.

Kevin takes a cigarette from his pack of Marlboros. He flicks his lighter for both of them.

"What are your future career plans?" my mother asks, exhaling a plume of smoke.

Kevin smiles and exhales competing smoke rings. They waft toward the ceiling. He sips his Kahlúa and cream and takes his time answering. "I want to be a rock-and-roll star."

I break into astonished laughter. Natalie is unamused. Kevin is unperturbed by her eye-roll. I needn't have worried. He's irresistible. They flirt and succumb to each other's charms. My brothers like him, too. Tensions abate. Family visits include Nancy, Aunt Anne, and Uncle Leonard. Marc finishes college, moves home, and after a few years, he joins Larry in California.

Seven years after my father's death, Natasha sold the house and moved into an apartment. Our dog Roxie came to Boston to live with me, while my mother made friends with half the occupants of her floor. She filled her life with work, family, friends, theater, and museums, added travel and romance, and built a vivid, colorful life despite financial constraints. I graduated from law school, worked with a small feminist firm, and realized that my relationship with Kevin had to end. The following winter, I accepted a job developing and providing services for victims of juvenile crime in Portland, Maine. I left Boston and Kevin.

Though Natalie was an intelligent, well-traveled woman, she believed civilization was centered in Manhattan and ended in Massachusetts. She wasn't pleased when I moved to Boston, but Maine—a state she thought primarily populated by deer, moose, and forest rangers—that was entirely off the map. As a young woman, she could not wait to move away from the rural Catskills to live in sophisticated Manhattan. From her perspective, my choice was ridiculous. She felt that no sane Jew whose forbearers barely escaped Russia would choose to live in a state with vast stretches of frozen landscape. But that is where I wanted to live.

My breakup with Kevin precipitated earlier loss issues for me. I began therapy with a female social worker in private practice. My mother, immersed in her own struggles, was not empathic. Phone conversations became safer than visits. If Natasha became accusatory or verbally abusive, I learned to hang up.

"You're so weak. Oy, I should live so long to see you work out your issues with me in therapy. Your father ruined you, treating you like a queen. Well, he's dead now. Too bad for you, I'm the only parent you've got."

I stopped visiting, which further enraged my mother but protected me from feeling even more emotionally shredded. We had become entrapped in my mother's worldview. I saw her as my victimizer and myself as her victim. She saw me as her victimizer and herself as my victim.

During these years, my mother completed the elusive college degree. I do not remember if I was invited to her graduation or whether I declined to attend. In retrospect, I feel a deep sense of regret about missing the opportunity to celebrate such a notable accomplishment with her.

It was about this time that Natalie decided she wanted to be called Natasha. I assumed it was her way of acknowledging the assumption of a new identity as an independent working woman as well as a nod to her Russian heritage. She continued to hold a good job with benefits and security, and she began to date. The psychics she consulted never illuminated her star-crossed romances, nor clarified her connection to men with coronary conditions. A number of men she dated died of heart attacks, including the man with whom she had her most passionate romance, a dashing, wealthy, white-haired, blue-eyed executive. Smart, intellectually stimulating, and opinionated, he was a perfect match for Natasha. After dating for years, Natasha inexplicably ended it. On the evening he met her for dinner to request a reconciliation, he suffered a heart attack. She called rescue and accompanied him to the hospital. He died there a few days later.

———•———

I am sitting in my dining room at a pine table snagged at a yard sale, sipping mint tea, looking at a hideous twenty-year-old orange velvet sleep-sofa, which came from the den in my family's house. I hate the sofa, but I need the sofa. I call my mother.

"How nice of you to finally decide to visit." Though I am thirty, still immersed in therapy, and feeling more grounded and stronger, my stomach clenches. I have avoided her.

"It's Thanksgiving," I say. "You asked me to bring Joe down to meet you."

"And it's about time. You haven't been home for a year."

I stare out the bank of windows beside me. Red and yellow leaves cascade from the trees, blanketing the sidewalks. Fall sunshine illuminates the room. The windows in my railroad-style apartment are drafty, but I love the place—the bull's-eye molding, the maple floors, the large rooms, the high ceilings, the distance from Portland, Maine, to Long Island, New York.

"Everyone will arrive by two o'clock for the Thanksgiving meal. When should I expect you?"

"We're leaving at five o'clock in the morning. We should arrive by noon. We can help you set up."

"Everything will be done long before then." I hear the accusation in her voice.

"Okay. We'll help you clean up. It will be great to see everyone." With relatives present for the holiday, my mother is more likely to behave.

A week later, Joe and I stand in the early morning mist, packing my yellow Ford Fiesta. I settle Roxie in the back seat on a blue blanket. "We have everything?" I ask Joe. "Maps, water, snacks?"

"Yes." We've been dating ten months and are hosting our wedding at a friend's Victorian home at the end of January—just immediate family and close friends. My mother has been on a particularly hostile streak for a year, and I considered not inviting her to the wedding. She hasn't met Joe yet and only knows he's in medical school and grew up in Philadelphia.

The car rattles over the bumpy New York roads. Drivers cut each other off, honk, curse out their windows. Crushed cans, flattened paper cups, and plastic bags blow across the road. High rises erupt in the distance. I begin to bite my nails. I am not sure I can handle my mother's hostility. I remind myself that Joe is with me, that my therapist is on call.

"Put in the opera tape," Joe says. "The arias calm you down." He lifts his hand from the steering wheel to stroke the top of my head. I'm instantly soothed.

"I'd like to drive by our old house before we go to the apartment. Is that okay?"

"Sure. I'd like to see it," Joe says.

We turn off Southern State, pass Mercy Hospital, where my father died, turn onto my road, Roxen, where stately Tudors and Colonials sit on spacious lawns. Elegant trees arch over us, creating a leafy canopy, immersing us in red, green, orange, and yellow.

"Pull over here." I point to my fieldstone house with chocolate-brown shutters. Roxie is excited, thinking we're home. I take her out to pee. She pulls toward the house. My heart pulls toward the house. "No, Roxie," I say, picking her up and settling her back in the seat. She licks my hands. My eyes well up, tears spill over. I return to the front seat, light a cigarette, suck in the smoke, push down the pain. "I wish my father was still alive. You would have liked each other."

Joe reaches for my free hand. "I wish I could have met him."

"Thanks for stopping." I exhale a trail of smoke, stub out the cigarette. Life is so different. I have no place in my family. The only home I'll have is the one I create. "Better head to the apartment," I say. "Luckily you'll be meeting my loving relatives, not just my mother."

We drive to the other side of town, just beyond the shops. The streets are wide, the concrete sidewalks carefully tended. Large trees shade the streets. Flower gardens frame the front of each elegant three-story brick apartment building. Balconies hold flower boxes filled with fall blooms.

We park behind the building. Roxie's nails make clicking sounds as we cross the tile floor. In the mirrored walls of the lobby, I see Joe, dark-haired, mustached, and handsome in a head-turning way. He's wearing khaki pants, a tweedy vest, a wool sports coat. My mother will like his looks. I'm wearing fitted jeans, high leather boots, a black sweater, dangling silver earrings. My mother will not like my looks. She'll comment sarcastically on my prematurely gray long hair, my casual clothes, the fact that I am wearing eyeglasses instead of contact lenses.

Roxie is as reluctant to enter the tiny elevator as I am, but we squeeze in, exiting to the smells of cooking on the third floor. My mother opens her door, dressed in brown slacks, a cream-colored blouse, gold jewelry. Her hair is cut short, dyed brown with blond highlights. She looks slim and beautiful, as usual, her makeup perfect. She waves us into the narrow hallway of her apartment, fussing over Roxie, who is licking and yipping in delight.

"Hi, Mom." I kiss her cheek. Her nostrils flare. Her embrace is brief. Her rage is palpable.

"Mom, this is Joe. Joe, this is my mother, Natalie or Natasha."

"Hello, Natalie," Joe says, smiling as he extends his hand.

She takes his hand, does a cold-eyed scan. "Hello, Joe. Do you need to freshen up?" She turns, points Joe to the guest bath. "Jane, you can use my bathroom. Put your bags in the den."

I know from experience we'll be tortured all night by the metal frame poking through the mattress of the beige sleep sofa. Joe and I use the bathrooms and meet in the hall. I lead him to the sunny living and dining room, banked by a wall of windows. We sit on the green velvet sofa my father lay upon while his heart muscles died. The doorbell buzzes. Aunt Anne and Uncle Leonard arrive with my cousin, Nancy. They exclaim over me, over Joe, offer hugs and kisses all around. They want to know everything about Joe, about me, about us. Anne holds my hand, smiles broadly, laughs. Leonard leans toward Joe and tells jokes. Nancy asks excitedly about our wedding plans.

My mother carries out a platter of chopped liver. Joe rises, takes it, and sets it on the coffee table. He moves to my father's club chair, reupholstered from plaid to a more feminine fabric.

"Everything smells wonderful," I say. "And this is delicious." I spread chopped liver on a cracker. "Anyone want some?" Everyone assents, and I am spreading chopped liver on multiple crackers and handing them around. Leonard helps my mother with drinks.

Natalie settles on the French Provincial chair and lights a cigarette. She looks at Joe and laughs. It isn't a warm laugh. It's her haughty laugh. "I thought you were Chinese," she says. "Janie said your name was Pi."

"It's not *P-i*," Joe says, intuiting her error. "It's *P-y*. My background is French and Polish."

"We're Jewish, you know, from Poland and Russia," my mother says. "There was no love lost between the Poles and the Jews." She stubs out her cigarette, stands, and strides into the kitchen.

Joe looks bewildered. I smile ruefully and say softly, "At least she didn't come right out and accuse your relatives of being Nazis."

My aunt waves her hand through the air. "Ignore Natalie. She's angry about everything these days." Anne looks at Joe and smiles. "She doesn't mean it, really. You'll like her when you get to know her. She's just acting badly today."

Anne joins my mother in the kitchen. Leonard stands by the kitchen entrance telling my mother jokes. I look at Joe and Nancy and say, "I wish I had an Ativan or a Valium, or that I still smoked pot. The only drug here is chocolate." A pressed glass bowl on the side table is filled with my mother's favorites, Hershey's Kisses. I bend over, reach in, and take some, pulling off the paper flags, peeling off the silver foil, popping them in my mouth. Soon I feel calmer, slightly high from the chocolate. The doorbell rings, and Nancy gets up to open it. Joe pulls me close on the couch, kisses me. More relatives arrive. They're warm and welcoming. My mother is a block of ice. When everyone leaves, Joe and I offer to clean up.

"That would be just fine," my mother says. "I'm beat. I want to watch TV in the den." She cajoles Roxie into trotting behind her.

The door to the den slams shut.

Realizations assault me. I miss my father. I long to see him napping in his chair, sharpened Steinbrook Lumber pencils in the pocket of his flannel shirt, the scent of Old Spice and newly sawn lumber wafting off his neck. I want to be in our house, not in this apartment where my mother's grudges for my supposed failures to respect or support her precipitate scorn and condescension. It is not the apartment that makes me anxious, it is the utter disintegration of what once felt like the safe harbor of my family. It is my mother's barely disguised hatred for me, stoked by my failure to join her demonization of my father for dying and failing to ensure her financial future. Maybe she blames me for his heart attack. I don't know. I only know that since his death, I have never felt completely safe with my mother.

———————

Joe and I marry a year from the day we met, in a small ceremony. It is hosted by a friend who is renting a large Victorian house on Portland's Western Promenade. We have invited only immediate family and close friends. The ceremony takes place in front of a roaring fireplace during an ice storm. My mother behaves. Joe, though not Jewish, meets some of her criteria: he's handsome, intelligent, well-mannered, and attending medical school.

———————

After a few years of traditional legal practice, I knew that law was not my passion and began evening classes in a master's program in social work. My mother happily announced that I should have listened to her qualms about law school, but I never regretted my legal training. It has added immeasurably to my life, though social work has been my passion. I practiced psychotherapy for almost three decades, adding mediation training to my repertoire. All therapists have to do their own work, lest their unresolved personal issues impair their ability to help their clients. Both my personal work and professional work allowed me to delve more deeply into mother-daughter issues.

——————

By my mid-thirties, I feel bushwhacked by longing for a baby. Joe and I eliminate birth control but don't conceive. My gynecologist, a national sensation in holistic medicine, suggests diet and meditation. Joe has noninvasive tests. He is fine. She doesn't recommend testing for me.

We rent an apartment on the second and third floors of a two-family house. The owners occupy the first floor. In July, I feel lightheaded and queasy. My pregnancy test is positive. We are ecstatic, but our joy is cut short when my general practitioner examines me.

"Your test is positive, but your physical exam is not normal," he says. "I'm concerned this could be an ectopic pregnancy."

"What's that?"

"The embryo lodges in the fallopian tube instead of making its way to the uterus. If the tube bursts, it's life-threatening. I'd like to set you up for more tests."

I call my holistic gynecologist. She examines me immediately and reassures us. "This is just an early pregnancy. You don't need more tests. Just relax."

My general practitioner is furious. "Ectopic pregnancies can cause hemorrhage and death," he says. "She is wrong to reassure you without ordering some tests. Please, don't take this risk."

"Give me a week or two," I say.

"You may not have that long."

He is right. Ten days later, while resting on the top floor of the apartment, excruciating pain flings me to my knees. I know my fallopian tube has burst. The searing pain is as intense as my shame—for trusting the wrong doctor, for letting longing overcome common sense. I navigate the stairs, stop to call Joe and then a friend.

My landlady is on our front porch. "What's wrong? Your face is gray."

"I think my fallopian tube ruptured. A friend is coming to take me to the hospital."

"We're not waiting." The daughter of a physician who often found bloody patients waiting on her front porch, she pulls her car onto the lawn to collect me.

I am wheeled into the emergency room, put into a johnny, attached to an IV, and whisked from here to there, perhaps for an ultrasound or an X-ray, I'm not sure. I am focused on a different experience, one for which I hardly have words because it comes from a place where spirituality, normal reality, and sensation intersect. It escapes the vocabulary at my disposal to clearly describe. The experience belongs to the world of luminous things, the space between life and death, the thin curtain separating us from those who've died. I feel the part of me animating my being—awareness, consciousness, spirit, or soul—detach from my physical body. It slides out, and without taking on a discrete form, hovers close by, intermittently slipping back into my body, where pain and urgency combine with the antiseptic smells, the clanging sounds of metal gurneys, the intensity of the bright lights, and the activity taking place around me.

Joe arrives and takes my hand. I meet the surgeon, a round teddy bear of a guy.

"You need to get me into the operating room," I say. "I keep leaving my body and I'm not sure how many more times I can get back in."

He looks at me with incredulity. "Can I just touch your belly?"

"Sure," I say. "But call the anesthesiologist. You have to hurry." He nods. Then walls rush by. I am wheeled into surgery. "Don't let me die," I say.

He takes my hand. "I haven't lost anyone yet."

I throw up into a metal pan in the operating room. Then fleeting, momentary awareness. Floating, again, out of my body. Then a bed, a window, Joe asleep in the chair beside me, clasping my hand.

I've lost a lot of blood. Joe's mother comes up for a week to care for me as I recover. She irons, reads to me, and talks, quietly. When she leaves, my mother comes up to care for me. She revisits old wounds and vents a storehouse of anger. She acknowledges making deliberate choices to hurt me, in retribution for choices I've made that have hurt her.

"How could you not invite me to Joe's conversion to Judaism? Even if it was a small ceremony, I should have been here."

"You've been so mean to us this year, Mom," I say. "Joe wanted the weekend to be filled with love. He didn't invite many people. And this was Joe's choice. You haven't been very welcoming to him."

"Too bad," she says. "You should have invited me. And because you didn't," she continues, smiling, "when it came time to organize a celebration for your brother and his new wife, I decided to schedule it for that same weekend. I told you it was the only weekend I could get the venue, but I could have done it the following weekend. I didn't want to. I wanted to make it difficult for you to come. And your failure to attend was duly noted by everyone in the family. So there!" Her smile is triumphant.

I am still so weak from surgery that I need help walking down the steps to the living room. I need help walking to the bathroom. Yet I cannot believe this woman is my mother. I don't care if I have to crawl to the bathroom. I cannot wait for her to leave.

My recuperation takes months. Tests reveal a blockage in my remaining fallopian tube, a congenital malformation, probably a consequence of medication my mother took to avoid miscarrying me. I feel submerged in a lake of grief, yet when I paint, I am surprised to see images that offer an unusual view of the operating room during the surgery. I begin to reckon with the reality that part of me slipped out of my body to float above the operating table during the procedure. I am filled with amazement and gratitude for my life.

———•———

Infertility proves challenging. I focus on what I can control, beginning a private psychotherapy practice with a feminist orientation, working collaboratively with friends, diving into a satisfying career. Joe and I begin to study a healing modality based in Jewish mysticism. I continue to work in therapy on the intractable conflicts with my mother. But the healing training softens me. I develop more compassion for myself and my mother. I see my own role in our conflicts more clearly. I become less reactive to her provocations, recognize the depth of her childhood wounds. I read books about narcissistic parents, the way children are affected and recapitulate their own injuries on others. I work on my own personality fractures. The Kabbalistic Healing training becomes crucial five years later.

My mother phones on a bright fall day just before the Jewish holidays. "Jane," she says. "My chiropractor found a lump in my abdomen. My gynecologist ignored my complaints for the past five years, and now I have advanced ovarian cancer. I'm scheduled for surgery."

"I'm so sorry," I say. "Joe and I will drive down to be there for the operation, and we'll stay for a while afterward."

My mother recovers well from the surgery and begins chemotherapy. Her many friends work out a schedule to drive her to treatment. Our phone calls change in frequency and content.

"Joe," my mother says, "this is what my oncologist said. What did he mean?"

"Jane," she says, "I need you to come home for a few days. I always feel better when you're here." I fly home more frequently. We are more often affectionate, loving.

Joe and I drive down for a visit. We carry the suitcases upstairs, and Joe goes back to the parking lot to move the car. My mother looks at me appraisingly. "If you don't lose weight and start coloring your gray hair, your handsome husband is going to have an affair with his nurse."

My immediate response is to laugh, though I am aware of feeling shocked and hurt. "Joe's nurse is a gay man, Mom. It's not likely they're going to have an affair."

After my mother's first year of chemo, I ask an oncology nurse for a few moments of private time. "Could my mother handle a trip to Santa Fe? She's always wanted to go."

"If she wants to go, take her," the nurse replies. "This may be her only chance."

That summer, Joe and I take my mother to Santa Fe. Marsha flies in to meet us, and we spend time with Nancy, who has made a permanent move to New Mexico. It's precious time, filled with laughter, shopping, delicious meals, and splendid sunsets. During the next four years of chemo, my mother often wants me near. I continue therapy to work on untangling years of complex interactions with my mother. I am able to recognize my contributions to that complexity more clearly. Our time together is often sweet, but conflicts remain.

———•———

The following May, Marsha and I arrange to meet in New York for a long visit with my mother. After lunch in a restaurant, we return to my mother's white Volvo, shining in the bright sun of a perfect spring day.

My mother settles behind the wheel. I settle into the passenger seat. She dons sunglasses.

"Those are great sunglasses," I say.

"You like them?" She peers in the rearview mirror before removing them. She hands them to me. I am wearing contact lenses, so sunglasses are useful.

"Try them on," she says. "Larry sends boxes of them from Hong Kong. He gets them for next to nothing on the street."

I slip on the sunglasses and turn to model them for her and Marsha.

"They look lovely on you," Natasha says.

"Those do look great on you, Janie," Marsha adds from the back seat.

"Would you like to keep them?" Natasha asks.

"Are you sure you want to give them away?"

"Of course. I have plenty."

"Great," I say. "I'd love them."

Natasha smiles as she brings her face close to mine, and in a voice suddenly tinged with utter contempt says, "You always were so greedy."

It is as if a snake inside her rises up and hisses the words through her mouth. I never know which personality will emerge, not day to day, week to week, or minute to minute. In time, I come to see how my mother, like all of us, contains unhealed parts of her personality. Some are very young parts. They're split off, not integrated into her adult self, and uncontrollable. Her behavior is painful to me, but it must be so much more painful for her.

By spring of 1999, I've pushed my mother's oncologist to make a long-overdue referral to hospice, which can provide care, equipment, and a social worker. Marc and I meet with the social worker a number of times to talk through some challenging issues, like my mother's refusal to be buried with my father. She wants her body taken from New York to Virginia to be buried with her brother and sister-in-law. The social worker helps my mother make the final decision to be buried beside my father in New York. During that spring and early summer, I fly to New York often. For my mother's seventy-ninth birthday, my brothers plan to take over. Larry will fly in from Hong Kong, and Marc will drive up from New Jersey. I'm with my mother for the week beforehand but plan to return to my home in Maine before her birthday. My clients have been patient with my frequent absences, but I have a responsibility to them, too.

I am sitting on the living room sofa, sipping tea and staring out the bay windows at the flowering fuchsias on our front porch. A wave of guilt and longing washes over me, and I turn to Joe, who is sitting beside me. "This is going to be her last birthday. I should be there."

"You should," he says, standing up and walking toward the kitchen. "I'll call the airlines." A few minutes later he returns. "You're booked on an early-morning flight. You'll get to the apartment by ten o'clock. And you'll fly back at nine o'clock tomorrow night."

I stand up to kiss him. "Thanks, honey. I'll call Marc and ask him to keep it a surprise."

It's a warm, clear summer day. The morning flight goes off without a hitch. Larry has arranged for a car service. Marc answers the door when I press the buzzer. My mother is sitting up in her brass bed, surrounded by vases of fresh flowers.

"Oh, Janie!" she says with a surprised smile. "I'm so happy you came back. Now you're all here. What a wonderful birthday!" She's wearing the gift I left for her, a pink bed jacket. "Look how beautifully this fits me," she says. "I love it." She's weak but has put on makeup for the occasion. She pats the bed for me to sit beside her. She reaches for my hand and holds it as we talk. Marc's humor brightens the day. Larry picks up food from the local deli. I help my mother to the dining room table. I've set it with her good china. It's a lovely last birthday.

Ten days later my mother calls while Joe and I are at a graduate seminar for our healing program on Cape Cod. "You need to come home," she says. "I'm so weak that I fell. I'm dying."

I phone hospice and my brother Marc. Then I call my cousin Nancy. "Can you fly in from New Mexico? My mother says she's dying. Hospice says they don't see that, but patients usually know. Marc and I will need your help."

Joe and I drive to New York. He stays for a few days. Marc, Nancy, and I move in for the duration. My mother stops eating, drinking, and talking. Nancy and I share my mother's brass bed as my mother hovers between life and death in a hospital bed beside us. We wash her, wet her lips, and change her sheets. A ceiling fan whirs overhead, as ineffectual as the window air conditioner against the insufferable summer heat. Marc's humor keeps us sane. We grow closer. I slide onto the bed beside my mother. I hold her, caress her, sing Hebrew prayers to her. My dear friend Simma joins us. Hospice provides an aide. The days seem both precious and endless.

Larry sends money. Marc and I go to the funeral home to choose a casket and make arrangements. The gravesite is prepared—my father is buried there. Natasha dies on August 4th, the anniversary of my ectopic rupture and near-death experience. Marsha flies in from Los Angeles and rings the doorbell a minute or two after my mother has taken her last breath.

I am completely exhausted, but for once in my life, I feel that I've done enough.

Relatives arrive. The night before the funeral, I lie in my husband's arms and wail, filled with grief for so many things: my mother's suffering, our long-standing conflicts, the sweet periods of closeness we shared in the last years of her life. I also feel enormous relief. Her death has extinguished an intractable struggle in a complicated relationship, but my mother's influence is not extinguished. We remain in relationship. I hear her voice, sometimes in my own. I see a trivet at an antique store and think of her. I attend a play I know she would have loved. I see her expressions on my face. I bake when sorting through problems. I struggle with irritability and moodiness. As issues arise in life, I check in for tune-ups in therapy. I understand her more clearly. My compassion for both of us grows. I carry her DNA. The imprint of our relationship still marks me—in ways that are good, and in ways that are not.

More than eighteen years have passed since my mother's death. I still feel relief. Freed from the complicated pain of our interactions, I can see the woman she was in relation to others more clearly now. I can celebrate her many strengths, her varied skills, her gifts, her humor, her affection, her intelligence, her love for people. I also understand more clearly the fractures in her personality, but most importantly I can see the wholeness of the woman she became, living the life she was given and transforming what she could into the life she desired.

Reflection: "Natasha"

During an afternoon workshop with Pat Taub, sponsored by Maine Writers and Publishers Alliance, I recognized how many stories I held in memory about my mother. Jenny Radsma's invitation to sign on for a longer exploration sounded like a wonderful opportunity to explore mother-daughter issues with a group of other writing women, especially since I'd spent innumerable hours on both sides of the couch, as a client and as a therapist, doing just that. I knew my mother's history, like all of our histories, shaped the woman she became and the woman I became.

Through this collaborative process, I came to see my mother more clearly and objectively, recognizing why so many people loved her, realizing how she loved and helped so many. I came to understand how complex and multifaceted she was, to accept that while she had many gifts and was quite beloved, it was not solely my fault that our relationship was so fraught. It took many years and much work for me to depersonalize her criticisms, to understand that her hostility and eruptions emanated from her own anxieties and depression, the unhealed parts of her personality, and sometimes from the side effects of medications. Through my own therapy, and through writing, I saw more clearly how the wounds of her childhood were carried into her adult life. I understood the multigenerational history of trauma in my family and its impact on my mother. Over time, I saw more clearly the stresses in my parents' marriage and realized the impact those stresses had on my mother's relationship with me.

Through this journey with my writing friends, my collaborators, I began to truly value all my mother taught me—through example and direct instruction: to create a beautiful home, to take pleasure in entertaining, to value relationships with friends, community, and family. She taught me to extend myself to others, to laugh, to read, to appreciate art and theater. She taught me to relish life, to crawl back from tragedy and loss, to make the best of situations, to use humor in the midst of the darkest days. She taught me about style, fashion, jewelry, china, and treasure-hunting in junk shops. She taught me to cook and bake with imagination, fearlessness, and flair, using recipes as starting points. She taught me how to love.

Natasha had a personality so big there was no containing her. Though our relationship was often painful in my adult years, I now more clearly understand the forces leading to the distance between us. I recognize, too, that for a woman who loved glamour, style, beauticians, gossip, and tall tales, my seriousness must have been both confusing and tedious. And as I have come to see more clearly the ways my choices and behaviors were hurtful to her, I feel deeper compassion for us both.

I must also acknowledge my inability to write about Natasha as a mother from a place of identification and personal experience. I have never been a mother. I imagine I would have recapitulated at least some of my difficulties with Natasha with my own children.

The era in which Natalie parented contributed to some of our struggles. I did not grow up as she did, with grandparents, a mother, and uncles who gave up everything to flee to a new country, nor did I live in a small town where many of my peers died overseas in a world war, nor did I feel the shame of being Jewish in times when Jews were hunted and murdered en masse. But the effects of those traumas seared my ancestors, my mother, and her generation, and they filtered down to me. Fear, shame, and a lack of a sense of safety in the world create chronic anxiety. Trauma was not well understood in my mother's era, nor was it treated with the compassion and skill that are available today.

If Natasha lived today, her talents could easily be put to use in a corporation, but Natalie wanted to be a mother. She wanted to nurture a family, to be a wife, to create a lovely, welcoming home. Of course, those goals were promoted as the right goals by society, so I might simply say the era in which she lived both constrained my mother and allowed her to fulfill some of the roles she desired.

And this is the stuff of life. It is the thread among our shared stories. There is no perfect mother. I don't know how well I would have mothered or how well I would have stood up to examination in an essay such as this one. In my generation, psychotherapy is normative. Not only have I practiced as a psychotherapist for almost thirty years, I've been a client for many years as well. I am much more aware of my flaws and fractures than my mother was of hers, and I consistently work to heal what I can and temper the effects of those I can't. Natasha was certainly a "good enough" mother. She rose above innumerable obstacles to fully engage with the world, bringing light and laughter, love and nourishment through her voice, her curious and sharp mind, her humor, and—of course—her talents in the kitchen.

I am grateful for my collaborators on this journey. Our work together has enlarged my vision, enlightened me, and allowed me to honor my mother in ways she truly deserves.

The Questionable Letter

by Cheryl Gillespie

The plump manila envelope sat unopened on my kitchen counter. After twenty-eight years, I had finally worked up the nerve to send for what was in it but not the strength to look inside. What if it wasn't there? The theory I had clung to for so many years would be blown to hell. It took me a couple of days to find a good time to open the packet. I moved it around in the house to different spots. To the side counter by the refrigerator. To the dining room table. I waited until I was alone. These notes detailed the four months my mother spent in the Augusta State Hospital, a psychiatric hospital in Maine, more than a half century ago in the fall of 1948. They would be too emotionally upsetting to share with my husband or daughters, at least at first.

That late summer afternoon in 2012, I fell deeper and deeper into this pile of photocopied papers for at least four hours. The stack began with my mother's involuntary commitment to the mental health institution. The clinical description of my mother, then twenty-three years old, was bluntly objective with phrases such as "body very undernourished, but no vermin noted though very untidy. Uncooperative, spoon-fed." Handwritten notes from nurses were obviously not intended for the eyes of the patient's daughter. I had anticipated they would be hard to look at, but my reaction was much stronger and more visceral than I had imagined. I felt like I was at the scene of a car wreck with no control over what was happening.

I pored over interviews of my mother that were mixed with testimonies of close friends and relatives, including my father. Curt observations by a doctor were in a challenging, handwritten scrawl. Careful records of weights and blood pressure readings, along with shock treatments administered, were hastily printed by different hands on a single chart. Someone actually quoted my mother as saying "I am going to get out of this dishpan alley somehow." I paused and wondered if the inclusion of this notation reflected a medical person's sense of humor. A comical, naïve description my mother gave to a doctor concerning her roommates not acting normally on the ward made me laugh out loud, and some of my tension eased momentarily.

I hit the bottom of the pile after reading a letter my twenty-four-year-old father signed for the doctor in which he promised to bring my mother back to the hospital if she showed any signs of regression. The one document I was hoping to find was missing, though. There was no letter signed by the psychiatrist verifying my mother's sanity. I had spent my life clinging to the notion that such a document existed. I grew up hearing about this official letter. What was I to think now? How could I resolve my feelings about my mother's illness? I felt betrayed.

I have spent most of my adult life trying to unfold the mysteries surrounding my mother. We were not speaking to each other when she died in 1984. She called a friend for help instead of me the day she collapsed alone in her house. As she lay semicomatose in the hospital for a couple of days before she died, I felt angry with her. I stood stoically at the foot of her bed. Friends hovering nearby tried to get me to talk to her. They told me even though she did not respond, she possibly could still hear me, but I had nothing to say to her.

My denial about her impending death was so strong that I drove home and called a center that provided constant care and asked about the availability of a spot there. I had always worried about my mother and figured I would continue to do so. I was genuinely surprised when I got a phone call telling me she had died a day later. I remained upset with her for a long time. I believed no one understood what I had been through with her, particularly in the last couple of years of her life. My husband was probably the closest person who could best understand, but he was young with parents who were vibrant and still working. He had them to turn to, but I was at a complete loss. I was also pregnant with my first child. I worried about losing the baby as I had experienced a miscarriage a few months before. The odyssey of repressed anger, resentment, and grief I started traveling often consumed me.

Upon Mom's death, Holly, one of my favorite maternal cousins, attempted to comfort me. "Don't think of the trying last few years of Grace's life," she said. "Instead, remember the 'old Gracie' before she became so ill."

I never told Holly this before she herself died of cancer, but the trouble with her advice was that I never knew which Grace I was apt to be dealing with at any given time. The unpredictability of my mother's behavior was one of the most challenging things about her. As many people do, Grace saved her most difficult behavior for her immediate family. Beyond my father, my brothers, and myself, few people knew all the sides of my mother. No one outside of my nuclear family knew of this "letter of sanity" that I grew up considering very important to our family's existence. I had to cope with the irony of an outwardly popular parent who was hell on wheels at home.

Grace was born at the wrong time. When she was a young woman in the 1940s and 1950s, people did not talk openly about mental health issues or being hospitalized for such problems. She tried to follow these societal rules, but since she truly believed she was an example of a cured patient, she would sometimes talk about her travails with mental illness. It cost her dearly. She was stigmatized and suffered loss of respect and job opportunities because of her actions, yet she gallantly tried to educate prejudiced people and commiserated with other sufferers of mental health issues. How different that part of her life would have been had she been a member of her granddaughters' generation! Although they never met her, both of my daughters visibly bristle at the stories I tell them of the discrimination their maternal grandmother Grace experienced. Thinking of her bravery concerning those issues still gives me chills.

One thing my mother did not talk openly about was the abuse she suffered at the hands of her alcoholic father during the first twelve years of her life. Hints of this would come out of nowhere as I was growing up. For example, one day when I was about ten years old, I was helping her put up new curtains in our living room. On a stepladder, she was struggling with cramming the curtain rod into the curtains I was feeding her as I stood by her feet. The back door opened, and we were startled as my father was not due home this early.

"Good God, Cherie, take these curtains!" Mom whisper-shouted as she threw them down on my head. "If your father catches a glimpse of legs with my housedress up my thighs like this, I'll pay for it with the son of a bitch later."

"What?" I asked as I pulled the mess of curtains and rod away from my face.

"You'll learn soon enough about what abusive bastards they can be, kid."

I had no time for any more questions as my father came into the living room and swooped me up in a hug. My mother scurried to the kitchen.

Another time not long after that, my mother and I were driving down a road near our house to visit a woman my mother liked to help. She pointed to a dirt road that led off into the woods and announced, "That's where your father raped me when we were dating. I was only fifteen. You have to be careful with men. They're all the same. Bastards!"

Once again, I had no time to question her as we arrived at the dooryard of her friend, and she jumped out of the car and hollered, "Come on. What are you waiting for?"

After my mother's death, her two older sisters decided to act as surrogates to me and my young family, even though one lived in California and the other in Connecticut. One traveled to a camp in Maine every summer, and the other joined her as often as she could. They called me. They sent packages to me for my first baby. One summer day while pregnant with my second baby, I left my three-year-old daughter with a babysitter and went out to lunch with the two of them. We planned to drive an hour up to central Maine where I would show them where their biological parents were buried. I knew they had not grown up with my mother and her younger brother Ira John or their brother Kenneth, but I was hazy on the details of their separation. I decided this would be a perfect opportunity to quiz them about some things.

"Do either of you remember my father being abusive to my mom?" I asked over my lobster roll. Aunt Cora and Aunt Flippie looked at each other and then at me. These two sixty-something ladies soothed me. My mother at five foot three had been the tallest sister. Although short, they all had a sturdy bear shape. My mother appeared a combination of the two sisters' looks. I always told people if one put Aunts Cora and Flippie in a bag and shook it, out would come my mother Grace.

"Are you kidding me, dear?" said Cora. "Your father? He never raised a hand to her no matter how much she fussed at him. Why?"

"Mom told me he raped her while they were dating."

"Oh, dear, I don't think so," said Aunt Flippie.

"Her own fucking father raped her!" Cora said. "She always transferred guilt, didn't she, Flip?"

Flippie tried to mutter something about not knowing exactly what went on in my mother's biological home, but her older sister Cora outshouted her. Cora, a former Wac or member of the Women's Army Corps, spoke bluntly.

"Our father Kent was a drunk who abused Gracie and our mother Myrabelle. I didn't even want to look at him at our mother's funeral, but relatives forced us to kiss the bastard on the check. Jesus H. Christ, do you remember, Flip?"

"So you were at Myrabelle's funeral?" I asked.

"Yes, we were, dear," said Flippie.

"Mom always said her mother died of neglect during an asthma attack in the sanitarium," I noted.

"What? Who told you that?" asked Cora. "She died of congestive heart failure. I read her death certificate," announced Cora without waiting for me to answer.

I began to realize that some information my mother had shared with me was not exactly based in reality. I asked about the breakup of the family.

"I'll remember it forever," Cora told me.

"I remember that day, too," added Flippie.

"My mother always said she was a nursing infant, and that was 1924. Heavens, how old were you two then?" I asked.

"Cora, weren't you five years old?" asked Flippie.

Cora nodded and said, "Yes, and you were only three, Flip. Do you really remember it?"

"I remember feelings of it even though memories are shadowy," whispered Flip. "But you tell her, Sis. Your memory would be better."

Cora started, "I was starving and cold as usual. It was the month after Grace came along. She was born at the end of October, and it was cold in that shack in Windsor after her birth. I was supposed to be watching sister Flippie and brother Kenneth while Mother was sitting in that old rocking chair trying to feed Grace, but I was fussing at her about not wanting another baby. She said things like

'Babies just come, Corabelle. Can't do anything about it.' She was so sick she had a hard time getting out of her chair. Young as I was, I was scared.

"She had just asked me to check the fire in the woodstove that night when we heard a commotion in the yard," continued Cora. "Mother told me to grab Flippie and Kenneth and scoot into the bedroom and slide under the bed. That's what we always did when Father would come home from a bender. 'Push way against the wall,' she said, 'so your father won't see you. You know what he's like when he's drunk, Corabelle. Keep everyone quiet. Put your finger in the baby's mouth if you need to.' She put your mother and a blanket in the box she had been using as a bassinet and tucked it in with us."

"I remember being under that bed," Flippie chimed in. I listened as Cora continued.

"By the time she was out of the bedroom and back in the front room I heard voices, but none of them was the old man's voice. I just stayed under the bed. Didn't know what to do. Sounded like more than one man was talking to Mother. She hollered for me to come out with Florence and Kenneth. Knew it was serious when she called us all by our formal names. She hollered for us a second time, and I rolled out from under the bed and pulled up Sis and Brother. I left Grace in the box. For some reason, she wasn't howling. We three stood at the bedroom door in order of age. Ken must have been about two years old. Three men looked back at us. Lord, we must have looked like a set of canisters, one slightly larger than the other, but none of us taller than the latch on the door we stood next to.

"Mother was crying. I recognized one of the men. He was the reverend who used to call on us to talk to Mother. He always seemed upset with her. He was kneeling at Mother's knees and talking to her that night. The other men stared at us and made comments about how bad we looked. They used terms like 'filthy rags' and 'not getting enough to eat.' Then they grabbed us. One grabbed Flip and Kenneth, and one latched onto me. Mother really started screaming then. I bit the man who held me. I remember him fussing, but he didn't hit me. The reverend must have noticed his uplifted hand since he told him I had seen the back of a hand one too many times already. They turned to take us out the door. Grace started to cry then. The man holding me asked the reverend about taking her, too, and the reverend simply replied no. Told him they'd go back for her when Myrabelle had a chance to get her 'weaned.' Remember not knowing what the reverend meant by that. He said they'd upset Myrabelle Murray enough for one night. They took us to a car in the front yard. Finally let me have Sis on one side and Brother on the other as we sat in the back seat. Flippie, you cried, but Kenneth never did. Funny about that. He just clung to my side. The reverend came out after a few minutes and told the man behind the wheel to get going. I remember the reverend was crying, and the other man sitting with us made a comment about it. I had never seen an older man like that cry before. Obviously, they never went back for Gracie. She was left behind."

"And she was there for twelve years?" I asked.

"Oh, yes, Cherie. Ira John was born when she was eight years old. We were allowed to see them occasionally. They were twelve and four when relatives finally took them. Myrabelle became so ill she was placed in hospital care at that point," explained Flippie.

I was overwhelmed with this information and sat pretending to eat for a few moments as my aunts did the same. I would have other chances to question these ladies about family history. The day had become too heavy for more grilling right then. It was my first inkling that my mother's sisters knew she had problems. This was the first day I remember feeling empathy for my mother.

One of my mother's favorite stories about her childhood pertained to a new glass washboard someone had given my grandmother Myrabelle. Grace claimed time and again with paradoxical glee that at the age of eight she had knocked out her drunken old man Kent by jumping up on a stool and breaking this board over his head. She always announced that he had been "messing with her again." Unfortunately, Myrabelle, complacent with her husband's behavior, was only upset with Grace for ruining her new washboard. I never knew how to react to that story. I was still grade-school age when she started sharing this tale. Was I to be impressed by her audacity, or was I to understand how difficult she had it compared to my easy life? It didn't matter because Grace would always announce with indisputable certainty at the end of the retelling that all men were bastards, and the subject would be changed.

In the late 1950s on a trip to Perry's Nut House in Belfast, Maine, Grace found a knickknack in the gift shop that consisted of a five-inch horned man standing on a base that read "Men are beasts." My father forced an uncomfortable laugh as he purchased it for her. He didn't say much as he drove us all home. My cousin Holly happily displayed this figurine in her china cabinet for years after my mother died. She was surprised that I didn't want it as she thought it was a great joke.

When my mother was eight years old and her brother Ira John was born, their mother was quite physically disabled with remnants of polio and asthma, among other things probably cardiac in nature. Gracie's alcoholic father Kent would leave the family for days at a time. Not producing enough milk for the new baby boy, Myrabelle asked Grace to walk to a neighbor's farm situated two miles from their house. There she would be given a pail of goat's milk. One day, coming home from the journey for this supplement, Grace met with a mean German shepherd dog that bit her on the left cheek. The owner of the dog realized Grace's family could not afford a doctor, so he brought her to a horse doctor who lived nearby. The result was a deep, crooked scar she carried for life. When she was in a self-deprecating mood, she would call herself "Old Scarface." Her version of the story was that the dog had mangled her face when she was only four years old and had accidentally fallen over a fence into its yard.

It was not until years after my mother's death that I found out from Ira John about the goat's milk and her real age at the time of her confrontation with the dog. He talked about how guilty he always felt. He told me, "Our mother always said, 'All Grace worried about was spilling that pail of goat's milk before getting it home for her baby brother.'" This was another example of my mother altering history to transfer guilt from one person to another. She obviously didn't want any blame for her scar to fall on her baby brother.

The year Grace was twelve, her mother Myrabelle became so ill that she couldn't get out of bed. Grace tried to cope with caring for her mother and her four-year-old brother Ira John as best she could with the help of a neighbor and friend known as Jackknife Fred. Jackknife was a poker buddy of her father and lived in a shack behind their house after winning some bet Kent could not pay off. Luckily, Jackknife was kind to Grace, Ira John, and their mom. My mother often talked about this friend cutting wood for them and bringing food, even if it was sometimes just squirrel. He didn't let them starve like Kent did. A few years later when Grace would ask relatives to take her to visit Jackknife, she would be told that he was a bad influence and not someone a young lady should befriend.

In their small community, word about Myrabelle's ill condition traveled quickly, and soon Grace's two paternal aunts arrived to gather her mother and take her to a sanitarium. Left alone, Grace and Ira John were told to take care and wait for a relative to pick them up.

The experience was obviously traumatizing for my mother, who told me over and over again about being in her mother's bed with Ira John while waiting for someone to come for them. She would start the story with: "It was in the middle of the night, and I couldn't sleep. Ira John had finally dropped off but was sleeping restlessly. I suddenly was startled by a presence just above my head. Then I relaxed when I noticed it was my Aunt Edie, you know, my father's sister. I was so glad to see her. She started to pick up Ira John, and I began to get up, too. She hushed me and told me to stay in bed. I told her I wanted to go with her, but she explained that her husband Uncie was not ready to take on a half-grown girl. When I protested, she told me to give her some time. She was sure she could talk him into letting me join them soon." Edie never did, and my mother waited a few more days alone until someone from her mother's side of the family came and picked her up.

After that, my mother was passed around to well-intentioned maternal relatives who appreciated the "help around the house." An intellectually brilliant person with the tenacity of the toughest central-Mainer, Grace eventually became the perfect housekeeper and babysitter for her maternal uncle's family, which included four young girls. She was the classic overachiever at school and the darling of her teachers. She became the first female recipient of the Bausch & Lomb Honorary Science Award upon graduating from high school in Winslow, Maine.

While still in school, Grace worked at a photography studio. Her favorite part of the job was retouching negatives for the photographer. She marveled at how blemishes could be erased and other problems could be concealed. Fixing these things seemed to give her hope, and she loved to talk about it for years afterward.

Grace skated into her adulthood, holding it together, until a series of unfortunate events in 1948 knocked her down. She was twenty-three. After marrying my father Albert, she lived with him and his parents on a farm in Benton, Maine. With a husband who insisted "withdrawal" was the only acceptable form of birth control, she gave birth to two boys within seventeen months much to the chagrin of her mother-in-law.

I was a young teen before I realized the significance of my mother's "bale of hay" story.

"Steve was not supposed to happen," my mother would begin. "The nurses told us at the hospital that mothers who breastfed had less of a chance of getting pregnant. I was still breastfeeding Wayne as best I could when I got pregnant again. Mother Grant announced that we couldn't afford a second baby. What was I to do with it? I went out to the barn and lifted bales of hay until I almost passed out." My brother Steve would simply listen in silence when our mother recounted this story over and over as we grew up. Other troubles followed.

Soon after the birth of my brother Steve, my paternal grandfather Grant died of a heart attack at age sixty. He left my father Albert with a farm deep in debt, which was devastating for the young couple. A small house my father had built on a side lot of the family farm for Grace, himself, and their two young sons was sold, put on skidders, and hauled off down the road a couple miles. Years later my mother sat on the steps of a playhouse my brother Steve built for me at our childhood farm in Winslow and cried about how it reminded her of her little house that she lost to the Grant fiasco. I reluctantly spent time in the playhouse haunted by the sight of my distraught mother. Pictures of my little house still bring forth that uncomfortable feeling for me of not understanding my mother's emotions about it at the time.

Grace and Albert lost the family farm in Benton, Maine. Grace's mother-in-law moved in with a sister-in-law, and Grace and Albert bought a tiny house in nearby Winslow. Two boys in diapers were a challenge for Grace, who became gaunt and anemic. One day, Albert came home to find Grace unconscious on the floor with Wayne and Steve unattended. Friends tried to watch her to help as Albert held things together, but she attempted suicide twice, with the second try being a dramatic jump out of a third-story bedroom window at the house of a friend who was trying to care for her. Although Grace recovered physically, this attempt left her in an impossible state that seemed beyond Albert and the caring friends who had been aiding him.

In the fall of 1948, Grace was committed to Augusta State Hospital, a huge, formidable stone institution that housed approximately two thousand patients with a variety of problems, from mental illness to substance abuse to mental disability to misunderstood menopausal issues. One psychiatrist was there to care for all of them with the help of two interns. Grace suffered primitive diagnoses and a great deal of misunderstanding. Thus began her "four months in hell," as she referred to it. She purged her wretchedness by telling tales of her time there in the hospital. I was her most frequent audience even at an age when I had no ability to comprehend what she was telling me. Her medical records I received years later helped me begin to understand what had actually happened to her that eventful fall.

Grace entered the psychiatric hospital in a straightjacket. She was not even taking care of her personal hygiene. She was diagnosed with dementia praecox, catatonic type. Not responding much to anyone for almost a month, she was given a series of electroshock therapy treatments to bring her out of her severe depression. After twenty-one treatments, she was coherent and began therapy. Relatives and family friends sent letters to her doctor concerning the abuse she had received as a child at the hands of her father. They seemed to want the doctor to understand that her condition was an unfortunate circumstance beyond her control and not an illness that ran in the family.

Her constant refrain at the hospital was: "I need to go home and take care of my house and my boys. I'll be good and do my work." Time and again in the hospital records it noted that Grace asked attendants and doctors if her children were going to be taken away from her. She worried they would be taken by the state like her older siblings had been years before. She decided to submit to what she was told was her place in life as a wife and mother. She promised she would accept the hard work of raising her boys and caring for her home.

In the hospital, Grace met a fellow patient named Cheryl Lee. Cheryl confided to Grace that someone in charge was forcing himself on her, and then she hanged herself in the bathroom. Four years later, I became this dear lady's namesake. There was only one brief mention of Cheryl Lee in the hospital notes I received, but no reference to her suicide. I know I represented the grave injustice that Grace could do nothing about but always regretted. This name has weighed heavily on me at times. My father never approved of it. As a child I really did not understand the gravity of the story about Cheryl Lee, and I would have preferred to be a carefree Deb or Sandy.

According to hospital records, Grace became submissive in the hospital to the point that she allowed my father to slap her across the face after she sassed a nurse in front of him. This was something I never saw him do later. She turned twenty-four shortly before she was discharged in my father's custody and sent home. My father did not keep his promise to bring Grace back if her symptoms reoccurred. Her life was a cycle of mania and depression, with periods of normalcy mixed in. These "good" times appeased us and allowed us to weather the difficult episodes, for the most part.

My mother's cousin who lived with her as a child has informed me many times that the Grace who went into the hospital never came out. She has said, "We didn't get our Gracie back." I have often wondered what my mother was like before the hospitalization. How had she been altered? I tried to look through the bitterness that encrusted my mother and imagine what she was like as a young person.

At times, Grace was a great mother and even a Sunday-school teacher. She would bicycle with my brothers and me. She had a loyal circle of friends. Then there were the periods when she would not get out of bed for days on end. I always felt that I had some control over her moods and would try to cheer her up by doing different things like staying home and serving her tea. I loved to cook with her. She was an incredible pie baker. As she created her apple pie or lemon meringue masterpiece, I would watch at the side of the kitchen table. I inherited pie crust scraps as she trimmed her pies. It was my job to sprinkle these pieces with cinnamon and sugar and roll them into twists that Mom would bake with her pies. I loved those days.

I began to notice that there were times of the year that she was more depressed than others. My mother's depression was severe at Christmastime. The December I was seven was no different. Carpentry work was scarce for my dad, so he and my brothers busied themselves selling trees and wreaths to supplement the family income. We understood that the money was to go for essentials. My brothers said nothing about the very few presents we received, but I was silently disappointed. I swam in some hand-me-down black snow pants from a cousin. I wore them daily to school as it was a bitter cold winter that year. Mom apologized to me several times about the necessity of wearing these pants. I tried to tell her I didn't mind, that my friends and I spent all recess sliding on our butts down a hill on the side lawn of the elementary school. Those baggy snow pants worked great for that, but she didn't seem to hear me.

Shortly after that Christmas in January, I stayed home sick from school. This was a frequent occurrence that landed me the nickname "snot rag" from my brothers. Sitting at the kitchen table with the family remedy of saltine crackers soaked in tea in a bowl in front of me, I was startled when my mom entered the room and plunked a large bag down in the middle of the table.

"For God's sake, Cherie, sometimes I'm absolutely friggin' useless, I swear," she announced. "I completely forgot about these damned things. Hid them in too good a spot."

"What?" I sniffled.

"I got these for you for Christmas and forgot about them. Should probably hold them a couple weeks for your birthday, but what the hell. Your grandmother Myrabelle would always say 'We could be dead tomorrow so enjoy things today.' Look inside the bag, sweetheart."

Now, I loved it when my mother started swearing. It was a sign she was getting feisty and coming out of a period of depression. I grabbed the bag and peeked inside. The things at the top were of the clothing nature, so I tried to smile at Mom and look appreciative.

"Keep looking now," she said with a devious grin.

I pulled out a box I found at the bottom of the bag and peered at it. My mom took it from me and opened it while she blurted out, "I had a set like this when I was little. Think it was a gift from Aunt Bertha. Christ only knows what happened to it. Mom, Ira John, and I had to farm ourselves out to whoever would take us during the winter when that son of a bitch of a Kent would leave us high and dry. Probably got left someplace."

Kent was my deceased grandfather. I figured he must have been an evil-looking little creature with horns from the way my mother always talked about him. Mom seemed to be far away for a minute or two, then she shoved the box in front of me, almost knocking over my bowl. I fished around inside the paper wrappings that emitted a chill from the unheated upstairs of our old farmhouse and pulled out a child-sized teacup. More cups and tiny saucers followed, until finally I hit pay dirt with an adorable little teapot. Everything was real china with delicate pink flowers decorating the sides. I immediately worried I might drop one of the pieces and break it. I looked up at my mother. She sat in the chair next to me holding a cup and saucer in her hand with a look of enchantment on her face.

"Shall we have tea, my dear?" she asked.

"Indeed!"

We sipped tea and ate saltines spread with grape jelly. My bowl of soggy crackers was pushed aside and left uneaten. I almost forgot my cold until I had a sneezing jag. I apologized as I blew my nose, but my mother didn't notice. She simply brewed a second tiny pot of tea that we enjoyed as we stayed close to the kitchen oil stove that kept us warm.

At other times, the least provocation would send Grace into a raging tantrum. My brothers and I knew to stay away from her then. We waited until she had calmed down and was singing. That was our cue she was all right to approach.

When my mother's mood was upbeat, she would make many plans about changing her life. I was her confidant at these times, and she shared more than what was appropriate for a young girl to hear, including details of her sexual relationship with my father. My dad was painted as a beast by Mom during these monologues. She would not let me visit my paternal relatives during her manic times. My brothers could go visiting them with my father, but I was not to be tainted by these horrible people. To this day, I feel I did not get to know my father like my brothers and even my husband did. I still struggle with resentment toward my mother because of this.

My mother fought bitterly with my father, and when she became really enraged she would throw in his face the fact that he had committed her to Augusta State Hospital. I never knew what to think about that. She would rail about how he ought to have his brains fried twenty-one times because maybe it would do him some good. She would also talk about her letter of sanity if he questioned her moods.

Although I really did not understand it, this "sanity letter theory" would sustain my brothers and me when we were stigmatized by people outside the family. One late afternoon when I was about ten years old, I had a silly fight with a friend on the bus. When my brother Steve and I got off at our stop, which was about an eighth of a mile from our house, this friend and her sister hung out two bus windows and chanted several times, "Cherie's mommy's crazy!"

Steve and I stood looking back in humiliation until the bus stopped. The bus driver hollered at them, and they pulled themselves back inside as the bus rolled away. I glanced up the road to check if my mother was watching from the window where she sometimes perched while waiting for us. I wasn't sure if I was glad or not that she wasn't there.

"Stevie, what do you think Mom will say about this when we tell her?" I asked.

Steve grabbed me by both shoulders and put his face in mine. "Cherie, you're not going to say anything about this to Mom! Do you want to upset her? These neighbors are ignorant. Mom was in a hospital for a breakdown years ago, but she has a letter of sanity now. Just ignore those idiots."

I really wanted to see this letter, but I did not dare ask any more about it.

Different versions of my mother's medical history circulated in the family. This confused me dreadfully. My mother said her family doctor had always thought she had a blood clot at the base of her brain. This was the cause of her erratic behavior and breakdown when she was twenty-three. The blood clot could have been a result of the severe beatings that she had sustained as a child at the hands of her abusive father. This doctor's theory was that the twenty-one shock treatments she was given in the fall of 1948 at Augusta State Hospital had dissolved the clot and allowed her to recover. I liked this theory for years as it allowed me to think that she wasn't really mentally ill. There was a physical aspect to her problems, and it was not a condition I had to worry about inheriting.

Whenever I tried to question my father about the blood clot idea as a teen, he became very uncomfortable as if he were hiding something. I also wondered why he said nothing to her when she raged at him about committing her to the hospital. He did not say a word to anyone about the family doctor's theory. He just continued to protect my mother as best he could. He gave me what hints he felt comfortable giving. My mother tried to divorce him three different times, and due to legal fees they lost their farmhouse as a result. Between separation numbers two and three, they started looking at little project houses to buy to get out of the small, uncomfortable apartment we were living in on Sand Hill in Winslow. They were tired of being the token Protestants in a French Catholic neighborhood. I was thrilled as these houses were in the same neighborhood as a close school friend of mine. My father noticed my enthusiasm and pulled me aside to speak privately.

"Cherie, don't go thinking we're going to actually buy one of these houses now," he said in his quiet, cautious tone of voice.

"What do you mean, Dad?" I asked.

"God only knows, your mother won't stay in this good mood for long. I can't afford to buy another house. I've lost too much as it is. Try to understand, please."

I didn't ask about the houses or moving again.

My father pretended nothing was wrong even when my mother refused to get out of bed all day. At times he would physically carry her from room to room. He would be considered an enabler today and maybe part of her problems, but I thought of him as her savior. He tried to protect me from her illness. For example, on the morning of my wedding, my mother was upset. She did not go with me to the farmhouse where I was to get ready with my maid of honor and friends. I was determined to have the wedding proceed and was not going to let her ruin it. I was surprised at how startled friends were about my calmness concerning my mother's absence at this supposedly important time. My maid of honor's mother fussed over me and commented about my mother's absence. This intrigued me. I felt my mother had always provided challenges to other family members' plans, and this was just another incident. It seemed no big deal to me. Mom arrived in time for the service with my dad at her elbow.

My brothers reacted differently to our mother than I did. Wayne was six years older than me, and Steve was four years older. I now realize that Wayne probably always saw our mother as ill. He would question her about her moods and actions to the point where she would slap him in rage. Steve was more her confidant even though I always noticed that he, too, worried about her as if something was really wrong. Enabler or protector, Steve was very loyal to Mom.

I never felt I was allowed to have an opinion about my mother's health. My mother bluntly told everyone she had me to try to save her troubled marriage, and it did not work. She was still miserable and would be glad when I was grown up and gone. I felt guilty about this and tried desperately to be the perfect daughter. I would feign illness and stay home from school to keep her company if she seemed depressed. I could make myself vomit on command. Steve once marched me back to our house from the bus stop and tried to tell my mother I was faking sickness. She told him to get back to the bus stop and mind his own business. She didn't care about my school absenteeism. I stayed home. We had tea and watched soap operas as usual. It seemed to make her happy, and that was what I wanted.

My mother's actions and requests of me when I was in my teens often worried me. I was frequently asked to go downstairs to the store underneath our apartment and shop for a few items to put on her running tab, a convenience small, local grocers used to afford customers. My mother knew if I went down and requested things the owner would not have the heart to deny me as he might deny her, as her tab ran very high at times.

One Saturday morning, my mother woke me up and exclaimed she needed my help.

"We need to help Barb with Everett. Quick, get your clothes on. We need to get to their apartment right away," she explained.

I knew better than to question her, so I threw some clothes on, and we drove the half mile to her cousin's apartment. My mother and Barb spoke quietly in the kitchen as I sat with Barb's four-year-old son in front of cartoons. I was startled to hear moaning coming from the bedroom of the tiny three-room apartment I knew so well from babysitting for Barb.

"Let me dress little John, and we'll be ready," said Barb as she and my mother came into the living room. "Everett's already dressed. He never took off his clothes last night. Grace, how can I ever thank you?"

"Get ready," replied my mother. She looked at me. "Cherie, Everett's not taking his Thorazine. Barb can't handle him. We need to help her take him down to Augusta State."

"What's he not taking?"

"Everett's a schizophrenic, Cherie. He's giving Barb a hard time about taking his medication to control it."

"Oh, geez, Mom, I didn't know that. So, I'll stay here with little John?"

"God, no. We need you in the car with us. Everett's a big guy. He could give us trouble."

"What will we do with Johnny? We don't want to take him there, do we?"

"We'll take him. We can all fit in the Volkswagen bug."

"Don't they have ambulances for this?"

"My little high-strung princess, grow up. We can do this." Mom's scowl was interrupted by Barb, who came back into the room with her little boy and tall, thin husband. We went outside and folded Everett into the front passenger seat. Barb, Johnny, and I crowded into the back seat. No one spoke, except for Everett. He muttered nonsensical things as he rocked back and forth in his seat.

It was a thirty-minute drive from Winslow to Augusta, and I was petrified the whole way. I was sure Everett would start acting out of control and cause a problem. Maybe even a car crash. As we sped along, my mother gripped the steering wheel tightly and spoke only in sound bites through gritted teeth to Barb, saying things like "almost there" and "hang on now." I noticed Barb was weeping. Johnny clung to his mother. Just as I thought I couldn't stand being washed in reality by Mom anymore, she made a sudden turn into a driveway. We had arrived at the hospital. Everett stopped making noises and looked scared. My mother simply grabbed his left arm.

"Everett, this is where you need to be!" she proclaimed. Barb patted him on his shoulders. With the help of my mother, she got him out of the car. I stayed with little John in the car and waited. No one asked me to do this; it just seemed right. I remember being shocked that my mother took someone she knew to this hospital. I had listened to her tell so many horror stories about this place. I never dared question her about this, and I still wonder how she justified helping Barb commit her husband Everett there when she had scolded my father for years for doing the same thing to her.

As a teen, I started noticing the different ways people reacted in my mother's presence. My paternal aunt Ruth was long-suffering and overly patient with Grace even when Grace went out of her way to irritate her with nasty remarks about my dad's family. My mother would fuss on the way home from a visit about how foolish Aunt Ruth was. "She wouldn't say *shit* if she had a mouthful" was an expression my mother would use to describe her sister-in-law. I loved Aunt Ruth, and it confused and angered me dreadfully to hear my mother criticize her. I wished my father would speak up for her, but he never did. My brothers were close to this aunt, too, yet they never questioned my mother's right to demean her.

My older brother Wayne died suddenly eleven years after my mother passed away. He was only forty-nine. As he had made the military his career, his commanding officer gave a eulogy at his funeral. I wanted Aunt Ruth to hear a taped version of it and brought it to her house in central Maine. At this point in her life, the family nemesis arteriosclerosis had taken its toll on her ability to think clearly, but she gripped the arms of her rocking chair and cried as she listened attentively to the officer's voice.

After the tape stopped, she rocked and chanted over and over again, "First Albert and now my Wayne. It's not fair. It's not fair."

"I'm sorry to upset you so," I tried to say, but she didn't seem to be hearing me.

"Sit with me, Cherie. Sit for a while with me. I don't know you. Grace hardly ever let you visit. Sit with me now."

I sat with her that afternoon. She told me how she felt she did not know me because my mother kept me from her as I got older, and my parents experienced three separations. This was the only time she ever openly expressed anger about my mother's behavior. I was astounded. I had not realized how she felt. We lost Aunt Ruth not long after that, so I was glad we had that time together.

I eventually began to understand that people who needed to deal closely with my mother usually ignored her quirks. People who did not see my mother often suffered her wrath after questioning her.

My maternal uncle's wife Alice tried to confront my mother about her problems when we visited them at their home, which was an hour away from our house. They inevitably ended up arguing as my mother would always start screaming at Alice and tell her she was a spoiled little girl who had no idea how she felt. Things became so difficult between them that we stopped seeing this branch of the family. My brother Steve, in allegiance to my mom, started talking about how overly religious these folks were, and how he wouldn't miss having to visit them. I missed them. This aunt and these cousins had been very kind to me.

Ironically, the cousin closest to my age from this family is the image of my mother. Her father and my mother looked alike enough to be fraternal twins, even sporting the same crooked grin. At a recent gathering after years of not seeing each other, she and I talked a bit about my mother. She was not surprised when I talked about my mother's illness. It did not startle her to hear my version of how my mother's life ended. Did everyone know about how ill my mother was except for me? Over our coffee cups, my cousin told me how her mother was bothered by how my mother treated me so harshly. It never occurred to me that people noticed her gruffness with me.

I wonder now if people were waiting for me to break down or fall apart as my mother had. In high school, I discovered that the adults around me treated me a little differently from other students. I would use this to my advantage. In my senior year, I started doing things such as running out of classes and hiding in the girls' room. I was delighted to find out that the administrators would not punish me for doing this, especially if I cried. Teachers did not call home with issues about me. Maybe they weren't eager to deal with my mother, who had developed a reputation for being difficult when my brothers preceded me in school. Many teachers let me slide by. I would get an occasional sad look of sympathy. Some were pleasantly surprised when I did something well.

In school, I had to learn to self-motivate as my mother did not have the emotional energy to care about my school achievements or lack of them. I also started the process of physically separating myself from my family as I finished high school. It was easy to do. I became very involved with a loving, protective young man who did not consider my family as unusual as I did. He accepted me. My brothers were out of the house. My boyfriend, who was an only child, loved both of them when they would visit. My parents were embroiled in their on-again, off-again tumultuous relationship. No one seemed to miss me. I became the cousin that people forgot. I noticed that my oldest brother basically did quite the same thing by going into the military and not coming home very often. My other brother Steve was the family-oriented one who visited relatives as often as he could, including dining with relatives who lived near the university he went to in Orono, Maine. Ironically, these were the same relatives whom he had dismissed a few years before for my mother's sake. Steve then proceeded to move to Mobile, Alabama, for a job upon graduating from college. He did seem to enjoy the distance.

Steve managed to convince my father to pay for my freshman year at our state university, even though Dad thought educating a woman beyond high school was a waste of money as I would just marry and stay home with babies. I gleefully packed amid my mother's protests. I was angry that she did not want me to leave after spending years complaining about having to raise me. I proceeded to marry my high-school sweetheart the next year in 1971 and left my parents' household for good to live in Old Town where we both finished college. I went home as infrequently as possible, even when my mother started having severe cardiac problems. After all, my father was her caretaker.

In 1976 I took a teaching position in Chelsea, Maine, which is one town over from Windsor, my mother's childhood hometown where I had stood at my grandmother Myrabelle's grave for luck before my interview. I was ecstatic to get the job, even though it would be an hour-long commute from where my husband and I were presently living in Brunswick. The school principal introduced me to the staff as a person with roots in the community. One teacher well into her seventies asked who my relatives were. When my family was explained, this senior teacher bluntly announced that my grandfather had been the town drunk. She refused to speak to me for the rest of that school year, which was her last one before retiring. I got a very small taste of the shame and discrimination my mother grew up with during this experience. I was dumbfounded. My mother was still alive at the time, but I was never able to share this with her.

My father died unexpectedly in 1978 at the age of fifty-five, and my brothers and I took over Dad's job as Mom's caretaker as best we could. Mom had a brief period of time where she seemed happy and relatively healthy. She volunteered a couple of days a week in my second-grade classroom, and my students adored her.

"Grammy Grant is visiting today, so let's clean up the room," I announced to my second graders one school day.

"I love her!" announced chunky Troy over the cheers of classmates.

"Why, Troy? You don't usually like much around here," I teased.

"She gets me! Makes school more fun." With that, Troy was off to help neaten up the coatrack, and left me to ponder how she did such a thing with Troy and not me.

I was pleasantly surprised by her ease with students, but comments from fellow professionals about seeing who I took after as a teacher left me feeling disconcerted. Unfortunately, Grace soon developed congestive heart failure and became very ill. Being the only one in the state near her, I scurried to her house to get her to medical help.

Upon arriving at my mother's house, I found her sitting peacefully in her reclining chair. She was too calm.

"Mom, we need to get you over to see your doctor," I said as assertively as possible after noticing how swollen and blue her legs looked.

"I'm fine, dear. Just fine," she said while coughing. "Be a dear and go put on the kettle for tea."

"Mom, a couple of your friends have called me about how bad off you are. We really shouldn't waste time. I'll call your doctor's office."

"I'm not going today, Cherie." This was all she could speak without coughing. When the fit stopped, she added, "I'm too tired to get dressed up and go today."

"Mom, we need to get you out of the house before something happens."

"My little drama queen, what can happen? I'll die? I'm ready. I'm tired of this old life anyway."

"I can't sit here and watch you die, Mom!"

"Then go home, sweetheart. I'll be fine."

My heart seemed to stop. I sat and looked at her for a moment. I noticed she had supplies around her chair as if it was impossible for her to get up out of it.

"Jesus, Mom, I just drove an hour and a half to help you out."

"Then stay the night. You can have the bedroom to yourself. I've been sleeping here in my chair. It's comfortable with this darn coughing." And another coughing spell overcame her.

"You're having trouble getting out of that chair, aren't you?"

She managed to stop coughing long enough to scowl at me. That's when I realized that I was in for a serious battle. I had never won one head-on with her. My method of achieving what I needed to with my mother was to sneak around behind her back or simply take off and leave her to eventually accept something. I didn't have the time for that on this day. At that point, she had already died and been resuscitated so many times, I had lost count. She closed her eyes and appeared to be napping. I called one of the friends who had alerted me to her condition that day. The two of us decided that it wouldn't be wise to upset my mother in her condition, so I said I would stay the night with her and try to get her to the doctor's in the morning. This friend told me that if Mom was still giving me trouble she would send her adult son Neal to help me force her into the car. After I calmed myself down as best I could, Mom and I had tea. Or rather, I drank tea while watching my mother cough. The television blared in front of us, and the time passed.

Mom struggled to get up from her chair and walk to the bathroom before going to sleep that night. I helped her. I couldn't imagine how she had coped with her physical condition to this point. I spent a sleepless night in her bedroom around the corner from where she rested in her chair in the living room. I agonized over every coughing spell she had and worried about her labored breathing.

Daybreak found us eating cereal while I willed the clock to get to a point when the doctor's office would open. I called the office at eight o'clock. An overly patient receptionist tried to soothe me and said the doctor would receive my mother as soon as I could get her there.

"Mom, your doctor can see you right away this morning. How about we get ready and scoot over?"

My mother just looked at me.

"Mom, please?"

"I told you I'm all set now. I don't want to go to the doctor's. I'm tired of the battle. Let's talk about who I would like to give a few special things to now."

"Good God, Mom, what are you doing? You're too young to be talking like this!"

"I feel it's time, Cherie. Now I'd like those Friendly Village dishes to go to Lucille's daughter to finish her set. I know she loves them. Wayne's June can have the Blue Willow dishes since he got them for me in Japan."

"To hell with the dishes, Mom! I can't sit here and let you do this!"

"Let me go, darling. Let me go."

I called the friend who had offered her son as help. I couldn't tell if my mother could hear who I was talking to or not, as the phone was in her kitchen. I'm sure she knew what I was doing. When I returned to my mother, she was sitting with her eyes closed, but she was breathing. I glued my eyes to the television screen. Neal arrived within minutes and came into the kitchen from the back door.

"Grab your purse, kid," Neal said. "I'm going to pull Grace's VW as close to the front door as I can get it and leave the side door open. You jump in the car and keep it going. I'm walking Grace out the front and putting her in the passenger seat. As soon as I close the door on her side, take off and don't stop till you get to the doctor's office. Okay?" Neal actually seemed to be excited about this mission.

"Neal, what if she tries to jump out?"

"She won't. Ma thinks if she sees me, she'll know that everyone wants her to go and she'll cooperate."

"Oh, God. Well, she's in her chair in the living room."

I had barely gotten settled in Mom's VW when Neal came out the front door with her. She looked scared. He was struggling while trying to support her as she had such trouble walking.

"Take care now, Gracie. Mom says hi." Neal slammed the door. I gave him one quick, desperate look. He grinned at me and waved. I started driving. Neal was correct. My mother said nothing as we drove the six miles to the doctor's office. She had given in.

Her doctor was startled by her appearance and asked me to take her immediately to the hospital. The idea of calling an ambulance instead of taking her in a car surprisingly never came up. The doctor told Grace he needed to run some tests. She went with me to the hospital like an obedient dog. She started to smile and talk to the people at the emergency room. I relaxed somewhat. She was admitted and put in a room. I ran out after telling her I'd get some toiletries for her at the nearest drugstore. When I returned, her room was empty.

"Where's the patient who was just put in this room?" I asked a nurse in the hall.

"There was a code blue, I'm afraid."

"What?"

She must have realized who I was at that point. "They were successful at reviving her, and I believe she is in ICU." That is where I found her.

Mom met a charming cardiologist who talked her into having a pacemaker inserted. Friends and relatives came and told her that as someone in her mid-fifties, she was way too young to leave us. She nodded her head at them. My brothers both arrived from out of state in time to celebrate Mom's return to a somewhat healthy state. They went back to their respective homes right afterward, and Mom never did feel well again.

Years later, my brother Steve talked about how we should have respected her wish to die. How could we have let someone that young go? She never forgave me for forcing her to the hospital that day. Try as I could for the next five years, I never visited her enough, or did the right things when I did visit. Her erratic behavior had her friends calling me at all hours of the day and night with stories and pleas for me to do something. A friend called to tell me my mother met her at her door with a shotgun in her hands. Another told me that Mom had fled a gas station with the gas hose flying out of her car and causing a mess.

During one hospital visit, my mother's cardiologist slyly got a psychologist who was also a Catholic Brother to informally evaluate my mother's mental condition. This Brother proceeded to tell me that my mother was mildly psychotic, and she did not know the truth from the fiction she made up at times. I felt insulted by this. Did he not realize that I knew something was wrong with her at this point? Was it that obvious that I pretended not to know she was so ill?

My brother Steve and I found a congregate living facility for senior citizens and those with disabilities in southern Maine, which had a psychiatric nurse. Mom begrudgingly visited the facility with my brother and me and was even invited into a unit by a resident who was the mother of a teacher I worked with in Westbrook. This lady was lovely and spoke very positively of the place. The staff was willing to take my mother with her mental-health history, while other facilities were not once they spoke with her doctors. My mother accused me of trying to "have her committed again." Obviously, she equated this placement with her forced entry into Augusta State Hospital back in 1948. As my brother was paying her mortgage at the time, he informed her she was to try this place. He would close her house but not sell it. Unfortunately, there was a waiting list at this housing facility that was just a bit too long. They called to tell me of an opening for her a month after her funeral.

Grace left the world the way she lived for most of her life: she picked fights with people and insisted she needed no one's help. After several heart procedures to repair the pacemaker that never worked correctly, my husband and I tried to have her live with us in our house for a while. After the most upsetting tantrum she threw in which she declared she wanted to go home, I called both of my brothers. Over fifteen hundred miles away in Mobile, Alabama, Steve was very worried and didn't know what to tell me. Wayne, in Maryland, was more blunt with his advice. He said, "Take her home and let her have her way. You can't fight her anymore."

I followed Wayne's advice. I was pregnant with my first child at the time and worn out. My mother's health was infringing too much on my own health. Having lost a baby the year before, I was dreadfully afraid of what this battle with her was costing me. I brought Mom to her house, which was an hour and a half from mine and left her with some groceries. She would not say goodbye to me. I just left. Two weeks later I received a call from my cousin Holly. She had gone to check on Grace and found her face down in her living room. In her bathroom, an empty pill bottle rested on its side in the sink. Some of the cardiac medication it had contained was in the toilet.

My mother was rushed to the hospital and admitted. Holly told me she was unconscious, and there was no hurry to get there on my part.

I was planning to go up to the hospital early the next morning when my phone rang just before midnight. The sagacious cardiologist who had spent the last few years trying to help Mom said quietly, "Grace is comfortable in a regular ward. She is not aware of her surroundings. She is medicated and feels no pain. Is this okay with you, dear?"

I said it was. No mention was made of the pills discovered in the toilet at her house. No toxicology tests were ordered. There was no need to know. Grace lingered for three days before she left us physically. Still feeling anger and frustration in my caretaker role of her, I stood at the foot of her bed and watched her as I cradled my baby bump. I was still in battle mode with her. I missed her actual death since I went home to rest to appease my worried mother-in-law and husband and thought I needed to make plans for when Mom was released. When I received the phone call about her passing, I was in disbelief. Somehow I thought she would keep coming back. Some of her friends avoided speaking to me at her funeral as if I had purposely botched her care. I was buried in guilt concerning what I might have done differently.

After spending the past several years caring for her, I was left with an incredible hole filled with time and quietness. I played up my pregnant condition to the hilt and allowed people to care for and fuss over me. I sat on the lawn of my mother's house the day after the funeral and watched my brothers, my mother-in-law, and my mother's sister Flippie clean out her house in preparation for selling it. At one point I found my brother Steve sitting in the driver's seat of the truck he and Wayne had rented to haul stuff off to the dump. He was smiling and reading something he held in his hands.

"What's that you have, Steve?" I asked.

"Love letters. They're really something," he replied.

"Who wrote them?"

"Mom wrote them to Dad one of the times he was staying at Aunt Ruth's and she wanted him back. Want to see one?"

"God, no! Why would she write those? Always told me she hated him."

"You never really understood their relationship, did you, Sis?"

I turned and left him to the letters. I just could not handle talking to him about the subject at that point. I did not want to talk to anyone about my mother. I postponed grieving for her until after my daughter was born and settled into my life. I paid a price for that in physical and emotional ailments.

At a teaching staff meeting a month after my mother's death, I became involved in a game that was introduced to help a new principal get to know us teachers better. We were supposed to tell the stories of how we got our names. I was emotionally very raw. The new principal looked out at the group and pointed at me to start the activity. I was a young, pregnant thing who perhaps appealed to him. I was caught without my usual filter in place.

"Oh, my name is really unique. My mother did a stint in Augusta State Hospital, they call it AMHI now, about four years before she had me. I was named after a young woman who hanged herself in the bathroom after being raped by someone in charge," I said glibly.

After I shared this anecdote, the silence of my fellow teachers was disquieting, but the face of the new principal displayed absolute horror. It surprised me that adults were so shocked by this story. I began to realize I was covering my own unhappy childhood in shrouds of sarcastic, brusque comments, but I could not talk about many events from my early years without making a farce of them. If I did not laugh, I would cry, and that was too painful.

Later in the day, a friend and school counselor tapped me on the shoulder and talked to me about seeking therapy. At that point, I realized I had to try to investigate my mother's life and how it affected me instead of ignoring it or at times even running away from it. I did put it off until after I had the baby, though. I tried grief therapy and overwhelmed a nurse therapist with talk of my family. She quickly informed me that my problems involved more than just my mother's death. I went home and burned my mother's half-finished autobiography written on green surplus paper from a mill in Winslow in my woodstove. I cried and scolded myself for saving it from her house.

I kept trying to ignore my mother's life and its effects on me until I found my ultimate catharsis. On the heels of my older daughter investigating her grandmother's life for a school paper, I started writing Grace's biography about seventeen years ago. I have written and rewritten it several times. Each rewriting shows greater understanding and acceptance of her. Slowly, I am finding peace and renewed love for her, but I still fret over so many things.

I have always felt left out or slightly different from the people with whom I share my life. Never believed I quite belonged. At the age of sixty plus, I have become educated, relatively accomplished in my profession, and the matriarch of a successful family, yet I still feel like I am on the outside looking in more often than not. I don't know why. Is this a reflection of my mother's unusual status in her family? Is it merely the result of my birth order? Is this just my temperament? What is it that makes me feel excluded?

Upon reading some of my musings, my daughter Kelsey wrote the following: "My mom's writing about her mother displays two polar opposite emotions; she portrays my grandmother as both the heroine and the villain of her own story. There are moments in my mother's writing that expose deep love for the woman who gave her life. She recognizes that her mother was strapped with more than her fair share of burdens in her life and that despite her faults, she did the best she could. And yet, there are times when she still seems frustrated with the woman who criticized her, pushed her father away, and could be nearly impossible to live with. My mother seems at odds with these two seemingly separate versions of Grace. Did her mother do her best with what life gave her and love her children to the best of her ability? Or did she use her struggles as an excuse to display unwarranted cruelty to others out of bitterness?"

I struggle to explain to Kelsey how complex this mother/daughter relationship was. Is it possible to both love and hate someone very close to you? Should I just try to hate memories of my mother's illness? As a child, it was impossible for me to know when her behavior and comments were driven by an unhealthy mental state. Did she possibly use her delicate condition to manipulate people, especially my father? I certainly have toyed with being devious. Did I learn this from her? It is only as an older adult that I have reached the stage of maturity where I can look at my mother more objectively as a person totally separate from myself.

I do marvel now at comments from relatives and friends when they talk fondly of my mother's frankness and sharp-tongued sense of humor. A good friend Jo-Ann always laughs when she recounts how she met my mother for the first time when we were seventh graders. I brought this dear friend home from school, and we came upon my mother spading in a flower box and swearing a blue streak at the back steps of our apartment. Mom informed us that a neighbor's cat had "shit" in her flower box and was going to "friggin' kill" her plants! She paid no attention to my friend as she cussed. I stood aghast, but my friend—whose mother was a prim, devout Catholic—did not seem deterred. In fact, she recently enjoyed retelling the story over lunch as my stomach twisted. I now realize that my mom's quirkiness was sometimes perceived as fun by others who did not have to live with her. My family never spoke openly about being worried about her illness, so why would people have interpreted things differently? Our ruse in public worked too well.

My daughters have quizzed me about how I became the type of mother they know. To them I am so different from the mother, their grandmother, I describe in my writing. I think I looked for surrogates or models often. I loved some of my aunts. I would watch their gentleness with children. One of my maternal aunts was playful and loving when I stayed with her in the summer. A paternal aunt rocked me in her large wooden rocking chair when I was a small thirteen-year-old crying over new braces on my teeth. One of my mother's dear friends who watched me, often when my mother was struggling with difficult episodes, was a wonderful person and mother. I can remember watching her with envy as she sat in the same big, overstuffed chair with her husband while we all sat and watched television at their house. It astounded me that parents could be affectionate like that.

As a young teacher, I was blessed with older female colleagues who were incredible mentors to me. I gravitated toward and appreciated the wisdom of these women and learned a great deal from them. I must have been a good listener, as many of these teachers enjoyed offering help to me as a young teacher who was eager to have them share their knowledge. In recent years, it occurred to me that I have mentored several young teachers myself. Then I must admit that when my own mother was feeling well, she was an incredible teacher herself and must have shown me enough glimpses of the "good mother" for me to emulate. Once again, our relationship was a complicated paradox of feelings and interactions.

I have spent most of my life trying not to be a bother to anyone. I was the foster grandchild who refused to call my great-uncle's wife "Memere." I am still the biological cousin that the other cousins never really knew because I stayed with my mother instead of going with my father to family gatherings. Since both of my brothers died young of cardiac disease, cousins often forget to invite me to family events or even relay news of births and deaths. When I do go to family functions, relatives gaze at me like I am the ghost of my mother. My mother obviously puzzled them, and they probably have unresolved feelings of grief about her young death. I feel uncomfortable and usually do not stay long at such affairs. A sense of unfairness engulfs me. Is it my fault that my childhood family members all died young?

I brood about my anxiety and worry about signs of it that I see in my daughters. I watch my brother Steve's children and grandchildren for signs of problems. I feel guilty that I have allowed a long estrangement to take place between my older brother Wayne's two children and two grandchildren and myself since his death. My niece died in her forties after a troubled existence, and I struggle to accept this. I feel guilty if I do not take cautious care of my health or question some of the cardiac medications I am taking. Nieces remind me that I am "all they have left" of their dad's family.

Grace is still with me in many ways these days. I overcompensate for my childhood by doing things like buying a very expensive mother-of-the-bride dress and then anguishing over the price of it as I look at it in my closet. My older daughter Darcie recently picked peonies and hydrangeas for her bridal bouquet. These were two of Grace's favorite flowers. Darcie is also a quintessential lifelong student who downloads and listens to history lessons as she is doing her hair and makeup for work. Grace, too, was a studier when she was well. My other daughter Kelsey is a passionate champion of underdogs as her grandmother was. Kelsey loves nothing better than to debate philosophical issues as her grandmother did. Both girls have Grace's candor, which does not always win them friends! Grace would have loved so many things about them. They are both brilliant young women who question things in life and strive for competence in their work.

Grace sneaks out of me from time to time. It is not always one of her best qualities that bubbles out. As I get older, I would like to think that I can recognize negative behaviors that I have learned from Grace and catch them before damage is done, but I have done my fair share of apologizing to people in all aspects of my life.

Sometimes, some Grace sweetness emerges. The first time I rocked my infant daughter Darcie to sleep, I subconsciously started singing "An Irish Lullaby," and then I cried. Grace always sang that song when rocking a baby. Maybe she had loved me as best she could. I feel I have such a profusion of the upsetting memories that the good memories are often lost in them. I now visit the remaining few of Grace's friends and same-age relatives. I bask in their recollections of the good things they tell me about my mother. These memories allow me to put some of my pain in perspective.

After much deliberation, investigation, and time spent pouring out my thoughts in words, the importance of "the letter of sanity from the Augusta State Hospital" has finally diminished for me. Perhaps the letter existed. Perhaps it didn't. It "existed" for my mother when she needed it, and as a mature adult I can now understand why she needed this crutch at times. Maybe she was wise enough to realize how it helped us, as her children, in a very prejudiced world. I will simply have to accept that I will never truly know if it was real, and I will never have a twenty-first century diagnosis of Grace's problems and their causes. Does it really matter if she was suffering from a head injury, mild psychosis, or post-traumatic stress disorder as a result of her abusive childhood? Perhaps there was a physical aspect to her illness, but does that make a difference? I find peace in trying to appreciate how much Grace did accomplish in life despite what she was dealt.

Reflection:
"The Questionable Letter"

In the summer of 2000, I started writing about my mother Grace. By then my entire immediate childhood family was gone, so I felt compelled to record the family history. My mother had been the focal point of my family. We protected her, catered to her, and constantly worried about her, so I decided to start with her story. I was inspired by the fact that in her senior year of high school, my older daughter Darcie wrote about how her grandmother's life was greatly affected by the passing of a federal child protection law in 1920. This project was for an Advanced Placement English class, and she received recognition for it from Syracuse University. I wrote about Grace in the third-person point of view and treated my writing as fictionalized biography. I became her as I wrote, and the words flew out. If I got upset or too close to her in my writing, I could take off the mask of her and be me again.

I had always felt very alone about the fact that I had such incredible angst about my mother. Working with the writers of this anthology, I found an invaluable, cathartic outlet. I feel very blessed to have worked with such a wonderfully tolerant and caring group of writers. These women have come to know me better than many of my close friends, and I can speak to them openly about my mother without making my usual sarcastic, protective jokes about the dysfunction I saw and experienced.

I could not wear a fictitious "mask" and write my piece for this anthology in third person. Writing about Grace from my point of view as her daughter was an incredible challenge. It was painful. It was risky. I struggled continuously with this assignment until I sent away for Grace's hospital records from the fall of 1948 when she was a patient at Augusta State Hospital in Augusta, Maine. I received them in August of 2012. I pored over them many times. At first upsetting, these records have soothed many anxieties and answered several questions for me.

I am curious about how interested friends and family have been in this anthology project. Grace's life has been a mystery to many people. My mother's illness was kept hidden from so many of her relatives. My two daughters have been particularly interested in this work. Younger relatives seem to want to know this family history even if it leaves a sour taste at points.

This work has given me a new sense of significance and importance. I am now glad that my mother did share her feelings about her life and problems with me, even though it was difficult to hear and understand at a young age. I would encourage anyone to pursue this type of writing, though it can be agonizing and time-consuming. This work has brought me closer to my family than I have ever been, and I feel good about being able to share family history with them with a mature perspective. Grace has become a real person in my daughters' lives. They have enjoyed learning about this grandmother whom they never had the chance to meet.

My younger daughter Kelsey writes to me with the simplicity and generosity of a young person, and in closing I quote her: "I am not sure what happens when you die. I would like to think there is something more than this life, but I cannot fathom what that might entail. Wherever Grace is now, I hope she gets to see my family. I hope she gets to see my mother at school. I hope she gets to see her daughter reading aloud to children, teaching them grammar, reaching out to the students whom she can tell need a kind word or special nudge. I hope Grace gets to see my sister living her big-city life. I hope she sees her travel to overseas countries to do business. I hope she watches me swim. I hope she got to hear me doing a radio ad for my credit union or sees me leading a staff meeting at work. Grace was a smart woman who, with different parents, a different hometown, living in a different time, might have done great things. Though circumstance and hardship prevented her from reaching her full potential, there is some solace in the fact that each generation that follows her does a little better. I am not sure if my grandmother could have pictured a life for herself like the one I lead. A life with loving, stable parents. A life with a fulfilling career and her own apartment. A life with friends, an education, and happy memories. But I would like to think that the fact that I get to live such a life is the world's way of atoning for the injustice it showed to her."

The Essence of Mom *by Jenny Radsma*

"Mom fell sometime during the night," Frances says on the phone. "I'm on my way to the hospital." Given my mother's increasing frailties, this early-morning call isn't exactly a surprise. Just the same, my sister's news rattles me and makes me clumsy after we hang up. My hands tremble as I brush my teeth, and a sense of dread worms into the pit of my stomach. I think about my eighty-seven-year-old mother lying on the floor of her assisted-living room for who knows how long. Despite my sisters' repeated rehearsals with our mother to help her remember what to do in just this type of event, the pain and confusion from falling must have so disoriented her, she never thought to depress the call button suspended from her neck.

A fall is often the undoing of otherwise healthy elderly people, and my mother is no exception. She undergoes surgery later in the day to repair her fractured hip, and thereafter Frances updates me daily about what turns out to be a poor prognosis. On days my mother is alert enough, Frances holds the cell phone to Mom's ear. Her words are slurred, the residual of a stroke she suffered days after the surgical repair of her hip. Some two weeks into this ordeal, I hear her say in a dull, flat voice difficult to comprehend as my mother's, "Jenny, when are you coming home?" She pronounces my name with a Dutch inflection, "Yenny."

She often asks this question of me in anticipation of my next visit, but this time her question resonates as something deeper. She's weak and more vulnerable than ever before, and the reality sinks in that my mother is unlikely to regain the ground she lost from this cascade of events, that she will no longer be the person who asked me this same question only four months ago on New Year's Eve. That night, together with residents and visitors, we welcomed in the first few minutes of 2011. After singing "Auld Lang Syne" with everyone, Frances and I swallowed the last of our tea, then rose to put on our coats. Mom accompanied us to the foyer of her building. At the door, she leaned across her walker to kiss me. I hugged her in return and tried to impress everything about that moment in my memory. I took in her stooped back, gently strumming my hands along the washboard of her ribs beneath her sweater; I patted the short gray hair she curled with rollers every night, using the same sponge-and-bristle curlers she had used for over fifty years. I breathed in her clean smell, heard her uplifted voice, saw the perpetual white tissue peeking out from where she had tucked it up her sleeve. I felt her velvety soft cheek against mine. The gold wedding rings she wore, her own and my father's, clinked together with the movement of hands now shrunken by age. The sparkle in her eyes, her visible happiness and contentment—I imprinted it all.

As we said goodbye, Mom asked me, "When are you coming back?" pronouncing *when* as "ven."

She held my hands and I told her I'd be home in late spring, less than six months away. I promised to call every day.

These scenes race through my mind when I hear my mother, in the fog of dementia and postoperative pain medication, ask me on the phone, "When are you coming home, Jenny?"

"As soon as I can, Mom."

I am a college professor and with only a few days left in the semester, I pack my things and make arrangements to be away for an extended period of time—I find someone to proctor my final exams, someone else to tend my home. On the first day of my journey by car, I cross the international bridge spanning the shores of the St. John River from Maine to New Brunswick. I pull up to the customs office, where the officer on duty slides open the window and scans my packed Subaru.

"*Bonjour. Ou est tu habite?*"

"Fort Kent," I say, handing her the American passport card I received a year ago after becoming a naturalized citizen.

"Where are you headed?" she asks, switching to English.

"Calgary," I answer. Her face registers surprise at my destination some six provinces away. Then she asks, "What is the purpose of your trip?"

It's my turn to stare; how do I answer her? Do I tell her my mother is dying? That I want desperately to be by her side, to hold her hand and stroke her remarkably soft skin? I want to hear once again the stories and family lore I assumed she'd be around to tell me for years to come. I want to tell the customs officer of my disappointment not to be granted just one more summer to hear my mother talk to me in Frisian, her mother tongue, the language she passed on to her children, the *taal* in which she loved and scolded us, my sisters and me. Who else will call me "Yenny"? I thought for sure I'd have at least one more chance to feel her pat my knee and hear her say "*Lietse skat,* it's so good to be with you."

But these are not the details the officer wants to hear. With a slight shake of my head, I regain my focus: oh yes, the purpose of my visit.

"Vacation," I answer. After years of crossing the border, I know better than to give more information than asked.

I have nothing to declare, no alcohol, no tobacco, no fruit, no mace or pepper spray, and no gifts, just my clothes, my computer, and a few books, as well as my bicycle on the rear bike rack. The officer hands me back my card and wishes me a good trip. A few miles down the road, I turn left onto the secondary highway, and in less than two hours I am at Saint-Alexandre-de-Kamouraska in Quebec. I connect with the Trans-Canada Highway, which stretches across Canada from the east to west coast. In Alberta it passes through Calgary, directly alongside the hospital where my mother lies. The four days of travel before I will arrive leaves me ample time to mentally scroll across the years in which my mother and I have loved, admired, taken for granted, laughed with and at, argued with, been frustrated by, as well as hugged and comforted each other. My gaze takes in the fresh spring green of the Quebec landscape, the blue sky punctuated by hundreds of brilliant white snow geese, pulled by an invisible magnetism to their northern habitat. I observe the cycle of nature in living color, a fitting metaphor for my mother, who is nearing the end of her journey.

With little on the road to distract me, I register the heaviness within me. My thoughts revert back as they have so often these past six months to October, shortly after Mom moved into assisted living. Then two of my sisters, in the way of my oldest sister many years before, divorced themselves from the family. Over the past few years, as my mother's frailties and needs increased, so too did their mounting grievances about my mother's failings: her passivity and lack of initiative, the perception that our mother favored her younger daughters. "Don't bother me with anything more about Mom," one sister emailed the rest of us, while the other, "boiling with rage" my mother said, returned the briefcase holding our mother's paperwork. It was my sister's way of ridding herself of anything to do with the family, including the management of our mother's finances, a task she'd capably handled for many years. Certainly we sisters had our differences—we shared few of the same interests, and from time to time our individual sensitivities and temperaments contributed to misunderstanding and spats between us. Still, I thought we shared an affection for each other and an interest in one another's and our mother's well-being. I never imagined we could unravel so abruptly or so completely. Hurt, dazed, and shaken by this unexpected turn of events, Mom, Frances, and I spoke often to soothe and comfort one another, to try to make sense of this splintering within our family.

In light of such upheaval, we three needed to be together over Christmas and New Year's, if only to reassure ourselves that we remained a family, albeit a bruised and shrunken one, that we loved and cared for each other, that we trusted and could rely on one another. So I flew home to spend the holidays with Mom and Frances, and although we felt the absence of my sisters, our being together provided a needed balm. We picked Mom up and brought her to Frances's place; we lingered over savory meals; we helped Mom write Christmas cards to family and friends, including her absent daughters; we listened to favorite music; and we escorted Mom to various appointments. Every day we sipped tea together before driving Mom back to her assisted-living home. All of it helped to begin mending our battered souls. And although Mom wondered aloud about her missing daughters—"Why don't they call?" she'd ask—she nonetheless delighted in the time the three of us spent together.

In the days and weeks following our goodbye on New Year's Eve, I had reason to remain cautiously optimistic about my mother. She adapted well to her new surroundings at Wentworth, the assisted-living facility she moved to just in time to celebrate her eighty-seventh birthday. She engaged with the residents and staff she met and participated in some of the scheduled activities. Mom told me about the friends who dropped by, the tasty food, a card in the mail, an outing with her companion Pauline, visits from Frances and occasionally a grandchild. With regular meals, social stimulation, and attentive staff, her Alzheimer's fuzziness improved, and I felt sure we'd share in each other's lives for a few more years, perhaps even until Mom's ninetieth birthday.

As I near Quebec City, I direct my attention to the increasing flow of traffic. Without having to actually enter the city core, I soon leave behind the surge of cars and trucks and resume my reveries while continuing westward toward Montreal. I think about the complexities and contradictions of my mother's nature. At times, she showed remarkable determination and a will of steel, particularly with respect to her children's welfare, while at other times she caved in as easily as putty. She could argue vehemently in one situation and be as passive as a *doekje,* a dishcloth, in another. She retained lifelong friends but often relied on them to seek her out, and for as long as she drew breath, she formed new and meaningful relationships. Despite her polite manners, she felt little compunction to follow through with something if she "wasn't in the mood" as she put it, even if it meant canceling established plans at the last minute, impervious to the frustration and disappointment doing so caused those who had counted on her presence. She retained her faith in God, a mixture of evangelical and reformed theology, as pleased to sing "The Old Rugged Cross" as to join with friends in singing Dutch psalms with their metrical Genevan tone. When her age made going to church too difficult, she tuned in to a church service on the radio, delighting in the choir music and sitting still to pay attention to the sermon.

She raised five daughters with my ultraconservative father, held a somewhat more flexible worldview than him, but voted as he did. She couldn't be bothered to inform herself about election issues or candidates; instead, she relied on what my father said. He, in turn, considered her doing so a necessity because "otherwise, she cancels my vote," a notion at which my mother smiled but rarely questioned. To keep the peace, as she called it, she maintained a subservient role to my father, but she did so selectively, demonstrating a streak of independence in her marriage that befuddled my father. From the modest allowance he allotted her each month for groceries and household needs, she managed to save a small but growing pocket of money for herself. In a brown vinyl clutch purse she bought at the Salvation Army and stowed on an upper shelf in the kitchen, she kept several twenty-dollar bills, enough to make periodic loans to her maturing daughters to tide them over until payday from their part-time jobs. The monthly Canadian family allowance checks helped her to increase her tidy sum, from which my mother bought what she wanted and needed—a new coat, a pair of shoes, or an outfit, whether for herself or one of her girls—without the interference of my father and without having to ask him for extra money. However, my mother's sense of impending scarcity and her need to maintain her own "rainy day" funds never left her, a remnant from childhood hardships and the deprivations of World War II.

My mother was born in 1923, and her birth brought consternation, not joy, to her parents and four siblings who lived in a small northern town of the Netherlands. My mother's father lived with unremitting pain from a crippling back injury; consequently, he could no longer provide for his family. A few weeks after her eighth birthday, my mother walked home from school where her brother met her on the street. Their *heit* had died, he told her, but she was not to ask or say anything. In the way children do, my mother deduced from the swirling conversations over the next days and weeks that her father, fifty-one years of age, had ended his life, an act defying Biblical teaching that only the Almighty could decide how and when a person should die. The secrecy and silence shrouding her father's death shaped my mother for the rest of her life. She maintained a rigid code of privacy about our family matters, considering our happenings and conversations inappropriate for discussion outside of the family, which included the rows my parents often had before we drove to church on Sunday morning. Such arguments began with a side show leading to the main event.

"*Hé*," my father would say to my mother over our Sunday breakfast when he saw one of his daughters wearing the housecoat he had bought her a year or two ago, "why do you never wear it? So beautiful it is, but I never see you in it." In an unusually lavish gesture, for my father rarely bought gifts for any of us, he had presented my mother with a bag from Woodward's department store containing a beautiful emerald-green, full-length quilted dressing gown. Rarely worn by my mother and donned most often by her daughters, it served for a long while as the lightning rod for what bothered each of my parents about the shortcomings of the other. We children held our breath when my father brought up his gift to my mother. Her next comment would determine the direction the rest of the Sunday, perhaps even the week, would take.

If she said, "I like to save it and keep it nice," well, my father might grumble a bit—"What is the use in buying my wife such a beautiful thing?" But I could allow myself to relax a bit. Conversely, I tensed if I heard my mother say, "How you got it in your head to buy such a thing, no, I cannot understand. So stupid! If I spill something on it and have to wash it, all the newness is gone, ruined; what good is that?" Depending on her mood and whatever list of complaints she had accumulated about my father over the past few weeks, my mother, slicing cheese for her whole wheat toast, might add with a flushed face, "You never even asked if I wanted one. What I have is fine!" She'd point to the faded short-sleeved cotton gown overtop of her mismatched flannel nightwear, a safety pin in place of a missing button. Then revving up, she let him know how he could have better spent his money. "Helen here, she needs new shoes and you don't even notice. And you, with your shiny Sunday suit; what an embarrassment, you won't even buy a new one." At this point my father would begin to splutter, unaware he had entered a no-win argument.

"What? My suit is fine; the cuffs of my jacket are not yet even frayed!"

"And your shoes," my mother added, "so shabby, you almost walk beside them." Undaunted and unstoppable by now, she would invoke God into their pointless quarrel. "Do you think de Hemel likes to see you in church looking so humble, yet so stubborn and hateful to your fellow Christians? What you said to Mr. Groenewald a month ago, ach, I am still so ashamed I can't even look at him or his wife anymore. What they must think of us now, I can't even think of it."

"What? What did I say?" asked my father. Upon my mother's detailed recitation of his social flaws, my father, who failed to fathom how his ways so troubled my mother, would scoff at her ability to dredge up past gaffes he considered minor and long done with. "You! You always remember the bad, never the good." And he would recite a verse such as Isaiah 43:18, "Remember not the former things nor consider the things of old," his way of underscoring my mother's misguided penchant for dwelling on events of the past. "Why can you not learn from the Bible?" he'd go on. "The Lord says the troubles of the past are gone and hid from my eyes, Isaiah 65:16. Why can you not look ahead as God tells us to do?"

They tousled verbally some more across the breakfast table until my mother announced, "You can go alone to church; I'm staying home. Say what you like about why I'm not there, I don't care. That you can expect a blessing when you act like this, well, it's a wonder."

"Nobody needs to know," she warned us about these clashes with my father. "Say nothing," she admonished my sisters and me before we left home after these altercations. Obedience to my mother's persistent warnings reinforced for me that our family endured conflicts no other families did, that we risked shaming ourselves if others learned of our discord, that the ordered life of a God-fearing household as described in the bedtime stories my father read to my sisters and me applied to everyone else but not to us. Thus, from a tender age, I internalized and carried our family secrets, fearing that if I inadvertently divulged anything about our private tribulations to someone, I chanced disgracing my parents. I didn't understand why my oldest sister, Harmena, moved to her own apartment when she turned eighteen years of age, something unusual amongst our circle of friends, and my mother bore the crushing disappointment of a mother-daughter relationship gone sour. If people asked about her, I smiled and said, "Harmena's fine." I dared not reveal the tenuous relationship between my smart, attractive sister and our parents. Nor did I share how my mother cried and was sad a great deal of the time after her eldest daughter left home, that on days Mom mustered the energy to get out of bed, she merely went through the motions of her daily chores, and her unhappiness cast gloom over us all.

When a few years later my father determined his family would attend a better church, one more Biblically aligned with his shifting faith, I continued to smile when asked about this change by my own and my parents' friends. Talking fast and loud as I was wont to do and laughing nervously, I would stumble my way through what I hoped was an innocuous explanation. "Oh…my father, he just wants us to go to a Canadian church." I knew full well the tongue-lashing that would be rendered by my mother if I told the truth—that my parents quarreled all the time about my father's over-the-top obsession for "The Church," that sometimes she stayed in bed for the entire day, that doing the wash or cooking supper took more out of her than she had to give. My mother never considered herself depressed; only weak people gave in to their "nerves," the term used at the time to describe depressive symptoms. She did her best to "fight," as she put it, her glumness when it struck her.

How much did my father's ardor for the church tip my mother toward the depressive episodes that swamped her several times a year? Certainly it didn't help, and a periodic despondence shrouded her during my childhood. When about six years old, my youngest sister and I bathed together on a Saturday evening. My mother kneeled on the floor beside the tub to ensure we washed ourselves thoroughly, but she did so listlessly. Although she stroked our gangly arms and legs with the soapy washcloth in her hand, I wanted more of her; I wanted my mother engaged and playful with us, me and my sister.

"*Lekker* smelly soap, *hé,* Mom?" My naïve effort to break the strain and begin a conversation in the Frisian-English dialect we spoke at home resulted in her instantaneous laughter. My mother could not stop laughing, and for years she repeated my statement whenever she wanted a lift. The demands of child-rearing and the repetitiveness of her domestic responsibilities, day after day, week after week—cooking, cleaning, washing, ironing, mending, sewing—often added to her melancholy. As lengthening spring days ushered in the month of June, she lamented the approach of June 21 when the days would begin to get shorter. Our temperaments were so different. Some evenings, with the supper dishes washed and put away, I would proceed to bake a cake for an event the next day or set up the sewing machine to finish a project.

"*Ach,*" she'd protest, "at this hour? You're not serious!"

"Mom, don't worry; you don't have to do a thing. I'll clean every-thing up when I'm done." But despite such assurances, I completed those tasks under the duress of my mother's continued mutterings. "At this hour! How do you get it in your head?" For my mother, any oppor-tunity to cast work aside—evenings, Sundays, holidays—constituted leisure time for reading an absorbing book or watching a good show on TV after we finally bought one. My bustling about interrupted the calm routine she expected and depended on for her relaxation.

For a few years, after my aging mother's interest in shopping and her personal appearance slipped, I bought her new clothes I thought she'd wear. She thanked me for my efforts and chuckled at items she thought bold in color or unusual in style, but she contin-ued to wear the familiar trousers and blouses in which she felt most comfortable. Several times, when I arrived to pick her up for an outing, I did my best to hide my dismay at the mismatch of clothes she had donned for the day. Sometimes I approached the problem with directness.

"Mom, you can't wear that."

"Why not? There's nothing wrong with it." Her plaintive voice was a warning for me not to push her. During the cold seasons, the two layers of pants she wore for warmth clung to her thin legs with static electricity, the hem of one pair protruding beneath the other. The pilled saggy sweater she wore was an item she refused to throw away.

I did my best to cajole her into wearing something more attrac-tive. "Mom, where's that nice blouse that looks so good on you?"

"*Ach,* again not good," she'd say, slumping her shoulders as if having met with catastrophic disappointment, her voice beginning to whine. "I don't want to change; no, I have no mood to do that."

Her dispirited affect sapped me of energy.

With my mother's penchant for avoiding difficult topics, we learned in our household to circumnavigate the elephant in the room, as it were, favoring instead the pretense that everything was fine or soon would be. We argued loudly but rarely talked openly about what mattered most in my family: my father's crazed, religious zeal;

my oldest sister's abrupt move and her infrequent visits dwindling to none at all; how confused and disconnected my sisters and I felt since being uprooted by my father from the familiarity of our Dutch Calvinistic faith and the friends with whom we had worshipped for so many years. I felt out of place attending the suave, evangelical churches my father favored, first a Baptist church and a year later an Alliance church. All of it meant I wanted to grow up as quickly as I could so I could be independent and on my own, but in the meantime, I did not want to displease my father or disappoint my mother. As a family, we lacked the ability to talk about our conflicts and related griefs in ways that could help us mend or stave off additional emotional wounds. Because of their ongoing squabbles, I couldn't describe to my parents the embarrassment I felt with my friends. How could I explain to friends why I no longer went to the same church as them, not even the same denomination? Trying to do so only fueled my mother's anger toward my father. "See what you've done, what you make your children go through?" she'd spit at him when they bickered. In response, my father would claim his position of patriarch and spiritual authority, saying, "We must not be afraid to suffer for His name's sake."

I detested these arguments. One moment I exulted inwardly that Mom stood up for us kids, but in the next I hated how she clobbered my father emotionally. Despite that he almost always managed to retain the upper hand, I hated to see the bewildered, wilted expression on my father's face, all the while wishing he could be like a normal dad savvy to the needs of his kids. Consequently, I sidestepped my parents' circular arguments as much as possible, but my inability to deal with conflict persists. Although easygoing by nature, I recognize my tendency to acquiesce, to go along to get along, aware of my uncertainty and awkwardness in the face of touchy matters. I watch in amazement as friends tackle friction head-on and colleagues navigate gracefully through dissension in ways I never imagined possible. Conversely, when things blow apart like a volcano for others, I understand their lack of skill in coping with dispute. Conflicted emotions, mental illness, or interpersonal tensions—I am still learning that avoidance and procrastination are poor antidotes compared to transparency, honesty, and kindness. I am certain the current disintegration within my family is due in no small part to this long-held inability to talk about what's bothering us as siblings, with its roots stemming from our childhood.

In the aftershock of her sudden widowhood, my proud grandmother did her best to minimize the religious and moral condemnation of her husband's suicide. Few choices existed for single mothers in 1930s rural Holland, especially for women whose widowhood came as a result of a spouse willfully taking his own life. My grandmother, too proud to accept the charity offered by the deacons of the church, chose instead to disband her family, shooing her four older children to fend for themselves so she could rent a couple of rooms for herself and her youngest child, my mother. My mother expressed to me her sadness with how circumstances flung her next-oldest brother from the family home. At thirteen years old at the time, he coped as best he could as a hired helper on a nearby farm. Despite their meager arrangement, my mother retained a sense of home with her mother until she quit school and began working. In time, my grandmother provided my mother with a stepfather, *Pakke Jan*, whom my mother grew to love.

My grandmother worked as a housecleaner and supplemented her earnings by taking in other people's washing, scrubbing the dirty garments in the galvanized tubs that took up precious space in their already cramped quarters. On rainy days, of which there were many in that lowland country, the smell of damp laundry strung across the lines in their dank living space greeted my mother upon her arrival home from school, the clammy woolen underthings brushing against her arms and face as she changed her clothes. My mother helped out after school, ironing and folding aprons, trousers, dresses, and linens. She delivered the baskets of clean laundry to their owners and returned with the next batch of washing. Into the *spaarpot*, the piggybank, on the shelf, she dropped what she and her mother had earned for their labors. Those quarters and guilders helped to pay for their tea, bread, a soup bone, and once in a while some smoked herring or a few eggs. I can only surmise the extent to which my mother's meager beginnings contributed to her low moods.

I break my thoughts to glance at the gas gauge and decide to stop for fuel before approaching the roadways of Montreal. I park my car after gassing up and walk across the street of Saint-Hyacinthe to buy a cup of steeped tea at Tim Hortons. Before starting out again, I rummage in my cooler for something to nibble on through the inevitable stop-go urban traffic in which I will soon be absorbed. Behind the steering wheel again, I follow the exit ramp and am soon driving west on Route 20.

Midway through the seventh grade, my mother left school to become a maid for an affluent family. She never said much about her schooling other than that she had teachers who belittled children like her, youngsters whose parents held no influence in town because of their economic impoverishment. One teacher, she once told me, hit her hard on the head for some perceived misdeed, causing the barrette in her hair to break and fly across the room. "He wouldn't have dared do it to anyone else in the class," my mother said, "just to me, because I was poor and he knew he could get away with it. I could see it in his eyes." With her tender spirit, the injustice of the teacher's tyrannical act lasted for much longer than the throb from his hand across her head.

Many years later, my mother received a phone call from the Christian elementary school Frances and I attended. A teacher had punished me for not obeying her in the classroom, telling me I had to stand throughout the next class, penmanship. I considered this punishment grossly unjust and illogical. At morning recess, with a combination of humiliation and self-righteous indignation, I found Frances. As the older sibling, I was responsible for her, and I told her we were going home—now. Frances cried and asked, couldn't we wait until lunchtime? I agreed and we returned to our classes. She, however, upset and confused, told her teacher. Soon thereafter, the principal beckoned me to his office. He had called my mother, and on the phone, Mom, much calmer than I expected (given my disobedience to a teacher), told me to stay at school for the day; we'd talk about this matter when I got home. That evening Mom listened to my story and, without scolding me, said I needed to apologize, that the teacher, someone she was not particularly fond of, had to be respected. Aside from my displeasure at writing a note of apology to my teacher and the principal, what stands out for me from this exchange is that Mom understood my feelings, and for the next few weeks, I sensed a deeper affection between my mother and me. I knew my mother was at odds with my father about sending Frances and me to an expensive private school an hour and three bus transfers away from home when we could walk to either of two perfectly good public schools near our house. But in the strict European and Calvinistic family in which I grew up, children who voiced their disrespect or sassed adults in positions of authority needed discipline, not reward. Only years later, after my mother told me of her experience at the hands of her cruel teacher, did I comprehend the degree to which she understood my plight. But rather than allowing me to perceive myself as a victim, she used my altercation with my teacher as a way to teach rather than to punish: I learned to respect authority, to apologize when in the wrong.

Upon leaving school, my mother added her meager housemaid earnings to her mother's wages to help ease their situation. But it came with its own cost. Too often, Mom remembered, her employers and others in town, class-conscious as Hollanders could be at that time, made sure she never forgot her lowly station in life.

"Look, you didn't clean so good in the corners yesterday. Your mother depends on you, but if you don't do better, *ja,* I can always find someone else."

Mom took the barbs, she said, because that's what you did back then, but once or twice, unable to endure the insults directed at her, she quit a job, unwilling to listen to another put-down from the housewife who griped at her.

Even presumed gestures of kindness came with a stab. "Here is a dress my daughter outgrew," a woman would offer. "Too tall you probably are for it, *maar ja,* when you're poor, you can't be too proud."

Her sister Hinke, almost fifteen years her senior, ran a dairy farm with her husband, and as a young girl, my mother loved bicycling the few kilometers to stay with them whenever she could. "I always had a home with them, so long as I helped out. That's why my hands are so big," she added, stretching her fingers to demonstrate, "from milking all those cows, especially in winter, with my hands in and out of the cold water." Her hands, with their long, tapered fingers, were proportionate to her tall stature. But awkward as she felt about herself, Mom kept her hands folded in her lap, rarely gesturing with them in conversation as her daughters did.

As I matured, I grew to accept that some of Mom's exasperating behaviors did not occur in a vacuum, that the combined stigma of her father's death and the poverty from her childhood left an indelible mark on her. With her reserved, shy nature, the humiliation and uncertainty clouding my mother's early years caused her to be wary as an adult when in unfamiliar or uncomfortable situations, particularly with people she did not know or those who oozed a confidence she could not comprehend. An unexpected question or greeting from someone she considered to be *deftig*, dignified— the well-educated *dominee* or minister, for example—caught her off guard. With flushed face, she shook hands with him and stammered a rushed response to end her discomfort. Because of her self-consciousness, she often needed bolstering. "Mom, you look great; the blue in that dress suits you so well!" Or if she declined an invitation to join one of her daughters for an event, a similar dance ensued. "Of course I want you to come along, Mom. I wouldn't ask you if I didn't. It'll be more fun if you come."

My mother disliked being the center of attention, but paradoxically, she also felt miffed if she thought someone ignored or overlooked her. "He's quite uppity," she said if someone brushed her off with a cool, perfunctory greeting. She never considered how her own aloofness or unease might influence such encounters. She loved being part of the large gatherings her friends hosted for their birthdays and anniversaries, but she made it clear that others shouldn't bother making plans for her hallmark birthdays. "A cup of tea with you people and a *lekker gebaakje,* something from the Dutch bakery, then I have all I want," Mom assured us.

Although her sadness and emotional needs often obscured her intellect and wit, my mother was anything but simple. Her strong Dutch accent belied her ability with English, a language she learned to speak, read, and write without formal instruction. She often looked up unfamiliar words in the dictionary or would ask us the meaning of a vernacular expression she'd heard. "What does it mean, to 'cut off your nose to spite your face'?" she asked at the supper table one evening. "I heard it on the radio. What a strange expression." She loved the interplay of words, whether in Dutch or English. In acknowledgment of someone's education and wise ways, she'd say with admiration in her voice, "That woman must have a good under-standing." When she saw a large overweight person, she'd say some-thing similar, a rueful smile on her face: "That man for sure needs a good understanding," referring to the durability of the man's feet and legs to uphold his large frame.

After an hour and a half, I've finished sipping my tea just as the nerve-racking metropolis of Montreal recedes behind me. Soon I am at the Ontario border. Before long, Ottawa, too, the nation's capital, is in my rearview mirror. My ruminations make the miles pass by quickly while daylight gives way to twilight. Before night-fall, I find a cheap motel room in Renfrew, but after sitting for so long, I decide to take a walk before settling. Doing so reminds me of how Mom impressed upon me and my sisters the importance of getting exercise, preferably in nature. Conscientious about maintain-ing her trim figure, Mom ate healthy foods and made sure to "get some exercise" right up to the day she broke her hip. She preferred walking outdoors, with my father before he died, then with a friend, or by herself if need be. Should one of her daughters be around, she took joy in her company. Then she'd point out the wonders of nature, whether a crow's nest in the clock tower of the nearby college, a colorful flower bed, or a dandelion pushing its way through a crack in the sidewalk. On rainy days or cold wintry days, for as long as she could, she walked down seven flights of stairs to check her mail, then trekked up the same stairs to her apartment.

With clear skies beckoning the next morning, I spot Tim Hortons a block away, and I buy a muffin and cup of coffee to eat and drink as I drive. I make my way back onto the westbound Trans-Canada, where I mull over the changes in Mom's daily routines that signified a decided shift in her usual well-being. During my visit that summer of 2010, I discovered that walking just a few blocks in the neighborhood tired her. Cooking, laundry, grocery shopping—all of her domestic tasks overwhelmed her. That she failed to lock the door alarmed me, for she had maintained a decades-long ritual when leaving her home—pulling the door closed behind her, turning the key, then trying the handle to ensure the door had locked. "Oh, just one minute," she'd say, holding her hand up to indicate she'd forgotten something. She would reverse the steps to check one more time that she'd turned off the stove before locking the door and jiggling the handle to be certain no one could enter without a key. For years she worried about someone breaking into her home, so her lack of concern that summer when I pointed out she hadn't secured the door indicated a serious departure from her usual careful routine.

The lack of attention to her hygiene also concerned me. She had always been so fastidious about her personal cleanliness, but I detected a musty odor when I hugged her. Her whole life, she refrigerated all leftovers rather than waste a thing, a carryover from the meagerness of her youth. But in the throes of dementia and with an apparent decline in her usual appetite, she haphazardly placed food—unwrapped and uncovered—in the freezer after sampling a bite or two from her Meals on Wheels tray.

"Mom, what's this half-eaten sandwich doing in the freezer?" I asked, holding out a freezer-burnt lettuce-and-tomato sandwich. "And what about this soup? It's not in a proper container; now it needs to be thrown away."

"They give me way too much food, so I eat it later," she said, snappish, irritated at my snoopy bossiness, oblivious to her failing abilities. She lacked awareness of how she only picked at her food, so unlike her usual mealtime delight.

Frances and I spent as much time as possible with Mom during that summer of 2010 and we alerted Helen and Joanne, my sisters, to her diminishing skills. Helen brought Mom some homemade Dutch soup on her way to work; Joanne helped out with laundry and dropped off meat-and-potato food packages. As always, Mom let her daughters know how much she cherished their company. A day trip to Bragg Creek in the Rocky Mountain foothills gave Mom no end of pleasure. On more than one occasion, Frances and I offered to take her out for afternoon tea, but she preferred to brew a pot herself. We went for a walk first, Mom arm in arm with us to steady her balance. Midway she rested on a bench at a bus stop, where she drew our attention to the birdsong she heard above the din of nearby traffic.

"Listen," she said, her hand raised, her index finger extended to quiet us. "Can you hear that little bird? Isn't it nice?"

When we returned to her apartment, she put the kettle on. One of us, Fran or I, scurried into the kitchen to make sure the cups were clean, since half-washed dishes in the cupboard were another indicator of Mom's diminishing attention. After the tea had infused, Mom set the tray on the coffee table. She poured us each a steaming cup, then reached over to pat each of us on the knee. "It's so nice to be with you people," she said, a smile on her face, warmth in her voice.

Over the course of my stay that summer, Mom visited at Fran's place, where I grilled chicken or salmon. When we ate at Swiss Chalet, a family restaurant, Mom ordered lemon meringue pie, her favorite dessert. I took her to meet with a lawyer so she could update her legal affairs, and together, Fran and I introduced her to the idea of assisted living. With the encouragement from a home-care nurse, she agreed to an aide coming in twice a week to help her bathe. Over the coming weeks, the risk of her living alone became ever more worrisome, especially when she spoke about my deceased father as if he were still alive, how he arrived late at her apartment every night and stayed until early morning.

"He says nothing to me and is gone to work by the time I wake up in the morning," my mother explained. She agonized about how to get him a set of keys when she moved to her next address.

That autumn, a room at Wentworth became available, a place my mother regarded as very *deftig*, posh. She chuckled to think she would be living in such a stylish, elegant place. "Imagine!" she told me on the telephone after I had returned home, "it has a spiral staircase and a fountain in the entrance! You've never seen anything like it!" During our daily phone calls, she described the many facets that caught her attention: the library, the treadmill, the white-tailed deer grazing on the lawns, and Sally, the elderly British war bride who sat at her table for meals. My mother blossomed with the attention she received from staff and, notably, she never mentioned my father's visits again, perhaps because she no longer needed his watchful eye over her.

In the interim months before our mother moved to assisted living, Frances located a companion to spend time with Mom a few afternoons each week. Fiercely private and independent, even as dementia gripped her mind, Mom resented the idea of someone "interfering" in her life. But with Pauline's gentle persistence, Mom began to look forward to their dates. Together, they visited friends, took walks in the park, chatted over cups of tea, and prayed together in Wentworth's chapel for, among other things, the sorrow my mother felt about her daughters being lost to her. Before long, Pauline became an integral part of her life. "She even warmed my hands between her own," Mom told me on a particularly cold day in January, "just like a daughter would do." And thereafter Mom welcomed Pauline wholeheartedly into her life, a relationship Frances and I continued to nurture long after my mother's need of Pauline had ended.

In northern Ontario, with little traffic on the highway that winds between lakes and through boreal forests, I give way to thoughts of my parents' romance, which began in late April 1945 when my mother, out for a walk, spotted the rakish young man she'd first noticed at church a Sunday or two ago. With the warm sun on her face, she could for the time being forget the chronic fears of occupation and a war that seemed never to end. The long, bleak *hongerwinter* was over, a winter in which thousands of Dutch people had died from cold and starvation. Best of all, the German army had all but surrendered and the end of the war was in sight.

To avoid conscription to German labor, my father, like so many of his countrymen, became part of the Dutch resistance. He took an assumed name, and using false identity papers, began work as a farmhand in Fryslân, a province in northern Holland where my mother lived. Finally, after more than four years of living as an *onderduiker,* literally an under-diver, he began to move about more openly without fear of arrest or death from a *razzia,* a raid by Nazi soldiers on unsuspecting citizens in their homes. For their first date, my father took my mother to a youth service at a local church. Nearly three years later in early 1948, they married and moved to Haarlem, where my father's family lived. Within four years, they had three healthy daughters—Harmke, Johanna Maria, and Hinke, who in Canada would become Harmena, Joanne, and Helen.

Postwar reconstruction in the Netherlands took a long time, and with no sign of a home large enough to accommodate their expanding family, my parents, with the assistance offered by their national government, immigrated to Canada. Although my parents were the first to do so on either side of their family, their decision became one more in the story of mass migration. Hundreds of thousands of Dutch citizens dreamed of starting anew in that young English-speaking country, a country that, during the war, had given safe haven to Princess Juliana, the future monarch of the Netherlands, and her children. After the necessary visas arrived in the mail, my parents packed their *kist,* the crate they jammed full of their hopes and the material goods they would need in that faraway land: clothing, a few furnishings, washtubs, a manual coffee grinder, and dreams of their own home. The promise of untold opportunities helped them to overlook what they would leave behind—their children's grandparents and "Het Wilhelmus," the Dutch national anthem—and the coming hardships they would surely endure, including a new language, frigid winters, and manifold uncertainties. But with the exuberance of youth and a devout faith in God, they never doubted they would rise above the difficulties.

A black-and-white photo taken on that day in late May 1953 when my parents set sail from Rotterdam shows them waving and smiling from the deck of the *Zuiderkruis,* a former troop ship, each holding a daughter. Tante Hinke, my mother's sister, stood on the wharf with the baby, her namesake, until the last minute. When a warning blare sounded from the ship, she and my mother, believing they'd never see other again, cried and bid each other a tearful farewell.

Out on the open ocean, Mom found her enthusiasm for the voyage short-lived. Racked by nausea for most of their ten-day Atlantic crossing, she placed her grateful feet on solid ground at Pier 21 in Halifax only to find she'd be on a train for yet another week, rocking her way from Halifax to Calgary. It was an unimaginable distance for someone from a country the size of a postage stamp. The Nova Scotia coast gave way to the lakes and forests of the Canadian Shield in Ontario, then the prairie provinces. Years later, my mother chuckled as she recalled the duress of that trip. "Helen, the baby, didn't like all that rocking back and forth either," my mother said. "She had diarrhea, and without anywhere to properly wash the diapers, they were so stained, I could never get them white again. By the time we reached the prairies, I began throwing them out the window." She laughed heartily to think of who might have come unawares upon those soiled diapers.

Eventually they arrived in Calgary, where the famed Rocky Mountains on the western horizon held them in awe, and where Mom's eagerness for this immigration adventure returned. Assisted by Dominee Hoekstra, a minister from the Christian Reformed Church who helped numerous Dutch immigrants settle in to their new situation, my father soon found work as a carpenter, and almost as quickly, a house to rent. Thrilled to finally unpack the *kist,* my mother felt waves of homesickness wash over her as she unwrapped the contents, each item releasing the familiar smells of a home and loved ones she had left behind. She pined for her mother and sister, crying at times when the mail failed to deliver their hoped-for letters, but she never regretted her decision to come to this country of extremes with its landlocked prairies, bitingly cold winters, and hot, dry summers.

"How strange—rivers without boats! I longed for fish—herring and mackerel. And I missed the wind and the smell of the sea," she told us. "Just the same, sunny Alberta is my home." She found the bright sun during chill weather invigorating, and the prolonged gray, rainy days of her homeland became distant memories.

During our phone conversations after she moved to Wentworth, my mother often surprised me with stories I had not heard before. Once she recalled how she and her mother sometimes walked together along the seashore behind the dike, the wind blowing their hair about. On one particularly warm day, her mother, my *beppe*, lifted her long black skirt to remove her shoes and stockings and wiggle her bare toes in the sand. "I kept watch so I could tell my mother if anybody else came on the beach."

When I asked why, Mom explained, "That just wasn't done then. A woman didn't walk barefoot, not even out of sight on the sandy shore." I realized how far Mom had traveled, not just geographically, but how much social change my mother had witnessed over her lifespan of eight and a half decades: from the introduction and novelty of the telephone to everyone owning a cell phone; from the awe of her first automobile ride at six years of age, belly pain and all, to the hospital for an appendectomy to men and women of any social standing—my mother included—driving their own vehicles; from few options beyond marriage for working-class women to her daughters and granddaughters pursuing professional careers of which my mother could never have dreamed.

I also realized that, in the self-centered way of children, I always thought of my parents' immigration as something that occurred in "the olden days." That they learned to speak and read English so quickly and as well as they did astounds me now, for I have no recollection of their inability to do so. As a child, I heard only their accented English and their awkwardness with the language. I'm embarrassed to think how my sisters and I lost no opportunity to point out their mistakes, especially our mother's.

"*Ach*! Again, not good," Mom would say, annoyed by our derision. With her Dutch accent, a *th* sounded like a *d*. "Vell den, Jenny, you need to learn me."

"Not *learn*, Mom, *teach*; you want me to teach you English so you can learn to speak it better." I can still hear my smug, smart-alecky voice, which embarrasses me now. Despite growing up in a bilingual country and despite my years of education, I have never gained fluency in another language.

Mom read stories aloud to us children, she conversed with Canadian neighbors, and she read Dutch and English books for her own pleasure as well. Even after moving to assisted living, with dementia punching holes in her brain, Mom read the daily national newspaper and leafed her way through interesting books. One day she found *The Rise and Fall of the Third Reich* in a hallway library. Describing as it did the horrors of a time she and my father had lived through, she read sections of it with great interest, for by that time she no longer read a book from cover to cover.

"That's quite a book," she told me on the phone, followed by an angry outburst: "Those dirty Nazis!"

By the end of the second day of my trip, May 3, my birthday, I want to get past White River, which, despite its rugged beauty, is desolate and remote. But when I finally arrive, I'm too tired to push on to Marathon, the next place on the map, another hour away. I find a motel room in this town, the birthplace, it turns out, of the bear for whom the storybook *Winnie the Pooh* was named (by a WWI serviceman who came from Winnipeg). I make my way to the café on the other end of the parking lot. While sipping a glass of wine and waiting for my salad tossed with anemic end-of-season vegetables, I call Frances. She tells me that although the doctors declared my mother's operation a surgical success, Mom faces a grim prognosis. Yes, Mom survived the surgery and the wound on her hip is healing well. But cognitively and physically, she is completely dependent and won't be able to return to assisted living.

"Drive carefully," Fran tells me, "but hurry. Mom is going downhill." With a quick "happy birthday," she hangs up.

As a child, I loved hearing Mom tell me the stories about my birth. Overdue with me, her fourth child, she experienced a precipitous delivery. "You were nearly born on the elevator!" The real shock, however, came immediately following my birth, when she was unable to hold her newborn as she'd expected. Her Dutch doctor explained the problem. A specialist needed to examine me, her Canadian-born child, because of an opening in my lip extending the length of my palate, an orofacial defect my mother had never heard of or seen before.

"I was so worried," she said. "How the doctors could make everything normal with you, I had no idea." Worried, missing the comforting presence of her own mother, and failing to grasp most of what the doctors and nurses told her, she cried. "But one day a nurse got mad at me, told me to stop crying, that for my baby something could be done; others were not so lucky. That was all I needed to hear." From there on, my mother's fears abated. Despite her apprehensions about the increased risk of aspiration from my cleft lip and palate, feedings went well, I gained weight, and the first of many reparative surgeries took place before I turned one year old.

Over the years, Mom took me by public transit to numerous appointments to meet with surgeons, dentists, orthodontists, and speech therapists. Because I otherwise enjoyed good health, these appointments became outings, free as they were of the worry a serious illness would have imposed. Often one or two of my sisters came with us, and when possible, we tacked on a shopping trip downtown or an afternoon cup of tea at a department store cafeteria. On the bus ride home, when I sat beside Mom, my tongue roved the metal wires and elastics the orthodontist had just fitted me with. We chitchatted together, my mother, my sisters, and me—about what to make for supper, the mending Mom needed to do after supper, the chores and homework we had to do before bedtime. In Frisian, Mom would say something comical to us about people on the bus. "Now that one there in the green jacket, he could go for three days without eating, and you still wouldn't notice it." We'd laugh together before Mom looked furtively around. "We better be careful," she'd say. "You never know who might understand us." This made us giggle some more. With the rocking and stop-go of the bus, my eyes would get heavy and I'd lean my head against Mom's arm until she would rouse me. "Jenny, we get off next stop."

Today, when I glance in the mirror at my facial features, I'm aware that the virtual absence of a scar on my upper lip, the neat closure of my palate, the even bite of my teeth, even the clarity of my speech are due to Mom's persistence on my behalf. In the days before publicly funded healthcare in Canada, my father, who managed the family finances, fretted about the costly surgeries I needed. In addition to meeting his tithes to the church and paying for my operations, he worried—would there be enough money to pay for the orthodontics I'd also need? But Mom, demonstrating her iron will in such matters, remained firm, leaving my father no recourse other than to agree that I would get the treatments I needed.

Years later, widowed, physically fragile, in assisted living, my mother was walking with Frances through "the avenues," as she called the long Wentworth hallways, when she suddenly stopped and leaned on her walker, tears coursing down her cheeks.

"What is it, Mom? What's the matter?" Fran asked in panic.

"To think when Jenny was born the doctors said she might never talk normal. And now look, she talks for a living. It's a miracle." Reaching into the basket of her walker for the large white table napkin she always carried with her, Mom blew her nose, dried her tears, and proceeded on her walk.

On the third day of my travels, I rise early to begin my day's journey. I drive through Marathon, past Sudbury, buying gas in Sault Ste. Marie, where a billboard announces this city as the home of Roberta Bondar, an astronaut. Eventually I drive through Thunder Bay on the north shore of Lake Superior. Over the miles I think about the change in our needs, that now it is my sisters' and my turn to escort Mom to her appointments. Although Frances and Pauline usually accompany her, I did take my mother to a few needed engagements when I was home a few months ago over the Christmas break. With her stooped back, swollen feet squished into boots, and her slow, shuffling gait as she pushed her walker forward, my mother looked so frail, not at all the strong woman who used to stand so tall and straight. But the strength of her personality remained intact. With fire in her eyes, she refused, at the hairdresser's, to let me dictate how short to cut her hair. "It's still my hair," she flared up at me. Upon the conclusion of a doctor's appointment, she slowly and painstakingly inched her way off the examining table. Aware that the doctor, Frances, and I each held our breath while watching her slow progress, she soon had us laughing aloud. "Don't worry, Doctor, I'm in no hurry!" she said, an impish grin on her face, no trace of her usual self-consciousness with such a *deftig* person.

Following her move to assisted living, Frances and I felt both relief and amazement at the ease with which Mom settled in to her new surroundings. Despite her physical and cognitive impediments, she coped well with the many transitions. Surprisingly, with the full bloom of her dementia, she now met change and uncertainty with acceptance and grace rather than with her usual worry and anxiety.

She considered the matched silverware and unchipped serviceware as "fit for the Queen," and she savored the three tasty meals set before her each day. She had staff to help her bathe, dress, and fix her hair; her room was cleaned a few times each week; and her laundry was also done for her. "Never in my life," Mom told me with an amazed chuckle, "have I had it so good."

Wentworth's Happy Hour every Friday afternoon also impressed Mom, both the live entertainment and the fact that Frances came to share the weekly event with her. During her younger years, my mother indulged at festive occasions with a dainty sip of wine or *advokaat* (a thick custard-like concoction made from sugar, brandy, and eggs), but otherwise she never held with "strong drink" of any kind. "Such a waste of money!" she decried. Fearful of becoming tipsy, and scornful of the foolish behavior exhibited by intoxicated people, Mom discouraged her daughters from imbibing in spirits. Just the same, when Frances showed up, a glass of wine in hand, to sit in the front lounge to listen to the music and share in my mother's company, it was a highlight for Mom as she sipped a cup of tea.

By late afternoon, distance signs to Kenora mean I am finally nearing the Manitoba border. I can make it to the other side of Winnipeg before darkness falls, where I will stop for the night. In the meantime, I consider how all her life, my mother hoped and worked for what most women in her circle did: a husband who loved her and whom she cared about in return, someone who could provide for his family, and with whom she could raise their children together. That was as much happiness as she could wish or pray for.

And my mother did pray. My father's religious extremes were not my mother's way, nor did she "preach" to or moralize with her family in the way my father did. Nevertheless, until the last decade of her life she went to church each Sunday, and for as long as she could, she read her Bible every day and offered her private thoughts and supplications to God. She overruled my father's strictures for what constituted acceptable Sunday activities and allowed us to read library books, not just Sunday-school material, and even do needlepoint. "I cannot bring myself to knit on Sundays because when I was *en* girl, that was considered work. I had *en* friend, though, whose father let her knit to keep her hands busy but she had to take it all out on Monday. So strict he was, she could not benefit from what work she did on Sundays," she told us, her way of stressing how lax things had become in the intervening years.

Joanne and I cleared our mother's few remaining possessions from her assisted-living suite when we realized she would never return to it. Among the cards and letters she had saved, in addition to her knickknacks and curios, we found numerous Bible verses and prayers taped to pictures and tucked inside books, their words strengthening her with comfort and hope. In her healthier years, when I or any of my sisters shared problems with her, she often passed on a Bible verse or a poem she thought appropriate to the circumstance. Although she prayed to the God of her faith, she preferred not to attract too much attention from a capricious deity who demanded obeisance, who blessed just as easily as punished.

Just the same, my mother accepted and understood that "the Lord's ways are not our ways." In one handwritten prayer, she expressed gratitude for her freedom from want and oppression, asked a blessing on the members of her family and those who suffered, and ended with her plea for a peaceful death.

The next morning, my last day on the road, I depart from Portage La Prairie, continuing west toward Regina, Moose Jaw, and Swift Current in Saskatchewan. All across the prairies, I observe farmers in their tractors readying the fields for spring planting and gulls circling over evenly plowed rows, the fertile smell of the newly turned earth wafting in through the air vents of my car. I think about how my mother prayed across the seasons for the farmers, that the crops they planted would receive rain and sun in sufficient amounts and at the right time so people the world over could eat from the abundance of the fall harvest. Whether her food was homegrown, store-bought, or harvested directly from the farm, my mother remained ever grateful for it.

My mother's city-raised children, who never milked a cow in their lives, drank milk from bottles delivered to the house in a truck, which stayed cold in our electric refrigerator. To minimize the loss and expense should we spill our milk, Mom never poured us a full cup. When a plastic tumbler tipped over, as almost always happened on the days when Mom had washed and waxed the floor, milk spread across the table and splashed onto the tiled floor. She wept as much at the waste as at our cavalier attitude.

"I could cry!" she wailed as she bent over to wipe up the mess. "To think what this milk would have meant during the *oorlog*, the war—you people have no idea!"

The Second World War aggravated Mom's childhood experience of poverty which, in turn, influenced how she raised her five daughters. Not a day went by she didn't consider us remarkably blessed to be wearing clean, well-mended clothes, eating three meals a day supplied from a full pantry, and living free from the threat of bombs and German raids. No matter how small the amount of food left over after a meal, Mom insisted we save it for the potlatch of leftovers we ate at the end of the week. Should I even think about surreptitiously throwing away a tablespoon or two of boiled potatoes, Mom sensed my intention. "*Nee, nee,* we don't throw good food away here; no sirree! What *en* sin!" With an ungrateful sigh, I placed the tidbit of leftovers into the Tupperware container Mom handed me, the faded pink plastic peeling at its worn bottom. If no saucers were available, I covered it with a used bread bag (plastic wrap was an unnecessary and wasteful expense), and placed the food in the fridge.

Like most of her working-class immigrant friends, Mom devised innumerable ways to wring the most from a limited budget. With the exception of coffee, she placed the cheapest brands in the grocery cart and bought as many sale items as possible, including the jumbo boxes of Kotex pads she ordered from Simpson Sears (wrapped in brown paper so neither she nor the delivery man would be embarrassed by the contents), and she sewed or mended the clothes her husband and daughters wore day-to-day. Every so often, she walked to the Salvation Army store to buy boots or other needed clothing that still had good use in them.

"If someone asks where you got it, you don't need to say," Mom said with stern, stiff pride, adding yet one more family secret. She assumed we were the only family who relied on secondhand goods, that other Dutch immigrant families always sewed their own clothing from new fabric or could afford to buy brand new garments. But unknown to my sisters and me was how deeply the stigma of my mother's impoverished childhood was etched into her being. When cousins in Holland passed along a photo of my mother's young mustached father wearing a somewhat tattered knit sweater, Frances asked, "Mom, your father looks so cool in that sweater. How come you never had a copy of this photo?"

"I do have it," my mother answered slowly, "but I don't like it."

To my mother, the photo reinforced the reality of a father who couldn't afford a suit for the photo he posed for, whose clothing emphasized the dire circumstances of her childhood, something not apparent to her daughter. Seventy-five years later, Frances saw a man, her grandfather, dressed in a retro sweater.

Perhaps because of the humiliation experienced from wearing other people's cast-off dresses, my mother purchased new clothing for our Sunday attire. Granted, she bought a size or two too big so we could grow into the new coat or dress to maximize its wear, and when we eventually outgrew the apparel, the next daughter wore it as a school outfit. Thus, on Sundays and weekdays, we all wore neatly pressed clothes with freshly polished leather shoes.

My mother's need for frugality evolved into fascination, and long after the need to buy used items had passed, my mother looked forward to browsing through a thrift store. She never lost the thrill of finding attractive clothing, useful housewares, interesting knick-knacks, and good books—all at bargain prices. And sometimes after rummaging through the bins of a secondhand store, Mom found a Royal Albert china cup and saucer or a crocheted doily, which helped to ease her from a low mood.

As Karen Carpenter used to sing, rainy days and Mondays always got Mom down. Doing the wash, her Monday task, involved a lot of manual work, even with the bonus of a wringer-washer and rinsing tubs, luxury tools she and her mother did not have when they took in other people's washing. While on our drive home from the Sunday evening church service, Mom bemoaned the end of the weekend, dreading the work that lay ahead in the coming week. "Too bad, *hé*, tomorrow already is Monday again. When we get home, you girls make supper ready and I go downstairs to put the wash in to soak. Make sure you give me all your dirty clothes," she'd add.

My father took literally the commandment to honor and keep the Sabbath day holy. He reacted in typical fashion. "*Ach, Sjoukje,* today is the Lord's day, a day of rest. Why can you not wait until tomorrow to do your work?" But Mom held firm, exasperated at Dad's inability to understand that sorting the laundry on Sunday and soaking a load or two overnight helped her transition more easily into the workweek.

Dad's fervor for the church and all things theological could also get Mom down. Although otherwise an affable, easygoing man, when Dad voiced his opinion about religious and spiritual matters, he did so vociferously and without reserve to his family and amongst his churchgoing friends. Initially after his arrival in Calgary, he maintained his Calvinistic beliefs of original sin and salvation, of infant baptism and adult profession of faith, but after a few years, he began to favor a more evangelical approach to the gospel. Dad's shifting beliefs meant a noticeable uptick of arguments at home and in social settings, which distressed Mom, and by extension, her children—my sisters and me. Several times a year my mother reached a breaking point with my father's argumentative ways. Perhaps on Sunday morning, at a coffee gathering following a church service, he raised his voice at our guests to criticize someone who favored attending only one, not both, Sunday church services, or he berated someone's lack of commitment to Christian education. Mom felt deeply the embarrassment of my father's boorishness. We could tell from Mom's pale face, the way she held her lips in a pencil-thin line, or the way she flung the next meal onto the table—soggy potatoes and overcooked beans—all the more tasteless because we knew that Dad had "done it again." We'd tiptoe for the next few days until Mom regained her equilibrium. In the meantime, should my unrepentant father dare to say anything, whether to defend himself or to cajole my mother, she hurled a scornful remark his way.

"*Ja,* and you think the Lord likes it when you say such awful things?"

"*Nee, Sjoukje,* what you say is not right. Ephesians 5:5 says wives are to be submissive to their husbands, and children to their fathers and mothers." Why Dad brought up this reasoning at such times I never understood. But both of my parents were adept at issuing to each other the same fruitless arguments over and over again, year after year, with the miraculous hope that the other would finally be compelled to respond to the correctness of the other's logic.

"Oh *ja?*" said Mom, her indignation rising. "*de Bijbel* says also that men are supposed to love their wives and to not bring their children to anger!"

But Dad knew more Bible verses than Mom, and he could hurl them back and forth like a ping-pong ball in a way that ultimately thumped his wife into angry silence. The next morning Mom, completely spent, remained in bed, unable or unwilling to prepare breakfast as she usually did. Dad made his own lunch while my sisters and I set out the brown bread and cheese we ate at every breakfast. One of us made a pot of tea to accompany our morning meal. Mom's absence at these times made us realize the vital role she served as the fulcrum of our family. Without her in our midst, and without actually talking about it, we all felt lost, trying our best to keep an appearance of normalcy with our stilted conversations. Getting out of her funk and back on track with her usual humor took Mom about three days. By the end of the third day, Mom asked if one of us had a joke to tell her, saying that she needed a good laugh. The joke didn't even have to be that funny.

"Jenny, tell that one again, the one about the butcher," she'd demand when I came home from elementary school, her mood clearly lifting after several days of gloom.

"What did the pig say when the butcher caught him by the tail?" I asked dutifully, and followed it with the punch line, "That's the end of me." Mom doubled over in laughter even though she'd heard the joke numerous times. A good belly laugh for Mom cleared the air for all of us, and we no longer had to tread as if on eggshells. In turn, Mom resumed her role as wife and mother, the balance in our household restored until she hit the next wall with Dad.

Despite my father's aggravating ways, my mother loved him, the man she would have married again, despite their differences. With their children grown and making use of the very opportunities for which they had moved to Canada, my parents settled into an ease they hadn't known since their courtship. They traveled to British Columbia during my father's summer holidays, and after he retired, my parents became active hikers along with several other longtime friends, tramping along the many trails of the nearby Rocky Mountains. By then my mother had returned to attending the Christian Reformed Church, where my father grudgingly rejoined her. My parents worshipped together, visited children and grandchildren, mourned when loved ones died, and sipped tea together in the carpeted enclosure my father had constructed alongside the garage, complete with a small aviary of finches and doves. When my father's vegetable garden was ready for harvesting, Mom appreciated the help he offered with blanching and freezing. A few months after my parents celebrated their forty-first anniversary, my father died from recurrent bowel cancer. My mother missed him, measuring time by its passage following his death, and without him she never quite regained her center.

"Dad has never seen this," she'd say when we drove by a new subdivision midway through development. "I wonder what he would say about it."

My mother's depressive episodes lessened over the years, although her melancholy never completely evaporated. If, in her widowhood, Mom spent too much time alone without the hugs and attention she received from her daughters or grandkids, or without enough social interaction with friends, then she could direct the nastiness of her dark mood toward whichever daughter happened to stop by to see her. Because Frances visited Mom most frequently, she bore the brunt of these moods, biting back her own retorts to prevent escalating Mom's negativity. But within fifteen or twenty minutes, Fran said, "something lifted from Mom and she became her usual self—fun and caring." Then they enjoyed being together as if Mom's dark side had never surfaced.

At long last, I pass the sign that says I have arrived in "Wild Rose Country," my home province of Alberta. Soon after, I stop in Medicine Hat for gas and a fresh cup of Tim Hortons brew. I lower the sun visor against the evening sun as I sip my tea, knowing I will make it to Mom's bedside before hospital visiting hours are over. Driving through the familiar panorama of southern Alberta, I am as good as home with just a couple of hours left to complete my journey.

In Strathmore, about thirty minutes from the city limits, I call Frances from my cell phone to let her know I'll soon be there. Before I hang up, she tells me where to park and how to find our mother's room. "Fancy things" like new cars and mobile phones both fascinated and frightened Mom. She never owned a micro-wave and never had an inkling of how to operate one. Computers were beyond her comprehension altogether: "*Ja*, how is it possible what *de* com-pewters can all do?" she'd say with her unique inflec-tion. "It's *en* miracle." By the time someone thought to give her a cordless telephone, it was too late to be of use to her. With a failing memory, knowing which buttons to push to make a call or retrieve a message escaped her. "There's something wrong with it," she kept telling Frances and Joanne, preferring instead her own familiar phone with its large numbers and coiled cord, a stool close by to sit on. If she expected one of her daughters to phone, she remained within earshot of the telephone so as not to miss the call even if that meant forfeiting other activities.

On a rise near the Calgary city limits, the snow-peaked moun-tains are visible in the distance. Soon the Trans-Canada Highway becomes 16th Avenue in Calgary, from where I reach Foothills Hospital, my destination. I park the car, run a comb through my hair, and make my way through the hallways and up the stairs of the building where Mom's room is situated. When I stand in the doorway, Mom recognizes me immediately. "You made it," she says with surprise and glee. "I'm so glad." I caress her face and simultane-ously she reaches for my hand to kiss it.

In the days that follow, I barely recognize my mother, shrunken as she is, disengaged most of the time. With left-sided hemipare-sis, she has a droopy left eyelid, which looks even worse because of the sticky ointment the nurse squeezes over her eye three times a day. Unaware she is drooling, she rarely wipes her mouth. She's unable to hold her head erect, her speech is slurred, and her aware-ness comes and goes like a flickering light. She is wraithlike from the weight she's lost. All her life Mom cringed at the thought of losing her dignity, of becoming a spectacle. But now, hospitalized and in the full throes of dementia, my mother can, when struck with fear or pain, holler with such volume and wildness that the nursing staff comes rushing in to see what calamity has befallen her. Mostly, though, she lies demure in her electronic Stryker bed, unconcerned by her total dependence on others to bathe, feed, turn, change, and medicate her. She lacks even the awareness of her evolving sightlessness, that colors dissipate and fade, then shapes and faces, and finally the light.

Mom's cognition evaporates like mist carried away on a warm breeze. Only the immediate present concerns her. "My dentures hurt," she says, and with her tongue she extrudes the new plate the denturist, only weeks before, meticulously fit for her comfort. When she wants something to drink we feed her thickened fluids, teaspoon by teaspoon, to prevent her aspirating. When she says "I'm cold," we rush to find her a warmed blanket. She no longer concerns herself with how we are doing, nor does she comprehend the news she will be moving to a hospice. This alteration in my mother devastates me and I mourn her loss, unable to will away my ever-present tears. In the weeks and months before she fell, I knew that each coherent conversation we shared was a gift. But I was unprepared for the day when my mother would never again take an active interest in my well-being, that I would never again feel irritated by her, not with her routine of locking and unlocking the door nor the question she asked that so drove me crazy: "Can you still do it?" She asks me this several times a year in reference to my work as a college professor, unable to imagine herself in a similar role, proud of my achievement but not quite grasping what exactly I do. Now I want to stand in the hallway and, like my mother, bellow loudly. "I want my mother back! What have you done with her?"

Frightened as she is by the jostling on the stretcher in the back of the ambulance, and then by the subsequent transfer to her hospice bed, I comfort my mother as she moans aloud in fear. Leaning against the bedrails, I hold her hand and explain the details of her new home—the gauzy curtains that filter the light through the window, the bureau, the armoire, the recliner in the corner. But Mom has only one concern. "There's something wet on my cheek," she says in Frisian, and with her stiff right hand she tries to wipe away what I realize are my tears falling on her face.

The hospice is close to where Frances lives, and I cycle the few miles to spend part of every day with my mother. She's unavailable to me most of the time, sleeping or lost in the netherworld of dementia. I can do little for her other than at mealtimes, when I feed her. Sitting by her bedside, I'm surprised to find how close to tears I am most of the time. Thinking about her, her strengths, abilities, gratitude, humor, her low moods offset by ready laughter, her criticisms and fears—they all stand out for me. Then I hear her voice as clearly as if she spoke the words from her bed, "*Fanke*, be *flink*," her pragmatic advice, and sometimes her admonishment, issued in the patois of Dutch, Frisian, and English that had become our family language, to be steadfast and strong in whatever trying situation my sisters or I find ourselves.

Despite the rift that has occurred in our family, my sisters make their peace with our mother as best they can. I encounter Joanne a few times while Mom remains in hospice care, and together we clear our mother's belongings from her Wentworth suite. Our conversations are friendly, but we skirt around the tear in our relationship. From Pauline, I learn that Helen also made a visit to Mom's bedside, and a few weeks after giving birth to her second son, my niece, Helen's daughter, brings Simon to meet his great-grandmother. Had she been aware of it, Mom would have delighted in meeting this newest member of the family.

The smallest of details lent sparkle to her life, even after the onset of dementia. And for all these reasons, I resent the blanket statement issued by her doctors, that their surgical hip replacement was a bona fide success. If Mom can't resume her life at Wentworth, what really have they achieved? Furthermore, the physicians, who see only an elderly woman in a bed, have no idea who my mother was. How can they know Mom's cologne of choice was *4711*, that she would dab some on a handkerchief for us children to keep in our purses should we feel the need to inhale a fresh scent during the day? I want them to know that the 1968 *Book of Knowledge* encyclopedia bought to help my sisters and me with our schoolwork provided my mother with forty years and countless hours of reading about countries and scientific phenomena she described to us with awe in her voice: "So interesting!" How can her doctors know that Mom liked something sweet to eat after waking from a snooze, that following a Sunday nap she broke up and served us all pieces of the scored chocolate bar she had bought for just this reason? Could they appreciate how she made Christmas special for her Canadian family with a decorated tree, wrapped gifts, and a turkey dinner, that she rented a television, over my father's protests, for the duration of the yuletide holidays? Do they know that to earn some extra money for herself and her children, she did housecleaning for many years? That along with my father, she fostered six babies? That for many years she volunteered to assist women with multiple sclerosis so they could spend an hour each week feeling weightless in a swimming pool? How could the medical personnel know that when her neighbor, Ann Unger, became noticeably unwell with a heart condition, my mother rolled her friend's hair each week? How could they know that Mom encouraged us, her children, toward new challenges, how she comforted us when we were upset?

Should I quit my job and go back to school? "*Ja, fanke,* girl, if you think you can, do it!" Once, when I voiced my misgivings about a new undertaking, Mom said to me, "*Fanke,* don't give up!" When I felt overwhelmed by a new job turned sour, Mom comforted me, "*Lietse skat,* dear one, when you come I make you some *Hollandse* soup." Although not a remarkable cook, my mother won hands down when it came to making a pot of soup, and almost every week she made some type of vegetable soup flavored with a soup bone or miniature meatballs and seasoned with a package of Dutch soup. Always, she urged me to be *flink,* to hold my head high and persevere.

Mom took great pride in her children. "Other people brag about their children, so I like to show off my kids, too," she said as our adult lives and careers evolved. But uncomfortable with openly boasting about her children and grandchildren, she instead put the photos and business cards of her beloved in places where she could point them out to company—under the clear plastic tablecloth or wedged in the frame of another picture. She also hung them with clothespins where she could. Upon knowing she would not return to Wentworth, I took on the task of clearing her things from her room. Her room remained as when, weeks before, the ambulance staff had collected her from the floor. Something flag-like suspended from the antenna of Mom's boom-box stereo caught my attention. In a ziplock bag attached to the aerial with a wooden clothespin, Mom had mounted an article clipped from the *Calgary Herald* announcing Frances's nomination a few months earlier for an Alberta teacher of excellence award. In this, her way, Mom proclaimed Fran's honor, and she could point out the notice to anyone who stepped into her room.

Showing off her daughter's accomplishment via a ziplock bag, using a bar of soap down to a translucent sliver, saving elastics and reusing twist ties, or slipping a list under the clear plastic tablecloth— all of it typified Mom. Never showy, she held with the notion that small was good enough. For as long as she was able, she completed domestic chores, such as laundry and cooking, because they were necessary. Other activities, knitting or crocheting, she undertook as satisfying pastimes because it made her feel good to finish something useful, but she rarely analyzed her thoughts or reflected on her feelings. When the Ladies Aid Society at church no longer satisfied, she quit going. A book was a good book because she liked the story, not because of the author's literary skill. She listened to classical music, which quieted her, but she felt no inclination to know the name of a piece or its composer. By tuning in to a French radio station she achieved two purposes: enjoyment of *mooi*—nice classical music—and remaining oblivious to the troubles in the world when the news came on in a foreign language. The beauty and simplicity of nature impressed and soothed her, but she felt no urge to learn the name of a flower or discover the science of its intricate botany. She loved her home and failed to understand the compulsion of others "to be always on the road" as she put it. Why would you go out to a movie or a concert when you could watch a perfectly good one on TV—for free?

Upon her move to hospice, Mom's death seemed imminent. One evening, Frances and I hovered around her bed, certain this night would be her last, but she roused after several semicomatose days. She began eating again, and for a few days the staff nicknamed her "The Phoenix." Days soon melded into weeks, which turned into months and eventually a year. Mom surprised everyone. She required complete care, and although her verbal skills all but disappeared, she nonetheless retained an ability to register simple conversation in English or Frisian.

During her year in hospice care, I sent a card every week that Pauline read aloud to my mother; during her visits, Frances often called me from the hospice. "Mom's having a good day, Jen; I'll put the cell phone to her ear." I'd chitchat to my mother, and on occasion her mumbled "*lietse skat*," her endearment for her children, brought me to near tears. Sometimes Frances told me about the big smile on my mother's face when I spoke to her on the phone. In my mother's last months, she uttered only garbled gibberish, but from her tears, Frances said, Mom knew her daughter Jenny on the other end of the phone loved her.

In the summer of 2012, a year after Mom's hospice vigil began, I drove back to Calgary once again but without the angst of the previous year. During my daily visits, my mother occasionally, with her contracted arm, reached for my hand and brought it to her toothless mouth, offering my hand a soft kiss. While sitting at her bedside, I mourned the mother I remembered who seemed gone, nowhere to be found. Once I glanced at my feeble mother lying in bed, so like an infant with her aimless gaze, but then I noticed how she retained a certain unmistakable mannerism. I watched as my mother lifted her hand to cup her chin between her index finger and thumb, and with this simple gesture, I recognized the inherent essence of my mother. Her gesture was as familiar to me as when I, a child, observed her reading, on a Sunday evening perhaps, when my parents, my sisters, and I would each occupy a spot in the living room—on the couch or in an easy chair—with our own respective book. Mom would sit in her chair under the swag lamp, engrossed in a book, grasping her chin between her fingers, clearing her throat from time to time in the way she did, mindless—or so I hoped—of the clock ticking toward Frances's and my bedtime.

Now I wonder: how and when did Mom become such an avid reader? What did she read when she lived in Holland? Who helped her get her first library card in Calgary? I never thought to ask her such questions. During my childhood, my sisters and I often walked on Saturday afternoons with Mom to the local library to exchange our books, carrying them to and from the library in a brown leather satchel she had squeezed into the *kist* so many years before. With a new supply of library books, we always had something fitting to do on Sunday, which kept us entertained and spellbound in ways a minister's monotone sermon never could.

For as long as I knew her, Mom kept a stash of books beside her chair. Whether biographies, histories, or novels written in Dutch or English, her stack included church and public library books, books borrowed from neighbors and friends, and books bought at a second-hand store. Her copy of *Afke's Tiental* remains on my sister's bookshelf, a book my mother talked about for weeks after finishing it.

"I wish you could read it," she said, mourning her inability to share fully the story and the emotions it stirred in her. "Too bad it's not in English." That Mom read English, Dutch, and Frisian seemed normal to me, as it should be. And I never questioned that none of us children ever learned or were interested to read my mother's tongue. That we had no schooling in Dutch proved to be little excuse given that both my parents learned to read English as soon as they arrived in their adopted country.

Among the English books she read, *My Brother's Keeper* by Marcia Davenport held Mom spellbound for days, and her used copy of Margaret Mitchell's *Gone With the Wind* so captivated her, Mom asked Dad to hide the book before he left for work so she couldn't be tempted to read it rather than attend to her domestic chores. But in the evening, with the book back in her hands, Mom made one of my older sisters responsible for hustling Frances and me to bed on time—without fighting—warning us not to bother

her and interrupt the gripping story for anything more than a good-night kiss. During those dark evenings, as winter snow and cold winds blew outside, Mom lost herself in the heated passions of the American South and the Civil War. When the book became a movie, she viewed it on screen, mesmerized by the compelling story and its characters. When the movie was broadcast on television, she watched it again. Each time she saw the film, Mom hoped that Scarlett wouldn't break Rhett Butler's heart. "That poor man," she sympathized. She wanted Scarlett to be a better person, but at the same time, she admired her verve.

"That woman really dared," Mom said, astonished by the fearless Southern belle who spoke her mind and did as she chose. Humble and timid as she could be, Mom rarely asserted herself in situations beyond the parameters of our home—except when it came to protecting her children. Then her ferocious maternal nature truly surfaced. Once, as children, my sisters and I came home sooner than expected from a nearby playground. Mom probed and learned from us that some boys had begun throwing rocks at whoever tried to use the swings or merry-go-round, using "swears" and calling us rude names. Mom marched off in her housedress and bare legs, uncon-cerned as she usually was about disguising the blue web of varicose veins running up from her shapely ankles. In one hand she grasped my little sister's hand, and in the other she clenched a baseball bat. Helen and I ran alongside to keep up with her, uncertain of what the unyielding look on my mother's face might mean. When we arrived, Mom, in awkward English and with a few coarse Frisian invectives, warned the boys that if she ever heard about them tormenting her children again, she would use the bat on them. We never encoun-tered trouble on the playground again.

Mom could, when provoked, let loose with some colorful language, whether in Dutch, Frisian, or English, but she never took the Lord's name in vain. Hearing someone *flokke,* swear, or reading blasphemous words in print offended Mom. "Why is that neces-sary?" she'd ask in annoyance.

I once opened a hardcover copy of Max Braithwaite's book *The Night We Stole the Mountie's Car*.

"Mom," I asked, "what happened to this book?" On almost every page, someone had used a black felt-tip pen to stroke out an expletive here, an oath there.

"Oh," Mom said calmly, "that was me. It's a nice story, but not with all those bad words."

She held the same attitude toward off-color jokes. A proper and moral woman of faith, Mom detested sexual innuendo, considering it unseemly and unnecessary. Should she hear us, her adult children, laughing at a "dirty" or suggestive remark, Mom would tune out, turn her gaze past us, then point to a tree or a bird in flight. "Look at that," she'd remark. "Isn't nature beautiful?"

Certainly, the day-to-day changes of the Rocky Mountain peaks visible from her west-facing apartment window gave her an ongoing sense of the grandeur of the natural world. But the smallest of details captured my mother's attention, whether the joyous song of a robin after a rain shower, a sparrow bearing a twig in its beak, or an ant crossing the patio dragging a crumb twice its size to its underground lair. On any walk I ever took with her, Mom never failed to point out a weed or flower pushing its way through a slim crack in a sidewalk. "Look at that," she'd say. "It's *en* miracle, isn't it?" I came to see those determined bits of nature as symbolic of my mother: unassuming but not to be overlooked.

The photo we hung of Mom on the wall in her hospice room, and later in the nursing home, showed her sitting outdoors on my sister's deck just a few years before her fall, her eyes bright with laughter, a smile on her face, a cup of tea in her hand. Although she was already in the early stages of memory loss, something my sisters and I didn't know at the time, the photo showed Mom at her best, physically and emotionally secure in the company of people she loved and trusted.

We displayed that same photo at her funeral. On January 2, 2013, Mom died in her nursing-home bed in the same unobtrusive way in which she lived. Christina, an aide who loved my mother, bathed and cared for her that day. During her afternoon visit, Pauline fed Mom lunch, gave her a hand and facial massage with olive oil, and read Mom's favorite Bible passages aloud to her. A half hour after being fed supper, before the nurse came with her meds, my mother slipped away from this life.

Mom did not want an open casket, so instead, Frances, Pauline, and I made a private visitation together. Upon our arrival at the funeral home, the attendant showed us where coffee and tea fixings could be had, and she then ushered us into the small chapel where Mom lay in the cheapest, humblest casket available—also her choice. And she *was* recognizable as Mom, at peace and laid out in a blouse and skirt from Frances's closet, her expensive dentures fitted back in her mouth and filling out her cheeks. After our initial tears, we congregated around Mom, talking to her, caressing for the last time her soft hands and face, and laughing together about shared memories. Before long we each had a cup of tea in our hands.

"Just what Mom would have wanted," we said, "a *gezellich*, cozy tea party together."

Mom relished the pause allowed by a cup of tea, a ritual she learned from her own mother, who likely took it on from her mother. *Beppe* always kept the teakettle on the back of the coal-burning stove, Mom told me, so she could add hot water when the tea got too strong. In like manner, Mom taught my sisters and me the role of tea in daily life along with how to brew a proper pot of tea. Upon our arrival home from school, Mom already had the tea things laid out on the table for my sisters and me. After a shopping trip, even before putting her parcels away, Mom filled the kettle to make a fresh pot. Hospitality for guests who stopped by meant putting the teakettle on when they arrived. I learned from my mother the therapeutic value of tea as a substance that could fortify, refresh, calm, or comfort. Drinking weak tea helped to resolve a gastrointestinal complaint, whereas a stronger cup of tea revived one's spirits. A cup of tea served as an opportunity to take a break, and it could also provide the transition between one task and another. "First we have a *lekker*, a nice cup of tea," Mom would say before putting the groceries away or beginning meal preparations.

Among the keepsakes on my mantle in Fort Kent is a silver tin, a gift Mom received from her mother in 1948, likely a wedding gift. She kept loose tea and a silver spoon in it, and although Mom got in the habit of using teabags just as her Canadian neighbors did, once in a while she craved an *echte* or real cup of tea. Then she'd spoon some tea leaves from the silver tin into the teapot, pour in the boiling water, and after steeping it for a few minutes, begin to sip a steaming cup of brewed tea.

One day in August of 2010, after we came back to her apartment following an appointment, Mom made me a cup of tea, which in retrospect I realized was the last time she did so. I resisted the initial urge to take over, agitated at first because I knew I could prepare the tea more efficiently, that I could be on my way sooner if I did. But I had nowhere else to be, no calls on my time, so instead I sat on the couch, allowing Mom to make the tea in the familiarity of her kitchen, willing myself to enjoy this time together. We chatted as Mom puttered about, waiting for the kettle to boil. She told me that Julie, a friend, had been by a few days before and left her some *Hollandse kranten*, the Dutch news magazines Mom still liked to read. She showed me a card she'd received from Trisha, a grand daughter, who had sent photos of my mother's newest great-grand-daughter. Propped up here and there on a shelf or tucked between the frame and glass of photos and lithographs were more pictures of her loved ones.

In time, and with careful steps, Mom brought in the tea tray, the cups rattling slightly in their saucers from her unsteady hand.

"Do you want anything for *bij* the tea?" she asked.

Without waiting for my answer, Mom made another trip to the kitchen to offer me some *speculaas*, spice cookies.

"*Hé*, what *gezellich*, a *lekker* cup of tea with each other."

It was so ordinary an event, drinking tea in china cups that had survived decades of use, but I recognized that afternoon ritual of tea as an extraordinary gift. Months later, as Mom lay in the hospice bed, I, while sitting at her bedside during my visits, drank tea from a mug heated in a microwave, my way to linger with Mom for just a bit longer before I went home.

And so it goes, the ritual of tea continues from one generation to the next to restore and sustain, and to keep mothers and daughters connected. As I sip my cup of tea at home in Fort Kent, I am grateful to remember my mother and equally grateful to have been her daughter. With no children of my own, it's my niece to whom I will pass on the silver tea tin, and it's to her I will say, over a cup of steaming tea, "*Lietse skat,* it's so good to be with you." And, I hope, she in turn will say the same thing to her daughter.

Reflection:
"The Essence of Mom"

What does it mean to love your mother? I pondered this question on my drive from Fort Kent to Portland, a six-hour trip, en route to the MWPA Saturday afternoon writing workshop, the catalyst for this anthology. At the time, my mother languished in hospice care a year after her admission there. Despite the vast miles between us, she in Alberta and I in Maine, and no matter her profound dementia and lack of awareness, I felt a close emotional bond with my mother. I wanted to pen her story, and the MWPA workshop provided a stepping stone with which to begin. The process to get from workshop to finished product involved a few years and became something of a personal challenge from which I gained new insights and great satisfaction.

My foray into creative writing began in the fall of 2006 when I took my first writing workshop. From it I learned how much I liked writing, especially crafting memoir stories. Some six years later when I began this essay about my mother, the writing came easily, and within a month I assumed, as only a novice writer can, I had completed the narrative about my mother. Because of the disruption of family dynamics some eighteen months earlier, writing it proved to be therapeutic, both as a way to jot down memories of my mother before they faded with time, and also to vindicate her memory from others in the family who didn't share my feelings.

In my excitement to have a completed manuscript, I emailed that early draft to two people who both loved my mother and are my most trusted fans, Frances, my sister, and Pauline, my surrogate sister. They sent me reassuring comments, but that's what sisters do for each other, right? Yet in our phone conversations and electronic communication, I could tell from their tone that the essay I had written was okay, possibly good, but not strong. Because of mounting demands on my time from work, the essay remained on the back burner of my mind, and as time allowed, I mulled it over and gave thought to what else it needed. But as part of the process of this project and thanks to comments and questions offered by my writing companions, murky details and obscure nuances gained the clarity and illumination they needed.

For me, this work meant facing a range of emotions and struggling through what I might otherwise have preferred to keep buried in the crypts of my mind. Dealing with the aftermath of my unraveled sibling relationships can still keep me awake at nights. For reasons known only to themselves, my sisters made the decision to go it alone without family contact. But like the Biblical story of the ninety and nine, my mother, despite her flawed memory, remembered she had five daughters and yearned for each one whose absent hand she could not touch. For as long as she had the capacity, she prayed for and never lost hope that the pain of love would once again turn to joy.

I vacillated about mentioning the family fallout in my essay and opted initially to avoid it. But in another writing workshop the instructor encouraged going where the "heat" burned in our personal stories. My companions in this project indicated I needed to include this family hurt, that the splintering of my family is part of my mother's story, that without its mention, her story becomes less honest. Indeed, the family fragmentation is part of what propelled me to write this essay about my mother, to thread together my mother's story and gain insight into what made her the inexplicable person she was. In the process, I have come to appreciate my mother more fully as a loving but imperfect person, someone whose early formative experiences bore lasting consequences for her children and grandchildren. My mother longed for peace and harmony in the family, and I, too, send out to the universe my hope that we sisters will someday heal existing hurts and forgive one another our past wrongs, that my sisters and I might begin afresh with one another, with loving candor and sincerity. But like my mother, I cannot imagine how to bring about this transformation.

Author Thomas King, during a CBC radio interview, spoke about the power of storytelling: "Who are we if not our stories?" he asked. His question resonates with me. Dementia strips a person of her memories, of her story, the essence of one's personhood. Who does my mother become if her story goes untold? And who am I if I fail to connect her story to my own—or that of my family? I endeavored to write "The Essence of Mom" as honestly as possible, my way of paying tribute to my mother's resilience and individuality. To do so, I looked at old photos with cousins in the Netherlands, some who I met for the first time; I dusted off nearly forgotten memories; blew the cobwebs from hidden details; and refreshed favorite and sometimes difficult recollections. In the process, I strengthened the admiration I hold for my mother, most notably an inexorable ability to remain her own person. I can only hope that my own story reflects similar strength, grace, humor, love, and a steadfast ability to be genuine and authentic.

Ellie *by Maggie Butler*

I came to know my mother mostly through her roles: daughter, sister, wife, and mother. These roles provide a natural and familiar framework for me to write about her life. Other things I know about her, or imagine I know, I learned through photographs or stories she told me.

The parts of my mother's life that I have included here are like mosaic tiles that, when placed together, suggest a likeness or an impression rather than an exact representation of a subject. In this case, the subject is my mother, Ellie, and the impression is my own.

My Mother as Daughter

When I was five years old, my family lived in a small town in Western Massachusetts. It's also when my mother's mother, Maude, came to live with us in our four-room Cape Cod house. Her health was failing and my mother, along with her two remaining siblings, agreed the time had come for their mother to be more closely looked after. Because my mother was the only one with a stable home to offer, it was a foregone conclusion where my grandmother would go to live. Ellie was devoted to her mother, and she didn't hesitate to look after her ma.

Maude was a first-generation Irish-American who was born and raised in South Boston, home to a robust Irish community. When she was barely into her twenties her first husband died, and she was left alone to raise their only child, a little boy named Joe. Several years later Maude remarried and had five more children: Ruth, Frank, Ellie, Tom, and Walter, who died as an infant.

When she came to live with us, my grandmother brought only one piece of furniture with her: a large antique Victorian curio cabinet that claimed considerable real estate in our tiny living room. In our family, the piece of furniture itself, rather than the objects in and on it, was known as "the bric-a-brac," and it remained in my mother's house many years after Maude died. When I turned eight, that mahogany behemoth became my nemesis because one of my chores was to dust it. Until then, my mother dusted it faithfully every week, in spite of relentless and explosive sneezing from her allergies.

"This was in my house when I was a child," she told me one day as she wiped the dustcloth over one of the shelves she'd just cleared, meticulously going into each corner and finishing with a swipe along the edge. It was just before Christmas, and earlier that day my mother had said the house needed a good cleaning for visitors, which I naturally presumed meant Santa. But I wasn't at all disappointed when I learned that my Auntie Ruth and Uncle Tommy were coming to visit that weekend. I was the apple of their collective eye and reveled in their love.

The phrase "when I was a child" caught my attention. I loved hearing stories about my mother when she was a child, even though I could never imagine her as a little girl like me.

"In Boston?"

My mother nodded. "We lived in an apartment over the store my father owned."

"What kind of a store?"

"It was called a tobacco and sundry shop."

I looked at the curio cabinet, which seemed enormous to me. "Was it a big apartment?"

My mother put down her dustcloth, sat down next to me on the red sectional sofa, and studied the bric-a-brac.

"Oh, yes, and it was filled with beautiful things." She told me about the carved mahogany dining room set and buffet, the wall tapestries woven in rich hues that hung from the walls, an elegant sterling-silver tea set, fine china rimmed with gold, and a sterling-silver flatware set that could serve sixteen people.

"I remember hand-painted porcelain vases that stood this tall." Ellie turned to me and raised her hand to a height that, if I was standing, would reach my shoulder. She looked back at the huge survivor in our living room. "It's all gone now."

"Where'd it go?" I asked, feeling as sad as my mother looked.

"My father sold it."

"How come?" I felt mad at my grandfather for making my mother sad.

When she turned to me, Ellie's eyes brimmed with tears that could spill at any moment. "He had to. We needed the money." She paused between her sentences, as though she had to stop for each memory as it arose. "He only got a fraction of what things were worth. It broke my mother's heart." Her tears fell gently. "It was a horrible time. Not just for us, but for everybody. It was during the Depression. I was a only a few years older than you are now."

"What's the Depression?"

My mother stood and picked up the dustcloth, cut from one of my father's old T-shirts. "That's enough for now. Go find something to do or I'll find something for you."

My mother was eleven when the stock market crashed and the Great Depression began. Her family considered her to be a sensitive child, and it's very likely that in addition to her own feelings of loss and insecurity, Ellie absorbed and carried those of her parents as well.

I'm not sure how my grandfather's shop survived or how he supported his family through that bleak period until 1938, when he died in his late fifties. But what I do know is that after his death, Ellie's life became even more difficult. Barely twenty-one years old, she had to assume the responsibility of caring for her now twice-widowed mother and her two brothers who lived at home. Tommy was still in high school, and Frank, who had a serious drinking problem, worked only sporadically. Joe and Ruth, her eldest siblings, did what they could to help their mother, but given the economic climate and the fact that they had families of their own, they couldn't offer much. Since Frank couldn't hold down a job, it was primarily my mother who supported the family on her meager secretary's paycheck. Fortunately, she had been trained at one of Boston's top secretarial schools and never had trouble finding work.

Ellie loved everything about working in downtown Boston. She found her work interesting and the buzz of the city exciting. She could meet friends for lunch, and sometimes after work they'd go window-shopping or to a movie. When she did shop, it was for bargains—often from Filene's Basement store, which allowed her to dress in the smart and fashionable clothes required for her workplace. Her looks and clothes were of paramount importance to her, and throughout her life she devoted a lot of attention to both. Being thrifty allowed her to indulge in her sartorial penchant and stay within her means, something I always admired about her.

In 1943, during the height of World War II and five years after my grandfather died, Ellie, Maude, and Tommy moved into a smaller apartment after Frank, who had a steady bout of work, moved out. They found a triple-decker house in Dorchester, the heart of the Irish diaspora in Boston. Directly opposite their first-floor back porch was that of the Scanlons, another Irish-American family with four sons. Their eldest lad, Billy, was fighting in the Pacific Theater, just like Joe, my mother's favorite brother.

In that close neighborhood, where friends and family always used the back door, it would have been impossible for Ellie to miss how frequently folks called in to the Scanlons. The cheerful atmosphere across the way was in stark contrast to her own home, strained by the problem of Frank's alcoholism and the reserve of her mother, a devout and pious Catholic. It didn't take long, though, before Ellie, who loved to socialize, was welcomed into the crowd at her new neighbors' home.

Just a few steps from her own back door, Ellie found a completely different way of being Irish Catholic. There, she met people who laughed and drank; shared cigarettes, food, and gossip; who partied and danced—as well as faithfully attended Saturday-night confession and Sunday-morning mass. She met people with names like Fitzy, Big Louise, Baby Lou, Pop, Babe, John Joe, Pat Joe, and Billy Boy. For all of them, the strong sense of community went a long way toward brightening those dark war years.

After their families had been neighbors for over a year, my mother and Billy Scanlon became engaged when he was home on leave, and this fun-loving clan became her future in-laws. She spent lots of time with them, and it wasn't long before most of her family— Ruth and her kids, Tommy, and even her mother—all became part of the crowd who squeezed into that Dorchester tenement, making friendships and creating a family that would last their entire lives. Growing up, my brother and I were often confused as to which side of the family an aunt, uncle, or cousin belonged. It didn't matter; we all blended into one family at Nanny and Gramps' house. I was an adult before I realized we weren't actually related to many of the people we considered family.

Tragically, the bonhomie and gaiety Ellie and her family discovered was quickly sobered when Maude received word that her son Joe had been captured by the Japanese and sent to a prison camp notorious for its brutal treatment of prisoners.

Joe, handsome and charismatic, had his wide-open future stolen by the war. Popular with his friends and family, he always had time for his kid sister, Ellie, and because of that, he held a special place in my mother's heart. Joe never recovered from the ill treatment he received or the tuberculosis he contracted in the prison camp; he died shortly after his release and return home to Boston. Traumatized by the loss, Ellie vowed that if she ever had a son, she would name her boy after Joe, whom she adored.

When my parents married and moved to Western Massachusetts, Ellie missed their family, especially her mother. In 1947, the drive from Springfield to Boston took over two hours, which meant there weren't many trips "home." There were even fewer visits by their family to my parents' little house, which was considered far away and "beyond the pale." My mother and father had left the clan, and the clan didn't travel beyond greater Boston. Even though my father was a full-grown man in his thirties, stationed at a Strategic Air Command base and held a top-secret clearance, it was still considered his duty as a son to come "home" and visit—a very Irish tradition for those who moved away from the family home.

In between their infrequent visits "down home," Ellie stayed in touch with the family through letters and cards, with an occasional photograph tucked inside those crinkly, white onionskin envelopes marked with "Air Mail" in blue and a border of red and blue stripes around the edges. When my father was transferred to an air force base in Bermuda, this correspondence became their only link to family.

Several years later, when they returned stateside and back to Western Massachusetts, the onus of responsibility was once again on my parents to visit their families back in Boston. This bothered my mother more than my father. She was proud of the home they'd made and longed to welcome her family there.

When my brother and I were seven and four respectively, and old enough for my mother to take away on her own, she brought us for occasional weekend visits to her mother, while my father stayed at home to work on converting the attic into bedrooms for us. During each trip, my brother and I were warned to be on our very best behavior. We complied, of course, concerned about the consequences if we didn't. We learned to be quiet and to tolerate boredom; being silly was not an option around my grandmother, Maude. Even though I'd only been on the planet for a few years, I understood that how my brother and I behaved had something to do with the dynamic between my mother and her mother.

The one memorable bright spot during those visits to my grandmother was a cut-glass bowl filled with butterscotch candies wrapped in yellow cellophane. The bowl sat on the side table directly next to my grandmother, and it was hard not to stare at it instead of looking at her or my mother when they spoke. Joey and I loved tasting those golden, buttery disks, sliding our tongues over the slight depression on either side of the candy. After we popped them into our mouths, we'd smooth out the crinkled wrapper, hold it up to our eyes, and look out at the suddenly golden world. We oohed and aahed and shouted "Look! Lookit this!" We'd invite Ellie and Maude to look, too, but they always politely declined.

"Okay, that's enough now. Throw away the papers and settle down," my mother would say. We complied, and the quiet of my grandmother's house was restored, punctuated only by the sounds of their voices and the anniversary clock ticking on the sideboard. We sat quietly until we were allowed to get up, to talk and to play. Spontaneity was a kenneled dog living inside me, longing for freedom.

My clearest memories of Maude are from the time when she lived with us. I remember her as stern and taciturn, a large woman who lumbered down the narrow hallway of our house with the help of her wooden cane, and who sat in my father's chair with impunity. The tiny-print floral dresses she wore had white collars and buttons down the entire length of the dress, which fell mid-calf. Sometimes when she was sitting, the tops of her thick, flesh-toned hose rolled down to just below each knee, peeked out from under the hem, exposing the blue-white color of her fleshy legs. Her glasses were rimless with gold arms, and her long hair, mostly white with tinges of yellow, was braided and coiled around the back of her head and held in place by strategically positioned tortoiseshell hairpins. Some of the hairnets she wore were the palest shade of yellow, and some were almost invisible, reminding me of a spiderweb.

Shortly after moving in with us, Maude was admitted to the hospital with pneumonia. My mother visited her every day, often returning for evening visiting hours. My father worked nights then, so my mother brought me and my brother along to the hospital with her. While Ellie spent time with her mother, we waited in the dark and immense stone lobby just inside the massive wood and stained-glass doors at the entrance. After my grandmother recovered from that bout of pneumonia, she returned to our house—and my eight-by-ten-foot bedroom, which we shared. Within a year Maude became seriously ill again, and this time my mother called an ambulance to come for her.

As far as I knew, an ambulance had never been on our street before—never mind at our house—and the flashing red lights drew the attention of our neighbors and passersby. Inside, obeying my mother's orders to sit quietly and stay out of the way, Joey and I sat bunched together on the scratchy, red living-room couch, our elbows and knees touching, while the drama unfolded in front of us. Filled with a mix of fear and curiosity, we watched the men in their crisp white jackets try to negotiate what looked to us like a cot on wheels through our small house. It felt like forever before they returned to the living room with my grandmother strapped to the top of the gurney. Their presence seemed to take up the whole living room. My father held the front door open for them to go through, but just before they went out, my mother stopped them.

"Wait just a minute," she told the EMTs. Then she said to me and my brother, "Come over here and kiss your grandmother goodbye." I can only imagine how my mother felt knowing this was the last time her mother would see her children, that we would never see our grandmother again.

After I dutifully kissed Maude on her soft, puffy cheek, she admonished me to "be a good girl for your mummy." Because I was six years old, her words and tone of voice sounded and felt like a threat. Decades later, though, this exchange would offer a valuable clue as I tried to come to terms with my mother and my relationship with her. In Maude and Ellie's world, the single most important thing a daughter could do—in fact, the key to pleasing one's mother and to be found pleasing by her—was to do exactly as her mother asked, and do it without question. Obedience was expected and demanded. It was how they measured love.

That pause in the doorway before my grandmother was wheeled out the door was the last time the three of us would be together, the last time three generations of hopes, dreams, expectations, and disappointments would be held in the same space. Maude died very soon after; unfortunately, her legacy lived on for too many years.

After my grandmother died, my mother gave all of her filial attention and affection to my father's parents—Pop, whom we children called "Gramps," and Babe, known to her grandchildren simply as "Nanny." With her own mother gone, Ellie willingly became their dutiful daughter, which never involved the fealty or work of being Maude's daughter.

Pop and his four sons all doted on Babe, who ruled her family from the throne of her upholstered rocking chair in the living room, a jar of multicolored sour balls and another of green smelling salts beside her on a metal TV tray. Relaxed and easygoing, Babe was often engaged in some witty, teasing banter with Gramps and her sons. Joey and I were drawn to them and the atmosphere they created; we wanted the warmth from their glow. My uncles and cousins, their wives, husbands, girlfriends, and boyfriends, plus all of *their* family and friends, along with *their* girlfriends and boyfriends, loved the *craic* at Pop and Babe's house, where there continued to be an abundance of food, stories, drinks, and cigarettes, and always room for one more. (*Craic*, pronounced "crack," is an Irish word that's hard to translate. *Fun* is close, but woefully inadequate.) There was always room for one more. My mother, young and attractive, found her place in this mostly male family. Weekend pilgrimages to Boston were bright beacons throughout my childhood and adolescence, not just because of the fun I had, but primarily because the strained relationship that existed between me and my mother left me feeling adrift and without a sense of belonging. Nanny and

Gramps, my Auntie Ruth, my uncles, and all my cousins—related or otherwise—anchored me in a place that felt safe.

Years later, when I was in my twenties, and for reasons that still remain a mystery to me, my mother felt a need to talk to me about her earlier life. I found this strange because over time, our strained relationship had developed into something I would describe as distant and conflicted. In fact, I assiduously avoided talking with her about anything other than superficial topics. The only explanation I can think of for these disclosures is that Ellie had recently joined Al-Anon because of what she called my father's "drinking problem," and perhaps that had something to do with these unprecedented conversations.

I was married, the young mother of two girls, a baby and a toddler, and lived with my little family in the small ranch-style house we owned about five miles from my parents. Occasionally, my mother would telephone in the morning and ask if she could come by for a cup of coffee later.

"I was wondering if you were going to be around this afternoon?"

I was around every afternoon so the girls could nap, which she knew.

"Yup."

"Well, I thought I might drop over for a cup of coffee if you're going to be there."

Her voice held a forced cheerfulness, like she was auditioning for a part and trying to catch the right tone.

"Of course I'll be here, Ma. What time?"

"What time are the girls going down for their naps?"

I was never comfortable anticipating those visits, because I never knew what to expect with her, and more often than not I was annoyed at having to give up an afternoon to my mother, when I would have enjoyed having the time to read or nap myself. As it became clear over time that she wanted, or needed, those afternoons to reflect on her life, I learned to listen while we drank instant coffee from green ceramic mugs and the afternoon sun brushed past my living room windows. Sometimes she would stay until the girls got up from their naps, but often she left before. My mother loved my daughters and welcomed any opportunity to see them, so it was unusual for her to leave without seeing them. It was as though she came with something on her mind, and as soon as she shared it, she needed to leave.

One particular conversation deeply moved me, so much so that my memory about it is still very clear. Ellie told me that when she was in her early twenties, her mother regularly sent her out, often late at night, to look for her brother Frank in the local bars and bring him home. Any bar in South Boston late at night was not a safe place for a young woman, but my mother went from bar to bar until she found her brother. Frank was always drunk, and it was no easy chore to get him home.

When I heard this story, I felt intensely sad for my mother—almost protective, but I was also outraged that Maude was willing to risk her daughter's safety to get her son home, especially since there was another male in the household who could have been sent out on what was ultimately a fool's errand.

"Ma, what kind of a mother makes her daughter do such a horrible thing? Why didn't she send Uncle Tommy out to look for him?"

"Well…because he was the youngest, I suppose."

"So what? He was old enough."

"I guess my mother protected him." Her voice was small.

"Yeah, but what about you? You should have been protected. Weren't you scared?"

"Oh, yes!" Fear came alive on her face. "It was late, and dark…" Her sentence hung in the air.

I'm embarrassed to admit it was with more accusation than tenderness that I asked my next question. "Why didn't you say no to her, Ma? Why didn't you tell her you weren't going to go out at midnight to look for your drunk of a brother anymore?"

Her reply was swift and firm. "I would *never* speak to my mother like that."

I could see it genuinely never occurred to her, even that afternoon, to refuse to do anything her mother asked, which gave me a laser-sharp insight about her idea of motherhood: A mother's wish, request, or demand must always be fulfilled. I understood in an instant why she seemed so frustrated and disappointed with me. Daughters do as they are told without question, even if it puts them in danger or places someone else at risk. My anger that day was mixed with sadness and a surprising tenderness toward my mother—Maude's daughter. It was the first time I'd ever felt compassion for her.

"What she did was wrong, Ma. She should never have made you do that."

Looking back, I wonder if sharing her memories with me was a peace offering for how she mothered me. Perhaps she hoped in showing me her wounds, I might show her some mercy, or, at the very least, have a better understanding of her. Those stories were a kind of emotional currency, the only thing she had to offer to coax me into a closer adult relationship with her.

It's my belief that my mother got lost in the background of all the drama in her own family. She was a "good girl" who didn't cause trouble and was always trying to please, but most, if not all, of the attention went to her older brother, a war hero, to her beautiful and talented older sister, and to her alcoholic brother. By her own admission in our afternoon conversations, my mother was a dutiful daughter who didn't get what she needed or wanted from her family, or from life.

As I write this, a sepia-toned school photograph of my mother comes to mind. In this one, Ellie is a sweet, gentle-looking little girl about seven or eight years old. Seated at a wooden desk, she wears a large bow atop her perfect Dutch boy haircut and a sailor-collared dress, so fashionable in the day. She's looking straight, but shyly, into the camera. To me, she looks sad, maybe a bit unsure of the attention of the camera, but glad to have it nonetheless. How I would love to know what that little girl is thinking. I want to take her by the hand and ask her to tell me her story.

My Mother as Sister

I never met my Uncle Frank—I knew him only from the small envelopes occasionally left on our dining-room table during my grammar-school years. My mother's name and our address were block-printed in pencil on the front of each one, and "New York City Post Office" was inked in a circle over a two-cent postage stamp. The backs of those weary-looking envelopes were never sealed. Instead, the flaps were tucked in to save postage. Inside, a folded one-page letter waited, always containing the same theme: Frank had found a new mission (homeless shelter), and could my mother please send him a dollar or two? I know this because my mother allowed me and my brother to read his notes. Frank was her brother; she loved him and felt no need to hide anything about him from her children. Ellie cried each time she got his letters, and within twenty-four hours she was tucking one or two dollar bills into an envelope with her reply. I have no idea what she wrote in return. Maybe because money was inside, Ellie sealed her envelopes. Or maybe she wanted to protect or reinforce her only connection to her brother.

My brother and I always felt Ellie's urgency to get her response sent as soon as possible. It took three or four days for his letter to arrive, and it would take at least that long for Frank to get his reply. My mother knew that ten days was a very long time when you lived on the streets of New York City. Usually we took her reply to the post office on our way to school the next morning, but sometimes my mother would drive to the post office with her return envelope on the same day she received her brother's request.

Frank was the tender underbelly of my mother's heart. When I was eleven and our family went to New York City for the Easter weekend, my mother insisted we go to several missions and shelters on Delancey Street so she could look for her brother. Of course she never found him, but Ellie couldn't bear to be in New York City without searching for him in the only places she knew. Eventually his calls and letters stopped. For my mother, the years of tracking him down in every bar in Southie, all her tears, all her dollar bills, and all her love couldn't save Frank. He died homeless, a "bum" on the streets of the Bowery, and it broke her heart.

Ellie's relationship with her sister, Ruth, was much more conflicted. In addition to her glamour, Auntie Ruth had a remarkable singing voice and performed in Boston's best nightclubs and on the radio. Her personality sparkled like the evening gowns she wore in her shows.

Ellie and Ruth's relationship added a new dimension to the term *sibling rivalry*. Alcohol and prescription medications fueled many horrendous arguments between them, which the family, including my brother and me, had to witness. No matter what the argument was about, it would return to one issue: Ruth always got all the attention, while my mother did the work of looking after their mother and brothers.

When Joey and I were little, my mother frequently took us for weekend visits to Auntie Ruth's house on Boston's South Shore. Many of those trips ended with them in an argument, prompting my mother to storm out of her sister's house, usually at night, with suitcases and children in tow. Sometimes their shouting woke us, and we'd huddle together in our bed in the first-floor guest room, waiting for what we knew would come next. When they fought, their vicious tones were chilling.

"Get up. We're going home." My mother's voice cut through the dark before she switched on the overhead light. We squinted in the harsh glare. "Hurry up. Put on your bathrobes and slippers." My mother grabbed her suitcase, snatching up our clothes and stuffing them in.

Invariably Ruth would show up in the doorway. "You're not going to drag those children out in the middle of the night, are you?"

"You shut up. I'm taking *my* children and I'm going home because you're making me do it! I won't stay here and listen to any more of your nonsense."

Predictably, the sisters would reach a detente before our car reversed down the driveway (though not always), and we'd stay the entire weekend—but not before creating the drama of making us climb into the back seat of a cold car, still in our pajamas, on a winter's night.

Although their relationship was tempestuous, my mother and my aunt shared many periods of calm and closeness, too. My mother's face and mood would brighten when she'd tell my father, "Ruthie's coming for a visit," or tell me and my brother, "We're going down to Auntie Ruth's this weekend." The fact is, as much as they didn't get along, they also enjoyed seeing each other. For entire weekends they smoked cigarettes (one of the few times my mother smoked), sipped coffee, and drank highballs in the evening, leaving behind bright red smudges of lipstick on everything that touched their mouths. They shopped together, gossiped, and flirted with any man who might cross their path.

I have no doubt they loved each other. Like most enmeshed relationships, theirs was intense, and when one or both of them reached their limit for closeness, an argument or incident provided some needed distance until the next time. Sometimes they wouldn't speak for months, because one or the other had finally done the "unforgivable"—whatever that happened to be at the time. I don't remember them apologizing, but that doesn't mean they never did. What they did do was move along to the next round of the same old cycle that spun them out and sucked them back in equal turns. Because I loved my Auntie Ruth so much and adored being in her presence, this roller-coaster relationship between her and my mother was especially confusing and upsetting to me. The thought that I might lose my aunt forever magnified those feelings.

A year or so after my grandmother died, my aunt moved to Springfield to be near my mother. To me, this was the best news ever. Auntie Ruth loved me and doted on me in ways my mother never did. Now my visits with her wouldn't be limited to weekend trips to the South Shore. I'm not sure exactly why, but Ruth no longer had her house or her nightclub bookings. She was twice divorced; two of her kids were married, and the other, a popular and committed bach- . elor, lived in Boston. Her drinking escalated around the same time, and I suspect this had everything to do with her change in circumstance and subsequent move.

Instead of living with us, Auntie Ruth rented a beautifully furnished room in an old mansion that was turned into a boarding house. She found a part-time job at the Arthur Murray Dance Studio. Living in a furnished room and teaching people to dance was a huge comedown for Ruth after the large and glamorous life she'd lived for so many years in Boston. It's very likely my mother helped her out financially, too.

During the time she lived nearby, Ruth was a frequent visitor in our home, and occasionally she babysat for me and my brother. Having an alcoholic aunt for a babysitter did have its upside—we got to stay up late and watch television while indulging in whatever sugary contraband she had managed to smuggle past her sister. My mother had very strict rules about what my brother and I could eat and when we could eat it, so we gladly gobbled up the candy or chocolates, taking equal delight in breaking the rules. One night when my parents were out at a dance, and well after Joey and I had gone to bed, I felt myself being gently shaken awake.

"Hi, honey." I opened my eyes to see Auntie Ruth's beautiful, smiling face just inches from mine. "Wake up, darling. I've got a surprise for you."

She sat on the edge of my bed holding a tray of Ritz crackers with peanut butter and a glass of milk. I don't know if she was lonely, crazy, or just drunk, but she obviously wanted company, and with a midnight snack like that under my little nose, I was happy to oblige. I sat up in my bed like a queen on her throne, and while I munched peanut butter and crackers, this glamorous former radio and nightclub singer serenaded me with "Love and Marriage," "Let Me Call You Sweetheart," and "'A' You're Adorable."

That magical midnight would have forever remained a secret between us if Ruth had had her wits about her and had gone back downstairs to put away the peanut butter jar and the cracker box before my parents came home. When they came in and Ruth wasn't in the living room, my mother called out to her.

"Uh-oh. Pretend you're asleep!" Ruth whispered.

I immediately got back under the covers and feigned sleep. I have no memory of what happened when my aunt was caught red-handed breaking my mother's rules, and three sheets to the wind to boot, but I'm sure there was hell to pay.

Ruth didn't remain in Springfield very long, which isn't surprising considering the quiet and unglamorous life she was living. She moved on to California, where she lived for several years before returning to Boston when I was fourteen.

From as far back as I can remember, my aunt and I shared a closeness that angered my mother. It was a source of conflict not only between the sisters, but also between my mother and me. I'm sure my mother felt left out, and it must have been painful to know I preferred her sister's company and sought out every opportunity I could to be with Auntie Ruth. Even though Ellie was jealous of my relationship with her sister, she allowed me to visit Ruth during summer vacations after she returned from California. I'm not sure how much of it had to do with my mother encouraging my relationship with her sister or if she just needed a break from what she considered to be her troublesome teenage daughter.

Despite my aunt's alcoholism, I always felt safe with her. I knew she loved me unconditionally, as did her three children—all of them close to twenty years older than me—and I thrived on the attention they lavished on me. I particularly remember my visit when I was fourteen because over the course of that summer my cousins, all married with children by then, told me how they tried to make it up to me for my mother's obvious favoritism of my brother.

One night at my cousin Arthur's house, after a dinner of heaping bowls of steamers and sweet buttered corn on the cob, we lingered around the table while the adults drank coffee or sipped whiskey. Ashtrays and cigarette packs sat casually amongst the detritus of dinner, and I was allowed to smoke right along with the adults. I felt so grown-up, so accepted, that if I close my eyes now, I can still conjure the feeling I had from that night over fifty years ago. During a lull in the conversation, Auntie Ruth asked me how things were going with my mother.

"The usual," I shrugged. Everyone there knew exactly what I meant; they'd seen my mother in action with me and my brother—particularly me.

My aunt looked directly into my eyes and reached for my hand. "I want to tell you a story, honey, about something that happened when you were only three. That means your brother would have been five or six." She pulled on her cigarette, then crushed it in the ashtray before she began. The four of us—Ellie, Ruth, Joey, and me—were going somewhere in the car. My mother drove, I sat in the car seat between her and Auntie Ruth, and my brother was in the back. My mother needed to run an errand and took my brother into the store with her, while Ruth and I waited in the car.

"After your mother and brother got out of the car," she told me, "you turned to me and said 'Auntie Ruth, I know my mummy likes Joey more than me, but that's okay.'" Ruth's eyes brimmed with tears as she finished telling me the story. "You broke my heart that day," she said, "and I've never, ever forgotten it."

The reason she told me the story was because that summer, eleven years after that incident, I still struggled with my mother's obvious favoritism of my brother and felt like an outsider—something I never experienced with Auntie Ruth or my cousins. With them I never once felt as if I wasn't one of "theirs" or that I was adopted, whereas Ellie frequently reminded me of my status.

Auntie Ruth eventually gave up alcohol and joined AA, where she met the wonderful man she married. They enjoyed decades of a happy life together until my aunt died in her mid-eighties. I adored her, and I'm so grateful I had the opportunity before she died to thank her for everything she gave to me, and to let her know the difference she made in my life.

My mother's younger brother, Tommy, gave me the same unconditional love I received from Auntie Ruth. Unfortunately, like Frank and Ruth, he was also an alcoholic. My mother came to his rescue, too, most notably when he came to live with us several times. With no job and nowhere else to go, Uncle Tommy slept on a folding cot in our cellar until he was able to get and hold a job. Even when he lived on his own but was still down on his luck, my mother would send him a few dollars, often by Western Union.

I remember some sharp words between my parents about Uncle Tommy's presence in our house. The cellar was my father's domain. Tools, coffee tins of nails, paint cans, paint brushes standing in glass jars of turpentine, the toaster waiting for repair—all of these were there on his workbench. The cellar door and hatchway gave him easy access to the backyard and his outside chores. I remember my father saying things like "I'd like to have my own house back to myself," and "He ought to get out of bed and go get a job like the rest of us have to." Other than that, I have only a vague sense of my father's unhappiness about taking care of my mother's family. Regardless of her husband's grumbling, Ellie was there for her mother and each of her siblings when they needed her. She never took money from the tight household budget, though; once again, she used her small salary as a part-time secretary to help them out.

During one of Tommy's nondrinking periods, my mother and a friend introduced him to Barbara, a warm and loving woman who was divorced with two daughters, only one of whom still lived at home. A lifelong bachelor until meeting her, Tommy married Barbara when he was in his late forties and managed to stay sober for about three years, until she died on the operating table during open-heart surgery. After losing Barbara, my uncle could not stay sober, and this time he had a stepdaughter to look after.

For my mother there was no question: He and my new cousin would come and live with us. This change in circumstance caused a lot of friction between my parents. There were now two more mouths to feed, and my mother didn't earn enough to support two new household members. A year after they moved in, my step-cousin quit school and got married at sixteen, and my uncle moved back to Boston, near Ruth, where he continued his battle with alcohol for another ten years. Thankfully, Tommy also got sober, close to the age of sixty. He, too, met someone in AA and remarried. Understandably, my mother's relief was huge.

My Mother as Wife

At the workshop where I met the other authors of this book, our first writing prompt was to think of a question we wish we could have asked our mothers. Immediately an image popped into my mind: a 1960s white convertible, flashy and big-finned with a red interior, parked on the main street of our little town.

Nope. I'm not going there.

While the other women were busy writing, I argued with myself about what to write. I squirmed in my seat like an anxious grade-schooler who didn't want to write the assigned essay. No matter where I looked in the classroom, the image of that car was right in front of me. Meanwhile, everyone around me seemed to be writing with ease and confidence.

This isn't working. I can't write about this.

I remember the physical sensation of my shoulders sinking into my body as I considered the logistics of how to gather my notebook, pen, coffee, and tote bag and slip out the door. I drew a deep breath to begin my exit, and that's when things inexplicably changed. It was as though my higher self, the part of me that relentlessly searches for peace and wholeness, found a space to speak: *This is why you came. This is why you're here. She was so much more than your mother. Remember, you came to find her, to find her story.*

It was true, and in so many ways I was ready for this. I simply didn't realize such a muscular fear could rise after I'd already made the decision—the commitment—to find Ellie, the woman whom I believed got so tragically lost in her own life.

I took another deep breath, and instead of slipping out the door, I picked up my pen. I hesitated for a moment, and with the same feeling of thrust I imagine one feels diving into a quarry, or out of an airplane, I wrote my question. *What was missing in your life, in your marriage, that made you go to a crummy bar with Pete when he came to town? A bar you had to know your kids would walk past on their way home from school, and recognizing his car, would know you were inside with him.*

Pete, one of my Auntie Ruth's many former boyfriends, was a large, overweight Italian man from Revere. I liked him well enough when he visited with my aunt, but when he came to visit my mother, I felt uncomfortable and didn't like being around him. Occasionally he would drive up to meet my mother after she finished her part-time job, and together they'd go to the more upmarket of the two dives on Main Street, a tavern where, as far as I knew, my parents or their friends wouldn't think of going.

If I walked home from grammar school with my friends and recognized his car parked in front of the bar, my cheeks burned with embarrassment. I was terrified one of my friends, or even the nuns, would somehow know my mother was in there, or that she might come out as we walked by. Shortly after my brother and I got home from school, Pete would drop off my mother and come in for a minute or two to say hello to us before heading back to Boston. While he was there, I worried my friends might see his car in front of our house and figure out my mother had been with him in the tavern.

There was another man from Boston, a former boss of my mother's named Allan, who also occasionally stopped by to visit my mother after she got home from work. Whenever he had business in Albany, he'd stop by on his way home and also left shortly after my brother and I got home from school. I never questioned why these men came to visit. I only knew that when my friends came home from school their mothers didn't have men visiting, and most of all, I knew for certain my friends' mothers didn't go to that creepy bar in the middle of the afternoon. I hated that my mother did this. I had no idea what those relationships were about, but I felt ashamed, and I also felt that my mother was somehow being disloyal to my father.

As the years went by, my mother made no attempt to hide her anger and disappointment with my father and her marriage. Comments to my father such as "We never go anywhere" or "Couldn't we for once do something interesting?" and "Am I going to have to live here, in this tiny house, for the rest of my life?" made it clear this was not what she'd signed up for.

Things started out well for my parents. As newlyweds they moved to Western Massachusetts, where my father was assigned to Westover Air Force Base. My mother was twenty-seven and my father twenty-nine when they bought that four-room Cape and established their first home almost a hundred miles away from their families in South Boston. It was the first time either had lived in a single-family house, and not only did they have a front yard and a backyard, there was a lake across the street, too. The move offered my mother freedom she'd never experienced before; with her new husband, she finally had a life of her own, and things only got better for them when my father got his orders to report to Kindley Air Force Base in Bermuda. My mother's dreams and my father's promises of traveling to beautiful and exotic places were coming true.

As kids, Joey and I pored over my parents' wedding photos, and we endlessly studied the pictures of them in Bermuda. They were a beautiful and stylish couple. My mother wore short-shorts, blouses tied in front, halter tops with tan lines showing, and bathing suits. The skirts of her elegant shirtwaist dresses were full, showing off her small waist, and her colorful strappy shoes and sandals matched her handbags. My father was often in his uniform khakis, but there are many photographs where he is wearing striped short-sleeved tees or tropical-print shirts and light linen pants. Some photos show them laughing on a sailboat, and in others they are laughing with a group of friends at a party. We found pictures of them with other couples at the NCO Club (for noncommissioned officers), dressed to the nines, dancing or sitting at round tables and holding martinis and manhattans. It's understandable why, as a young twentysomething and thirtysomething, my parents were always smiling. They were free and happy and living on a tropical island in the Atlantic, far from the war years and the lives they'd left behind in the United States. In these photographs, I see a young woman blooming and thriving after the overly responsible life she had lived, and it's very clear her young husband, my father, adored her.

During the four years they lived in Bermuda, they learned my mother was infertile, and with the help of the base chaplain, arranged to adopt a ten-month-old baby boy from Ireland. So many of the photographs of their time in Bermuda, as well as my mother's reminiscences, tell the story of a happy, almost idyllic life for the new family of three. Very recently I had the opportunity to look at some slides taken during this time, and my heart melted at the love and pride shining through my parents toward each other and their little boy. A year later, when their application to adopt another baby was approved, my father requested and received a transfer back to Westover AFB. They had rented their house while they were at Kindley AFB, but it wasn't long before they were settled back into the house they loved and waiting for their second child to arrive from Ireland.

When my mother left Bermuda, she left behind a close-knit circle of friends for a small New England community where she knew few people. Without her social circle and the support she'd enjoyed in Bermuda, it was a difficult adjustment for my mother to be home by herself with a toddler, knowing another baby—whose age was unknown to them at that point—was arriving in a few months. In 1951, Ellie traded a relatively carefree, fun life on a tropical island to be a lower-middle class suburban housewife in New England. She would have felt more like a military wife if they had lived on the base. Over time she made many friends, including some of her neighbors in the subdivision where they lived, and became active in her small Catholic parish.

Each year she hoped my father might come home with news of a European or Asian transfer, but that never happened. Her chance of any foreign travel ended when my father retired from the air force in 1959, a decision he made to avoid being separated from his family for a two-year TDY (temporary additional duty) in Thule, Greenland. As a hangar chief during the Cold War, my father was used to being sent away on top-secret or training missions throughout the United States, but this assignment was different. Seven hundred and fifty miles above the Arctic Circle was too far away, and two years was too long for him to leave his family. He retired after twenty-three years of military service. As a master sergeant, the highest rank he could attain without a college degree, he was at the top of his career ladder in the air force. Leaving the military gave him a pension for life and allowed him to earn better and much-needed money in a second career. When he took a good job with United Technologies in Connecticut, though, it meant my parents would stay firmly settled in their corner of western Massachusetts. Initially, I'm sure the increased income and promise of a brighter future made it easier for my mother to abandon her dreams of foreign assignments, but over time her disappointment turned to resentment.

After he retired from the military, my father was more than content with his life. He enjoyed working around the house, either making repairs or remodeling. He did all the landscaping and loved preparing and tending his vegetable garden. He left for work at five o'clock in the morning and returned at quarter to five each evening. This was his life, and it brought him great comfort and pleasure. For my mother, it was a completely different story. She wanted to experience a world larger than what she knew, larger than what her house could hold or her husband could provide.

During one of Ellie's afternoon visits when my daughters were very young and taking their naps, she brought up the subject of marrying my father. What struck me most about the conversation was what a non sequitur it was, how it came totally out of the blue. During these conversations—which felt more like confessions to me—my mother's tone of voice was dispassionate, which is not a word that usually comes to mind in regard to her. As a therapist, I now recognize it as a tone I would frequently hear from my depressed clients when they reflected on their lives.

"You know," she started, "when I married your father, I wasn't really in love with him."

It hurt me to hear this, but I also understood this admission was part of the larger truth of her life. My head reeled with questions. Why is she telling me this? Why does she come here and tell me these things? What am I supposed to do with this information?

I was quite young, but intuitively knew to simply offer her the space to say what she needed to say. She looked deep into her coffee cup.

"I'm sure that's true for a lot of people, Ma." I wanted to rescue her.

She looked out the window to the huge oak tree at the side of the house. "I was twenty-seven and didn't think I would ever get married. I didn't think I'd have another chance. Your father was handsome and in the military, so he could be stationed anywhere. He promised me we'd travel the world—that's how we'd spend our life together. And I believed him."

Her tone wasn't bitter. What she was sharing was beyond disappointment and deeper than resentment. Her loss and emptiness were heavy and delicate at the same time, and all of it filled the air we breathed. My mother sipped her coffee, cold by then, and stared at the braided rug.

"And look what happened. We've lived in the same house our whole lives. Your father doesn't want to go anywhere or do anything. Nothing has turned out the way I thought it would." There was a pause before she continued. "I've felt so alone."

We sat in silence with her loneliness. Allowing the silence was hard for me, but I didn't want to break the spell that afternoon. I wanted to hold the two of us inside this fragile bubble of suspended time and truth, where I wasn't afraid of her and we both had our guard down.

While some of my earliest memories are of loud arguments between my parents, just as clear are my memories of my father's attention and affection toward my mother. He often put his arm around her, or gave her a kiss for no reason, but I have no memory of my mother initiating any affection toward him. That's how I remember her—waiting for and expecting others to attend to her. Apparently, I wasn't alone in my observation. When I was a teenager, my best friend's mother told me the women in the neighborhood had nicknamed my mother "Queen Bee." At sixteen, I felt thoroughly vindicated by the fact that others saw what my mother was like. But if I felt vindicated, I also felt shame that my family was talked about in the neighborhood.

As I grew toward my teens, my parents' arguments increased. During the summer when my mother began a tirade directed at either my father or me, I ran from one room to the next closing the windows so the neighbors wouldn't hear, and this only made her angrier.

"Oh, so you're embarrassed by me? Well, you can go to hell." Her voice ripped with sarcasm as she raged. "Leave them open. I want everybody to know what I have to put up with in this house. Let them hear how upset you make me."

If he could, my father would quietly leave the room when my mother shouted at him, but she would follow, continuing her rant, trying to goad him into an argument. Our house was small, and there was no getting away from her. Ellie's rages were like storms you could see forming and growing on the horizon, knowing there was no shelter once it inevitably arrived. She made many threats to leave my father, but usually only went to her sister's house for a night or two, which probably accounts for those volatile trips to Auntie Ruth's with my brother and me.

Much of my mother's disappointment and frustration needs to be understood through the context of a time when opportunities for a woman to expand her life came to her primarily through her husband's job and/or hobbies. With very limited options to make her own way in the world or fulfill her own dreams, my mother was stuck. Instead of raging against the culture and institutions that kept her in such a constricted place, she directed her rage toward her husband and children, although my brother, the favored child, was usually spared.

Maybe it was her deep unhappiness, or maybe it was her undiagnosed mental illness that incited those rages in which she often lost control, lashing out—figuratively and literally—at anyone within striking distance. Her doctor's diagnosis was that she was "high-strung," and his solution was to prescribe her Librium, to be taken four times a day. She also took medication for a low thyroid issue.

As time went on, being high-strung was the explanation for my mother's behavior, causing everything from her temper tantrums to her need for frequent naps. It was the reason she couldn't handle the noise and activity of children. Normal everyday life often felt chaotic to her. Her unbalanced mental state and her addiction to prescription medications created her inability to tolerate frustration, which in turn made her volatile.

Today my mother most certainly would receive a different mental-health diagnosis. But any attempt to diagnose her, whether then or now, would be challenging because of the side effects of the medications she took, which no one explained or talked about. Common side effects of Librium are confusion, memory loss, hostility, irritability, and drowsiness, among others.

When I was a kid, our home life was like the movies my brother and I watched before supper, where a rumbling volcano was ready to erupt, and someone needed to be sacrificed to the volcano in order to appease the gods and avoid world destruction. Except on those rare occasions when he stood his ground, my father appeased the volcano until the day he died, and so did my brother. Most of my problems with my mother were rooted in my firm refusal to do so.

I don't remember my mother buying special gifts for my father or making his favorite dinner. My dad, on the other hand, saw to it that every special occasion was acknowledged. Birthdays, anniversaries, and Valentine's Day meant cards and flowers. Every Easter he ordered a lily plant from Bermuda for my mother as a loving and sentimental reminder of their newlywed years there. It was an expensive gesture in those days. Even as a kid, it made me sad that my mother never reciprocated such gestures. It took many years for me to understand and accept this was their balance, their dance.

We couldn't afford to rent a cottage or stay in a hotel or motel for family vacations. It was my mother's resourcefulness and my father's desire to appease her that sent us off on family camping trips each year, providing my brother and me with some wonderful memories.

The destination for our first camping trip was chosen a week after we all attended a camping show sponsored by the New England Family Campground Association. What I remember is typical of my parent's interactions when my mother wished to accomplish something and wanted my father's interest and enthusiasm to match hers.

It was after supper one winter night and as usual, I was in the living room watching a TV program with my parents. Ellie sat in her straight-backed chair surrounded by camping catalogues, reading and sipping one of her two nightly highballs while my father watched television and sipped his drink. They'd both had wine before supper, too. When he came home each evening, my father would pound down two small juice glasses of wine, and then pour another for himself and one for my mother to sip while he made supper.

"Billy, where do you want to go on vacation this year?"

"I don't care, honey. Wherever you want."

"Why can't I ever get a goddamned straight answer out of you?"

My father turned to her. "I really don't mind. Wherever you want to go is fine with me."

My mother looked back at the camping directory on her lap. "How about if we go to Rhode Island? There's a campground near the ocean, and if it rains there are plenty of places we could visit."

"That's fine," my father replied.

"That's fine," she mocked him. "Everything is always fine with you. I don't know why I bother with a goddamned thing for this family. I have to do everything myself. Nobody, NOBODY else cares."

Fast forward to the following summer and the Friday night before we set off for Burlingame State Park in Rhode Island.

"Billy, make sure you remember to pack the lantern. And did you remember to pay the bills? You kids stay out of your father's way."

My father was lugging things from the cellar and the porch out to the U-Haul trailer he had rented earlier that evening. With so much to do, Joey and I were doing what we could to help him. My mother was going over her many lists, each with its own title: Clothing, Food, Equipment, To-Do Before Leaving House, Games to Play, Medicine, and Miscellaneous. The deal was that Ellie made lists and my father, brother, and I gathered up and packed everything on the lists, except for my mother's personal items. Once we arrived at the campsite, she became the setup manager.

"I think the tent should go over here."

"It's not level over there. It has to go here," my father told her.

"Well, then, I'd like the picnic table over there."

"That's not a good idea."

"What do you mean? Why can't I have the picnic table over there?"

"Because it needs to be here, close to the tent and under the tarp in case it rains."

"Why can't I ever have anything I want?" My mother threw up her hands and gave one of her exasperated sighs. Meanwhile, my brother pounded stakes, my father pulled guy ropes, and I stood next to my father like his shadow, waiting for my next instruction.

And so it went until the car and the U-Haul were unloaded and we were finally situated. On vacation, just like during the other fifty weeks of the year, my father did the cooking and my brother and I cleaned up. It was a lot of work, but being on vacation made my mother happy, and that made my father happy, too.

On vacation, after supper was an especially calm and lovely time to be around my parents. The campfire crackled, releasing sparks upward toward the aromatic pines. Every now and then my father would take a log from the small stack of wood next to his chair, and lean over to place it on the fire.

My mother sat in her folding aluminum chair browsing through her tour books. "Tomorrow we can go to the beach, and the day after we can go to Newport," she announced to no one in particular. "That's where the mansions are."

"Can we toast some marshmallows?" I asked my father.

"Not too many," my mother answered without looking up from her book. Her voice was distracted and relaxed.

"Mm-hmm. That would be fine," my father said in reply to my mother's previous suggestion. He sipped his whiskey, and she sipped hers. My world was calm, enveloped by the smell of woodsmoke and pine.

Ellie could still be contentious and unpredictable, lashing out at my dad and me, but those aren't my most vivid memories of our summer vacations. Those few days of fun and ease with my family live much larger in my memory than any unhappiness. By the end of the two weeks, we had plenty of sightseeing and swimming under our belts. I still have photographs documenting those summer vacations: my brother and me next to cannons at various forts; on top of mountains, standing on either side of elevation signs; at the entrance to many campgrounds, pointing to the sign. There are photographs where we sit on blankets at the beach, eating sandwiches and squinting into the sun, our little bodies awash in sand and Coppertone. I'm glad I have these family memories and the experience of what felt like being a long way from home. I'm deeply grateful to my parents, especially to my mother, for those opportunities. She truly modeled where there's a will, there's a way.

Ellie was a party girl. She loved to dance, go out for dinner and drinks, and flirt—and she did them all as often as she could. My father loved to dance, too, and they were known to do a mean jitterbug.

When my mother got ready to go out, I'd follow her into our tiny bathroom, put down the toilet-seat cover so I could stand on it, and lean over the sink to see her reflection in the mirror as she put on her makeup.

"Can I help?" I'd ask.

"No. But you can watch. And be careful you don't fall over."

I took in every move of the ritual. Ellie dotted foundation all over her face, then carefully blended it, even over her jawline, and down to her neck. Next, after dotting liquid rouge on her cheekbones, she stretched a fake smile across her face to blend the color over the apples of her cheeks. Revlon Sapphire Blue eye shadow was her favorite; she drew the slender stick over each eyelid, then blended the eye shadow carefully and lightly with her ring finger. When she drew the mascara brush through her eyelashes, for some reason my mother always opened her mouth. Finally, she set the whole look with powder. But the last step, my favorite, came next.

"What color lipstick are you going to wear?" I asked, looking down at her small selection.

"I'm wearing this one, because it will go with my outfit." She opened a gold tube, twisted the bottom, and a beautiful shade of rosy red emerged. She picked up her small lip brush, swiped it over the lipstick a few times, and then outlined each lip with the color.

"How come you do that?"

"It keeps my lipstick from fading and gives my lips definition."

I had no idea what this meant, but I was intrigued. Once she was done outlining, it was time to fill in the rest of her lips.

"Can I wear some lipstick?" I knew the answer I'd get, but I always asked anyway.

"No, you're too young."

She arched the color over each half of her upper lip and then drew a broad stroke across the bottom, reversing a couple of times before closing her lips together tightly and moving them back and forth. I smiled thinking of my plan.

I knew what came next and handed my mother a Kleenex to blot her lips.

"Thank you." She tucked the tissue between her lips and moved her lips back and forth.

I reached for the Kleenex. "I'll throw it away."

My mother thanked me and took one last look in the mirror to examine her work. "There," she said. "Time to get dressed."

Still standing on the toilet seat and holding the tissue, I waited until she left the bathroom before I placed the lipstick-stained tissue between my lips and rubbed them back and forth as I'd watched my mother do. When I was done, I leaned over as far as I could to look into the corner of the mirror and admire the slightest hint of red on my lips. Ha! My plan had worked once again.

What was missing in your life, in your marriage, that made you go to a crummy bar with Pete when he came to town? A bar you had to know your kids would walk past on their way home from school, and recognizing his car, would know you were inside with him.

As I grew into my teens, what I considered to be my mother's inappropriate behavior bore a direct relationship to her increasing frustration and disappointment with her marriage. In 1968, I was still in high school and my brother was in the navy, stationed in Vietnam. It was the era of psychedelics and *Rowan & Martin's Laugh-In.* It was also the year my mother found a new, younger circle of friends who liked to drink and party. Just like her new friends, my mother wore white go-go boots and hot pants, but unlike her new friends, Ellie was in her fifties. The men wore polyester pants and shirts, wide open at the neck to show off their gold chains. Thank God my father refused to dress like them. Occasionally they would meet at our house before going out to dinner, and sometimes my parents hosted parties in our home. My father always seemed uncomfortable in their company, and after meeting them only once, I completely understood. I cringed around all of them. They were loud and laughed too much, and their conversations were often tinged with innuendo.

In 1969, when I was a senior in high school, I was humiliated to find that the bikini my mother had bought to wear to a pool party hosted by our neighbors was the exact same bikini I'd purchased for myself the week before. I was seventeen, she was fifty-two. It was more embarrassing than when she flirted with my boyfriends. Ellie always seemed to be in competition with someone for attention, and I frequently felt embarrassed not only by her, but for her. This overly flirtatious behavior diminished as she aged, especially a decade later in the seventies, when she became a born-again Christian around the same time she found Al-Anon.

At that point neither my brother nor I lived at home anymore, and my father's drinking had intensified as he tried to cope with my mother's unrelenting rages—now directed solely at him. She berated and blamed him for everything she believed was wrong with her life. As my father got older, I noticed he would become belligerent when he drank, which added fuel to an already out-of-control fire. My mother found bottles tucked away near his workbench downstairs and out in the garage, and marked them to keep track of his drinking. Ellie certainly didn't need another alcoholic in her life, but she had concerns well beyond that. My father had recently been diagnosed with diabetes, and drinking was one of the worst things he could do for his health. The breathtaking irony in all this is that my mother was completely blind to how her own drinking, especially when mixed with prescription medications, was contributing to her difficulties and our family's problems.

Shortly after joining Al-Anon, my mother found Jesus. It followed, of course, that my father would find Him, too. My mother's next step was to dragoon my father into the charismatic renewal movement of the Catholic Church, and their regular Friday-night date was a prayer meeting. Jesus might have made life a bit easier for my father in some ways, but now my mother had Bible quotes to hurl in her rage. She was now unequivocally convinced that God was on her side in all things, and He was disappointed in my father for letting her down so badly.

I left home in the summer of 1970, when I got married at the age of eighteen. With her daughter gone, and shored up by Al-Anon and Jesus, my mother didn't seem to suffer her emotional outbursts as often as she had in earlier years, although she was by no means done. I wasn't around to see her rages, and if she started one when I was present, I simply gathered up my children and left. I wouldn't accept her phone calls when she was enraged. I spoke with her only when she could speak calmly.

In the late eighties, I was living on the coast of Maine, three hours away from my parents. During one of their rare visits, my father took me aside.

"I'm worried about your mother."

"Daddy, she's the one person in this world who doesn't need to be worried about."

Normally my father would have smiled, happy to share a conspiratorial moment with me, but that day he didn't.

"Okay," I said, "tell me. What's the matter?"

He told me she was forgetting things. "She says things and doesn't remember she said them. I tell her things, or we go somewhere and she might not remember. She's not old enough to be acting this way, is she?"

At the time, my father was seventy-two and my mother was seventy. When I looked into those lovely, familiar eyes, I could see my father was more than simply frightened or concerned. I saw the thought of losing my mother was breaking his heart. I know he loved her, but over the years she had become something else to him, something more necessary, like the polestar around which he oriented himself.

My father, ill with a heart problem and diabetes, died just four years after that visit. During those years, even though I lived three hours away, I was the designated emergency contact person. I'd always taken on the role of caregiver for my parents. I made sure all holiday meals were in my home so I could include them, ensuring they wouldn't be alone. Just as I'd felt responsible for making them feel like "real" parents, I felt responsible for making them feel like grandparents, too. As they got older, I made sure their bills were paid, bought bright plastic containers boldly marked with the day and time for my father's many medications, followed up with doctors about appointments, and sometimes grocery-shopped and cleaned their house. My brother was divorced, recently out of rehab, and living with my parents during that time, struggling to maintain his new sobriety. My family leaned heavily on me for financial and health decisions, and my parents requested I be awarded power of attorney for both of them. My status as a last-year graduate student in an MSW program seemed to give them comfort as well.

In late February of 1992, I was wakened during the night by a call from my father's nursing home. The charge nurse spoke gently, but firmly. "You'd better come now." My father's body had begun the process of shutting down. The nurse knew I had a long drive ahead and wanted to give me enough time to get there while he was still alive.

"Is he conscious?"

"He's in and out."

"Have you called my mother?"

"No. We wanted to give you time first."

I didn't hesitate. "Okay, I'm on my way. I'll call her after I get there."

It was two thirty in the morning. I sped to Massachusetts, praying I would arrive before my father slipped in to a coma or died.

It was still dark when I arrived at 5:00 a.m. The window curtains were open, and the glass reflected the glow from a small table lamp across the room. My father wasn't conscious when I sat down beside him.

I am forever grateful to the staff who gave me the gift of time alone with my father in the wee hours of his last morning, just the two of us together in the soft, buttery lamplight. During that sacred time with him I offered my father my deepest gratitude for being so enormously proud of me and completely accepting me as his own daughter. I told him I was sorry he hadn't been celebrated and cherished by my mother, and that I thought he was a good man. I sang "Galway Bay" and "Daddy's Little Girl" to him, songs he often sang to me when I was young enough to curl up on his lap. I read him psalms and prayed with him, and although he never opened his eyes, I believe he heard me and felt me hold his hand. Now and then he struggled to say something, and I would tell him I was listening, that my heart could hear him.

When the sun came up, the nursing home came to life. The nurses and aides who had given me those precious hours with my father came in to check his vitals and say goodbye before the shift changed. At seven thirty I called my mother and my brother and told them it was time to come to the nursing home because Daddy was close to the end.

I can't imagine how the future looked to Ellie when she stood at the foot of her husband's hospital bed, watching him slip away. Aware of her increasing confusion and forgetfulness, my mother was understandably frightened of a life without the man she had relied on to manage the day-to-day business of their lives, had relied on for nearly fifty years to anticipate and take care of her needs.

Over and over she told him he needed to stay. "Who will look after me, Billy? I'll be all alone. I need you to stay." She cried and begged him not to leave her. After a half hour or so, I asked her to come out into the hallway with me.

My voice was low, and I could barely hide how annoyed I was. "Look, Ma, Daddy is dying. Do you understand? He's not going to get better or rally from this." My mother's eyes were wide as she listened. "His body is exhausted and depleted," I continued. "He has nothing left, but he's hanging on for you. Stop being so selfish, and for once in your life think of him."

I had her attention, but I felt like a principal with an errant student. "You need to go back in there and tell him it's okay for him to go whenever he's ready. Tell him you'll be fine and he shouldn't worry. Tell him you love him and want him to be at peace, so you're letting him go 'home' now."

My mother opened her mouth to protest, but I stopped her. "No, Ma. You need to do this, otherwise he'll linger, and he'll do that because he's devoted his whole life to taking care of you. Well, he can't take care of you anymore." I stopped and took a big breath. With a more gentle voice I said, "Come on. Let's go back inside. Let's go tell Daddy he can go now." She nodded. I took her hand and led her back into my father's room.

My mother walked to the head of his bed and stood in silence, staring into my father's face. It felt like the world stopped, but time continued on, second by second. Finally, she leaned over, her face close to his, and said, "It's okay, Billy. I'll be okay." She stroked his hair. "You should go now. You're tired. You've been a good husband and I'll miss you, but you can go now." It was the most loving thing I'd ever heard her say. My father died within the hour. I am eternally grateful that I witnessed my mother looking for—and finding—a place deep within her, a vein of compassion, from which she could offer an act of unconditional love to the man she took as her husband forty-six years before.

My father's death exacerbated Ellie's dementia, which had been diagnosed four years earlier. After we made plans to get together one afternoon, when I got to her house the porch door was locked. This was unusual, especially if she knew I was coming, but I felt comforted that she was taking the security precaution. I pushed the doorbell, and as I waited for her to answer, I noticed the amount of traffic speeding past the house. How can she safely back out of the driveway? I wondered. Then, she was at the door, smiling.

"Hello," she said. "Can I help you?"

Her demeanor and question surprised me. In the moment, I didn't understand what was going on, but I wasn't panicked. Even with her Alzheimer's diagnosis, it had never occurred to me that my mother wouldn't know who I was.

"Hi, Ma. It's me." I waited for her to laugh and say "Oh, for heaven's sake, come on in," or "I couldn't see you with that glare from the sun." But she said nothing, waiting only for this woman on her doorstep to explain what she wanted.

"I'm your daughter, remember?" It was a sincere question, and at the same time I was letting her know I was done with this. Enough already. When the slightest glint of recognition never came, that's when panic grabbed my throat.

"Ma? Hey, Ma, it's me." I couldn't use my name. I wanted her to find it, to find me.

My thoughts raced. If my father wasn't there anymore, and my mother didn't recognize me, how could I still be rooted or anchored in the world? If my parents were gone, was I still me? I didn't want the aloneness that was hollowing out my chest. "I'm Maggie."

"Oh," she said, but her blank look said she wasn't connecting the dots. "Would you like to come in?" Ellie unlocked her door and let in the stranger from her doorstep. Several minutes later, when I was getting the kettle to make tea, the light came back to her eyes. She knew her daughter was there, in her kitchen making her tea. "How are you? It's so good to see you."

During her decline, these episodes increased and her outbursts became more violent, too. Once, in a fit of rage and frustration, she threw a knife at my brother. It didn't come close to hitting him, but the act itself was a troubling shift in her already unpredictable lack of control.

Alzheimer's brought us tender mercies as well. Sometimes Ellie's disorientation left her softer and less combative—as though she were having a conversation with a stranger who had happened to drop by and visit her, and she, grateful for the attention, expected less and was thankful for more. I wish my father could have known that woman.

My Mother as Mother

Ellie became a mother for the first time in 1950, when she and my father collected my brother at Logan Airport in Boston. After spending the first ten months of his life in an orphanage in County Tipperary, he arrived in the US on a transatlantic flight from Ireland. Ellie became a mother the second time in 1952, when I arrived at Idlewild Airport in New York City. I was six months old and had spent the first four months of my life with my birth mother before she placed me in an orphanage in Dublin.

Three months had passed between the day my parents were notified a baby girl was available for adoption and the day I arrived in New York. After months of waiting, followed by a six-hour drive to New York with a toddler, the moment my mother dreamt about was in sight. With the addition of the little girl she'd been waiting for, her family would now be complete. But before she could hold me, my new family—my parents and older brother, an adorable, chubby, and good-natured three-year-old—had to spend several more hours waiting for my plane to arrive. From the photographs, I can see they were in their finest: my mother fashionably dressed in a lovely two-piece outfit with a matching hat and gloves, my father handsome in his dress blue air force uniform, and my brother wearing a coat and cap, shorts, knee socks, and saddle shoes. I can picture the three of them in the waiting area: my parents anxious and excited, maybe a bit nervous, taking turns walking and playing with my brother in the large but still confined space. With each plane that pulled into its gate, their anticipation grew while they thought "pretty soon" or comforted each other—"It won't be long now."

In those days, airports had no televisions. There were no portable electronics with movies and games, no mobile phones with earbuds, no duty-free shopping malls for entertainment and distraction— only the endless waiting. Once my plane did arrive and the passengers disembarked, my parents waited even longer for a stewardess to bring me from the plane and deliver me into my new mother's arms. Unfortunately for both of us, at that point I no longer wanted to be held. After leaving the orphanage, being passed from one stranger to the next, and flying for hours and hours, I wasn't the pink bundle of joy my mother had dreamt of. I was a jet-lagged, frightened, and confused baby with ears still aching from the descent. My mother interpreted my behavior as her adopted baby girl immediately rejecting her, and this set up a dynamic from which we would never recover.

I've always known I was adopted. I knew it long before I had any understanding of what the word actually meant—that came after an incident I had with another little girl when I was eight. We were walking home from school one day, scuffing our way along the dirt path that paralleled the busy street where we both lived. We were nearly home, having already passed the brick housing project we'd been told never to enter, and we could see my friend's large, gray colonial-style house with its stately front porch just ahead. Each day I continued beyond her house, past the lake and the cemetery where my grandmother was buried, to my house perched in the middle of a row of other small Cape Cod houses.

"My mother told me you're adopted," she said.

"Yeah, so?" I replied.

"She told me that means your mother didn't want you anymore."

Something clenched in my chest, and my entire little body stung. I'd never heard this before. It couldn't be true, I thought. But her *mother* said it, and mothers don't lie. Could it be true?

"No sir."

"Uh-huh. She said your mother had too much work to do and she didn't have time for you, so she gave you away."

I don't remember how I responded to her, or if I even said anything after that. I do know I began to cry when I walked past the cemetery, with something clenching my heart. I was still crying when I let myself into my kitchen through the back door. My mother was at the sink and turned when I walked in.

"What's the matter?" she asked, and I told her what had happened.

Until that day, to me "adopted" was simply another part of who I was: I had blond hair, I had blue eyes, I was Catholic, I was tall for my age, I liked Jell-O, I was adopted. For my mother, the time for explanations had arrived. Her voice was calm, steady, and kind.

"Well, what she said isn't true. I'm surprised her mother would say such a thing. I'm going to have a word with her." She went on to say my "natural" mother (as birth mothers were called then) wasn't married.

"You came from an unwed mother, and that meant you were illegitimate." She handed me a tissue. "And that meant she couldn't keep you. She put you in an orphanage so you could be adopted by a married couple."

I don't know if I asked her what *illegitimate* meant, but I certainly felt a sense of shame from the word, intuiting that being illegitimate was problematic in some way that was well beyond my eight-year-old comprehension.

Illegitimate. It didn't sound like a nice thing to be, and it seemed to me my natural mother and I were being punished for doing or being something bad. Ironically, my mother's attempt to comfort me and set the adoption record straight only deepened the sense of shame that firmly planted itself within me on my walk home from school that day.

Even though I'd always known I was adopted, because I had lacked any understanding of what it meant, I consider that day to be the day I found out I was adopted. It's when I understood deep in my bones that I was "other." It's when I learned I was a problem to be dealt with; I was someone who, with no "legitimate" place of her own in this world, was dependent upon other people allowing me into theirs, and this must somehow involve gratitude on my part. I also sensed what a precarious position this was to have in life.

That discussion with my mother opened a door to things I'd never thought about before, and a torrent of questions stumbled over each other. My little-girl mind wanted desperately to make sense of it all, but after that day, any questions I asked about my birth mother—who she was, where she was now, why she put me in an orphanage, if she ever wondered where I was—were initially met with impatience and later with accusations of ingratitude for all that she, my adopted mother, did for me. Any calm and kindness Ellie offered me during that pivotal conversation was gone. I was reminded that the "other one" gave me up, and it was she who adopted me, took me in, and was raising me, and that's what really mattered. Often she'd respond to my questions with "Why don't you care about me? I'm not the one who gave you up." Eventually I stopped asking.

My curiosity, so natural in all kids but especially in adopted children, wounded my mother, and with little impulse control she lashed out at me. Some words—*left you, gave you up, illegitimate, didn't keep you*—always stung and added to the feeling of shame I'd carry for many years. The way she said *her* or *she* when referring to my birth mother only reinforced what I learned that day in the third grade: there was something "less than" about the woman who gave birth to me, and I should be glad and grateful I'd been adopted because I could still be living in an orphanage.

When my grandmother came to live with us, this new living situation put a lot of pressure on Ellie, primarily because within my mother and grandmother's canon, whatever my mother allowed me to do or not do, and how she disciplined me, reflected the level of respect she held for her mother. Given her mother's diminished circumstances of having to share a small bedroom with a five-year-old, everything came into sharper focus. Under this rubric, how I behaved was a direct reflection of my mother's competence as both a good mother and a good daughter. While I was under her harsh and watchful eye, she, in turn, was under the no less harsh and watchful eye of her own mother.

My grandmother and I also had to share my small closet and bureau, leaving little room for two people's belongings. What this meant for me was that I had to carefully take out of my drawers whatever I needed without disrupting everything else, keep my two pairs of shoes in the closet on the floor next to each other, and have my toys either downstairs in the cellar or placed neatly in the back of the closet. My clothes were not to be left on the floor, and my dirty clothes had to be put in the hamper in the bathroom. Would my mother have expected so much of me if her mother hadn't come to live with us? There's no way to know. Certainly, she did need to ensure her mother didn't trip on any of my things and fall.

Small things became big things. If I stuffed my clothes or toys or shoes under the bed to keep the room clean and got caught, I would deny having done it because I didn't want to get in trouble. In the magical-thinking mind of a five-year-old, denying any knowledge of how those things got under my bed seemed a perfectly reasonable option. Once caught, I'd be punished first for doing it, and second for lying. With my mother, it wasn't that I was a kid who told a really dumb lie to stay out of trouble; I was a liar.

There was no room for being a kid and learning. There was only doing it right or doing it wrong, and little to no difference between behavior and character. At five and six years of age, I needed to be reminded more than once to pick up after myself. In my mother's mind, I was not forgetful, I was disobedient, and disobedience had to be punished. Punishments were often combined and included not being allowed to go out and play, having my toys taken away, not being allowed to watch a favorite television program, being made to stay in my room, or being sent to bed after supper. And, if she was angry, Ellie was also free with her open hand, not caring where it landed or how many times. Her view was that I should have to be told only once to do something. She sincerely believed I was cognitively and developmentally capable of holding her imperatives front and center, and never took into account the bubbling, racing, in-the-moment mind of a child. I was a kindergartener, and my house, my life didn't resemble anything like those of my little friends.

My brother's room was upstairs, out of the way of my grand-mother and everyone else, so the state of his room didn't seem to matter much. Plus he was a boy, and in our family that gave him a lot of leeway and privilege. Not as much was expected of him. He also learned early that if he did what was asked, didn't talk back, and stayed under the radar, he could pretty much do what he wanted and avoid my fate. For him, being compliant was a small price to pay for the freedom it offered.

It was around this same time my mother first threatened to send me back to the orphanage if I didn't obey (which meant keep my room clean, answer her properly, and not talk back by trying to explain my actions) or if I wasn't affectionate or forthcoming with her. The fact is, I was afraid of her. I was already on tenterhooks not knowing when she was going to explode in anger, and now there was an added threat; I didn't know when she might send me back to the orphanage. I knew an orphanage was where I came from, where children without parents lived. It was the place for children whose parents didn't want them.

When I was nine, my mother hoped our parish priest could persuade me to become a "good" and obedient little girl. "I'm sick of you making me so mad and so upset that I swear," my mother told me. "And then *I* have to go to confession because of *your* disobe-dience. I'm going to take you to Father Humphries. Maybe he can straighten you out. God knows I've tried, and I'm fed up with you."

True to her word, my mother brought me to Father Humphries, who led me into the parlor of the rectory, a bright room that smelled of warm wool and furniture polish, and had lace curtains in the windows. I was sure none of my friends had ever been brought here because they were such bad girls. I was scared to be in a place usually reserved for adults, and to be so close to the man who talked about sin and God every week. In church, I felt protected by my family and the distance between me in the pew and him on the altar. Now here he was sitting just a few feet away, perched on the edge of the chair opposite me. Father Humphries was in his seventies with a few tufts of white hair left and wore rimless glasses like my grandmother's. He had some sort of speech impediment that made his *s*'s come out of either one or both sides of his tongue, something that usually fascinated me, but not this afternoon.

"Now, Maggie, your mother tells me you are not being a good little girl. She tells me you are disobedient and don't do what you're told. I understand this is making her very unhappy."

I knew I was in big trouble. This man who was close to God and in charge of our whole church knew I was misbehaving; he knew that I was distant from my mother but not my father, and that I was a bold and naughty little girl.

"Not only are you making your mother unhappy—your mother who was so good to adopt you and give you a home—you're also breaking the fourth commandment, too. Do you know what that commandment is, Maggie?"

"Thou shalt honor thy father and thy mother," I mumbled.

"Yes, and we know it's a sin to break a commandment, don't we? And this is not pleasing to God. Now, I want you to be a good girl, to listen to your mother and obey her. Ask the Blessed Virgin to help you. You should be thankful that your mother found it in the goodness of her heart to give you a home. Most importantly, you must go to confession and ask God's forgiveness."

My mother escorted me from the rectory that day, confident she'd found the solution to my bad behavior, and I had the same heavy feeling in my heart that I felt the day I found out what it meant to be adopted.

At nine years old, I was a sinner for not keeping my room clean, for not immediately doing what I was told or for doing it wrong, for answering back, and especially for making my mother angry enough to lose not only her temper, but often control. It felt as though I was in a hole I could never get out of, because whatever I did was wrong or not enough.

One of the weekly Saturday jobs I had was to dust the house. If you want your house dusted well, don't ask an eight-year-old to do it. My mother would follow behind me, catching anything I missed, and when she found a spot, I would have to start all over again from the very beginning until I got it right. Sometimes this would take up my whole Saturday morning. She resented that I didn't do it right the first time and that she had to check up on me. I resented the fact that my brother and our friends were outside playing. Once I got it right, I would have to vacuum and dust my bedroom, which she would also have to check before I could go outside to play.

As a teenager, since the parish priest was unable to change my "incorrigible" behavior and I was too old to return to the orphanage, the threat of reform school came up from time to time. I didn't know anyone who went to reform school, but I'd often heard about kids from the nearby housing project going to reform school. My mother simply could not give up the belief that someone or something existed that could turn me into the daughter she wanted. Just to be clear—as a teenager, I never stayed out later than my curfew, which was always at least an hour earlier than that of most of my friends. This meant either my father had to pick me up from whatever dance or party I went to, or my friends had to bring me home and then go back out. I wasn't allowed to go out on school nights. At sixteen, I started working part-time after school and on Saturdays, and I gave part of my paycheck to my mother. I didn't drink or do drugs. I wasn't having sex. I never stole anything. I did my homework. On the school nights I didn't work, I had to go to bed at nine o'clock. The things that got me in trouble, that provoked my mother's rages, were not keeping my room picked up, tossing my school uniform on the floor of my closet rather than hanging it up, and having messy vanity and desk drawers. My mother went through my room on a regular basis, checking my drawers, even reading my diary. I still wasn't cleaning the house "properly," and I got caught smoking. And worst of all, I had an "attitude."

Around the time I became a teenager, I discovered within myself a new or previously unused ability. This superpower allowed me to hold back tears and keep my hurt and fear hidden. It was like a wall, and when I stepped behind it, it protected me. I thought I was safe. Ellie, unable to get a reaction out of me no matter how high she upped the ante, pronounced me "defiant." Defiant, safe—it was the same to me, and it became my MO.

One time my mother came into the kitchen when I was washing the dishes. She looked at the silverware on the counter waiting to be washed.

"What are you doing? You know better than that."

I knew exactly what she was talking about, but still asked, "What?"

"The silverware goes into the dishwater first to soak. The glasses are washed first, then the dishes, and the silverware is washed last."

"Why?"

"Don't be so goddamned fresh," she shouted, and threw the silverware into the sink. "Now, do it the right way."

"As long as the dishes get washed, what difference does it make what order I wash them in?"

"Can't you do one blessed thing right or without arguing?" She threw her hands up toward heaven. "Mother of God, what did I do to deserve this?"

"Look, if it's so important to you how the dishes are washed, why don't you wash them yourself?" I was on very thin ice, but I didn't stop. "You think I don't do anything right, nothing I do is ever good enough for you, so why don't you just do it yourself and make everybody happy?"

That was the kind of thing that pushed her over the edge. I saw stars for a while after exchanges like this.

When she asked why I was always over at my friends' houses and they didn't come to ours, I told her. "Because they don't like it here. It isn't any fun." Forced to explain why this was so, I said, "Because you're too strict, and there's no place we can hang out." Basically, I spoke the truth when my father and my brother kept their mouths shut. My brother's strategy remained the same as when he was a little kid—listen to what my mother had to say, do what she asked him to do (which still wasn't much), and then do exactly as he pleased. He often slipped out his bedroom window to meet his friends and stay out most of the night drinking and getting high.

My father frequently asked me why I couldn't be like my brother and say what my mother wanted to hear. I knew it might make life easier, but I couldn't. Something in me wanted to hold my mother accountable for her behavior. I was not prepared to accept responsibility for her behavior or her eternal salvation. I called her out on her favoritism of my brother, and I told her it was terrible the way she spoke to and treated my father. Needless to say, these conversations didn't end well.

I was appalled that my mother could explode and upset our household, abusing anyone who was in her way—either with her words or with whatever she could quickly grab—and when she was done, we were supposed to act like nothing had happened. We were required to hide our wounds. I didn't understand then that she was mentally ill, and even if I had, I still would have been trapped in an untenable situation from which there was no escape. And I still would have called her on her behavior.

When I was fifteen, my mother announced after school one day that she had made an appointment for me with a priest named Father Johnson.

"Who's he?" I said.

"He's the marriage counselor your father and I have been going to."

I was confused, and most certainly didn't want to talk to another priest. "Why do *I* have to go to *your* marriage counselor?"

"Because he said he wants to see you. Maybe he thinks he can do something with you. Good luck to him." I burned with indignation, but knew I had to go.

The following week, my brown and white saddle shoes echoed in the stairwell as I climbed four flights in an older downtown office building after school one day. The doors along the corridor were heavy oak below with opaque glass panels on top. Office numbers and the names of occupants were painted in black and gold lettering. When I entered Room 403, a small, neatly dressed woman greeted me with a voice that was more quiet than soft. I said I was there to see Father Johnson. She smiled. "He'll be with you shortly. Please sit down."

I sat in the small, stark waiting room feeling so out of place in my school uniform—a plaid wool skirt, knee socks, a button-down blouse and blazer. The schoolbooks I needed for homework were piled on the seat next to me. This was, after all, a place for married couples—it said so on the door: Diocese of Springfield Marriage Counseling. The room was very warm, but there was no place to hang my navy-blue woolen duffle coat, so I kept it on my lap and fingered the wooden toggle buttons. I didn't want to be there, and I certainly didn't want to be at home. I was anxious about this meeting, and the nausea I'd barely coped with all day was still there. During school, I had been determined to hide my gagging and retching, embarrassed and petrified I would vomit in class or in the hallway, and now I was terrified it would happen here. I imagined another priest telling me I was sinning and causing my mother to sin, and I'd better straighten up before I went to hell for causing my mother such aggravation—especially since she'd gone to all the trouble of adopting me and "making me her own." I thought about leaving, but knew if I left, my mother would find out and it wouldn't be worth what I'd have to go through.

I didn't understand it. My friends' mothers loved me. They invited me to dinner, to stay overnight. They laughed at my jokes, asked me about school. My Auntie Ruth and Uncle Tommy adored me and thought I was a great kid. Were they all so wrong about me? Did they miss something in me that my mother saw clearly? Was I fooling them?

The receptionist's phone rang. She answered and listened. "Yes," was all she said. When she hung up she turned to me. "Father Johnson will see you now."

I took a deep breath, picked up my books, prayed I wouldn't puke, and went through the door between the stuffy waiting room and whatever was going to happen to me next.

Father Johnson was a large man who sat hunched over his large desk. Cigarette smoke filled the air of the small office painted the same yellow as the reception room. Father Johnson's hair was silver and his eyes were hooded, making him look bored.

"Hello, Maggie. Come and sit down. I've been looking forward to meeting you." His voice was kind and not at all what I was expecting. I did as I was told.

"I asked to meet with you. Did your mother tell you that?" He drew on his cigarette, then smiled. When he smiled his eyes almost disappeared.

"Yes," I said.

He looked at me through the haze of smoke he'd just exhaled. "I wanted to meet you because I think you could use a friend."

And thus began one of the most important and meaningful relationships I had as a teenager. For many weeks I looked forward to going to Father Johnson's office as he tried to help me understand that I was not the problem and my father was not the problem. The problem, he told me, was my mother and her need for control, as well as her inability to accept any responsibility for what was making her unhappy. Shortly after I started going to Father Johnson, my parents stopped going to marriage counseling, but I didn't know why.

One week when I went to see him, Father Johnson was standing at the window looking out over the square opposite from the building. His large, soft frame was silhouetted by the sun shining in through the window.

"Hi. Have a seat."

I sat down, and he continued to look outside. I took a cigarette out of my pocketbook and lit it. On my second visit to him, I had asked him if I could smoke. He was so nice, and I figured I had nothing to lose by asking. Even if he said no, I knew he wouldn't tell my mother I asked. He said he didn't mind, and from then on we shared the hefty ashtray that sat on his desk.

"There's something important you need to learn, Maggie, which is that your mother isn't likely to change." He turned from the window and sat behind his desk across from me. By now he felt like a big bear of a friend whom I trusted. Sitting on the edge of my seat, I listened carefully.

"You see, I have a hunch you wake up every morning hoping this might be the day that things will be different, that this could be the day your mother is going to become nice to you, or maybe this is the day she's going to act like a mother." His words made my chest tighten. Like a skilled archeologist, Father Johnson had discovered something hidden deep inside me and was gently clearing away the debris it rested under. I felt exposed and vulnerable beneath the armor I had so conscientiously constructed. Sometimes I hated her, so why would I want anything to do with her? Father Johnson had found the tender place within me that still needed a mother, a place that I couldn't acknowledge.

"What you have to do is learn to accept that this is the way she is and find a way to live with her behavior as long as you're in that house." I cried because I knew what he said was true, and it all felt so hopeless. But more than that, it was the end of any childlike illusion I might have held that my mother would someday snap out of whatever was wrong with her.

For several months I went to see Father Johnson after school each week. At one point he asked me if I knew why my parents weren't going to marriage counseling anymore.

"I have no idea. Why would they tell me?"

"Well, I'm going to tell you why. It was because I told your father he needed to stand up to your mother, and she didn't like that. So they stopped coming."

"Oh," was all I could say. I felt as if I'd been allowed a peek behind a curtain I wasn't supposed to see behind.

"I'm telling you this because I want you to understand that your mother can't listen or hear anything other than what she wants to hear." I felt comforted and somewhat empowered that Father Johnson felt the same way I did—that my father needed to intervene with my mother.

Those visits with Father Johnson were a sanctuary, a safe haven for me. I'm sure it's where I developed resilience. I could tell him what was happening at home and share my confusion, shame, and horror over how my mother acted toward me and my father. He listened and often responded by saying, "Okay. So how are we going to take care of you?"

One afternoon, a couple of days after I'd seen Father Johnson, my mother announced I was no longer going to see him. "Why?" I asked. My heart was in my throat. I couldn't imagine not having him to talk to.

"Because I don't see any change in you, and I think it's a waste of time. You're not going anymore." She threw up her hands. "I don't know what the hell I'm going to do with you."

"He doesn't think I need to be 'fixed.'"

"Oh, no, of course not!" I could see the anger rising red from her neck to her face. "Everything's always my fault, isn't it?" And with that she launched into another tirade that lasted for hours.

The next day I called Father Johnson from school and asked if I could come in and see him. We made an arrangement to meet in a couple of days. I lied to my mother about staying after school for a project so I could go into town and meet with him.

As soon as I sat down in his office, I lost any composure I'd been holding onto. Sobbing, I struggled to tell him what my mother had said.

"I'm very sorry, Maggie, but I'm not surprised." He paused for a moment, looking directly in my eyes, and in his quiet, confident voice said, "You're going to be okay."

In that moment, it was hard for me to believe anything would ever be okay. I sat up straight in my seat and for the first time took a defiant tone with him.

"Yeah? How do you know that?"

His gaze and voice remained steady and warm. "Because you've done remarkably well given your circumstances with your mother. You're bright, and there's a whole future ahead of you, far beyond where you are now. That's how I know."

I needed to believe him. I sat back and let go of my defensive posture, allowing his words to find a safe place inside of me, a place my mother would never be able to find.

Father Johnson, my great friend, drew from his cigarette while clouds of smoke managed to escape from his nostrils. "And I want you to remember this: You do not have 'bad blood' like your mother has told you. You're a wonderful girl, and there is absolutely nothing wrong with you. In fact, you're strong. You're a survivor."

I left that day feeling a huge emptiness his words couldn't fill, no matter how desperately I wanted them to. I would not see him again for twenty years.

A few months after my second husband was killed in a car accident, I signed up for a weekend retreat for widowed and divorced women. I knew almost nothing about the program, but I didn't care. It was a retreat, it was spiritual, and I needed it. Once I was at the retreat and settled into my room, I found out that the person leading the retreat was Father Johnson.

On Friday evening, at the end of the plenary session, he told our small group of women that he would be in the sitting room, and anyone who wanted to speak privately with him was welcome. After the session ended, and while the other, mostly older, women were chatting, I took my opportunity. I knew he wouldn't remember me, but I wanted to thank him, to let him know he had made a difference in my life. I wanted him to know he had saved my life.

The door was partially opened. I knocked very gently before peeking around the door. "May I come in?"

"Yes, of course," he said through plumes of cigarette smoke and gestured to the chair across from him.

He sat in a large, beautifully upholstered armchair with his legs crossed. I sat down across from him in an equally beautiful brocade wing chair. I noticed a gap between his black sock and black trousers on his crossed leg. His elbow was on the arm of the chair, and his cigarette was in the same hand that rested against his temple. It was the first time I'd ever seen him sitting down without his desk and that big ashtray between us.

"Father, you probably don't remember me—"

"Of course I do," he interrupted. "It's good to see you again, Maggie."

"You remember me?" I was stunned.

"Certainly I remember you. How are you? And how's your brother, Joey?"

"He's married with way too many children," I said, which made him laugh.

After a moment, he cocked his head and dragged on his cigarette. "Why are you on this retreat?"

I sank into the comfort of being with my old confidant, my big bear friend. In only a few minutes I remembered who I was and where I came from, and I could believe that despite my current circumstances, all would be well.

Because I knew it would matter to him, I told him about a conversation I'd had with my mother ten years earlier, during one of those afternoon visits that felt like she was coming to me for confession, or maybe absolution. While we sipped our coffee, my mother said, out of the blue, "I was very disappointed with you." This caught me off guard, and I felt the same crush in my heart as when she told me she hadn't loved my father when they married. I waited, because from previous experience I knew she had more to say.

"You weren't at all what I wanted in a daughter. You didn't want to be cuddled or petted by me. You didn't like to play with dolls, you only liked those stuffed animals. You preferred your father over me."

I listened, incredulous and stock-still, not wanting to break the spell.

"I thought I would get a nice little girl who would obey and do what she was told. You were headstrong and had to question everything. I tried to make you obedient, tried to make you be a good girl, but nothing worked. I was sometimes afraid that I would break your spirit." She paused for a moment before finishing. "No, you weren't at all what I wanted in a daughter."

Tears, the stinging kind, filled my eyes. Like so many other times, but with less defiance, I willed them away.

"I've always known that, Ma. But it's good you said it."

I told Father Johnson that while she didn't say anything I hadn't heard her say before, the difference that day was that she wasn't raging at me. There were no blows or insults flying at me. Nor was there an apology; she simply acknowledged that I didn't live up to her expectations. It was as though she had finally given up and was trying to reconcile herself to the daughter she had. I told him even though it hurt me deeply to hear her say these things in such a calm way, I experienced a strange relief from her admission.

When I finished, Father Johnson's reply was, as always, something for my heart. He nodded slightly. "I'm so sorry." After a couple of moments, he pulled on his cigarette again. "And look at you now." His face and eyes broke into a smile. "I'll bet you're a wonderful mother."

There were many occasions when my father, my brother, and I witnessed my mother decompensate. It always started with a screaming rage, a not altogether unusual occurrence, but in these cases, she would reach a point where some inner switch was flipped and she became emotionally overwhelmed—had a "meltdown" as we'd say now. She cried hysterically, often hyperventilating. If my father was there, he might persuade her to lie down and take another Librium, and if that didn't work, he would call the doctor, who came to the house and injected my mother with a sedative. I could see my father's helplessness when this happened. Sometimes he just held my mother in his arms while she wept and repeated over and over again, "All I want is for someone to love me, and I want to love my family. Why won't they let me? What's so wrong with me that they won't let me?" I was never sure who she was addressing in these agonizing laments. Was it her mother? Or God? Inside this angry woman was a little girl who wanted, more than anything, to be loved and accepted for who she was, and to her it seemed no one was listening. Sometimes she would recover in a couple of days, but there were other times when she'd be depressed for weeks, still going to her part-time job but spending most of the time in bed.

At twenty-three I was a divorced single mother with a house, a mortgage to pay, and no car because my husband, who needed it for work, took it when he left. My little girls were three years old and eighteen months old. I received very little child support, and it was always late. I needed financial help, and when I finally got the courage to ask my parents they said no, because they had already lent my brother some money a short time ago. Oh, but of course, I thought, it's always Joey first.

A few days after I asked, my mother called me and said since she and my father had been paying taxes for years, I was certainly entitled to apply for AFDC (Aid to Families with Dependent Children) and food stamps. I was ashamed to be in this position, but I had no other recourse. I asked my mother to babysit and to let me borrow their car so I could go to the welfare office and apply.

"I'll ask your father to babysit and I'll pick you up. I'm coming with you—you're not doing this alone."

I hadn't told her how hard this was for me, but she knew, and just like she was there for her mother, her sister, and her brothers, she showed up for me. I was vulnerable and needed help; Ellie rose to the occasion without my asking, and I didn't push her away.

Welfare and twenty-five dollars a week in child support didn't offer a comfortable or promising life for my little girls. I needed to return to work. Again, I asked my parents if I could borrow money, this time to buy a car to get to work each day. They still couldn't help me, but my father said he would take out a loan from his credit union and I could give him the payments each month. Once I knew I'd have a car, I could look for a job.

My father looked after my daughters, and my mother sat beside me as I drove her car to my job interviews. While I attended each interview, she waited in the car and prayed. She never asked anything of me or offered any advice; she simply stayed with me. My mother loved me with her silence and by bearing witness to me as a young single mother trying to make my way in the world. If I could paint my early life, this act of unconditional love and kindness would be a large, luminous gold light with streaks stretching like open arms against a dark background.

Ellie was a deeply troubled human being who didn't receive the treatment and care that might have helped her navigate life less painfully. And for her, life was not only very painful because of her poor ego strength, it was fraught with deep disappointments she could never reconcile. I used to be sad that my mother believed her happiness depended on circumstances outside of herself, but then I came to realize because of her mental illness, it wasn't likely that she would ever find happiness or peace within. This insight gave me more compassion for her. Appropriate medication and therapeutic treatments such as those available now would have helped her create coping strategies to protect herself and those close to her. Back then, with the paucity of services available, we all suffered greatly, but Ellie most of all.

I moved to Ireland in 1993, and by then my mother was widowed. While I was living abroad, her dementia worsened, and she was eventually moved into a nursing home by my brother and social services. Because of her demanding, unpredictable, and sometimes violent behavior, she was estranged from my brother and had few, if any, friends left. Six months before she died, I returned stateside to check in on her. I found her on a ward with five others, sleeping. No matter how long I studied her face, I barely recognized the small woman with white hair under heaps of white hospital sheets and blankets as my mother. I was unable to move myself past the nurses' station.

"Does she ever have visitors?" I asked the duty nurse, my eyes still fixed on my mother.

"Let's take a look." She pulled my mother's chart from a stack on the desk, scanning the pages. "Yup. It looks like someone named Ruth and her husband, and a man named Tom, come every few weeks for a Sunday visit."

I was flooded with gratitude, and with tenderness toward Ellie. Despite their difficult and painful sibling histories, and even though Ellie had no awareness or understanding of who they were, my mother's sister and brother made the hour-and-a-half drive each way to regularly visit her.

I so love knowing this about the end of my mother's life: those two people who loved me so much, and who wanted to protect me from their sister, found a way to love her, too. While my aunt and uncle grew and healed with their sobriety, my mother continued to struggle with her demons of mental illness and addiction to prescription medications. Still, her sister and brother never let her go. When they needed help, she took care of them and made sure they knew they were not alone; they, in turn, stayed with her through the end.

There is a truth my mother and I shared, but never had the opportunity to acknowledge: A mother's happiness is a lot of responsibility and the heaviest burden to carry.

I hope my mother, and her mother, rest in deep peace.

Reflection: "Ellie"

When I began this project, I was steeped in newly found feelings of compassion for my mother, and it was from that place I set out to write an essay that would attempt to tell my mother's story. I wanted to write from the point of view of a woman who had traveled the difficult and painful journey of a mother/daughter relationship, and who, if she wasn't at the end of that journey, was at least at a comfortable rest stop that offered a wider understanding and deeper acceptance of the person who became her mother. I wrote page after page, fueled by the blessed peace of compassion—until I was stopped dead in my tracks.

In conversation with a close friend and one of the authors of this compilation, I related an incident from my childhood. Her response was quick and sincere: "I'm so sorry, honey. I had no idea you'd suffered so much trauma."

We are both retired therapists who have diagnosed and treated trauma in our clients, but until that moment I'd never considered any of my own life experiences to be traumatic. Painful things did happen in my past, and I moved on. I reduced the size of certain events to make them small enough to fit into my emotional backpack, put them in, and continued on my way.

I've been in therapy several times in my life, and no one ever used the word *trauma* to describe any of the life events I brought into those therapeutic hours. Then, last fall, suddenly and inexplicably, this one word spoken so gently by my friend completely upended my life. In that one moment, I recognized and accepted my own history of trauma. I also decided perhaps I'd been a little too hasty and generous with my compassion toward my mother. I couldn't continue with my essay.

I went back into therapy again and reopened difficult chapters of my own story. I allowed myself to see the huge, black amorphous shadow of trauma settling over me at different ages of my younger life and accepted my therapist's diagnosis of PTSD (Post Traumatic Stress Disorder).

How did I—especially as a therapist—avoid seeing this for so many years? Because in my family, as with many dysfunctional families, traumatizing events and behaviors were normalized. Over time I became used to the heft, the companionship of trauma, accepting it as part of the fabric of my life.

For those who look for it, or need it, there is a happy ending to this story—through therapy and the powerful modality of EMDR (Eye Movement Desensitization and Reprocessing), I experienced deep healing. The facts of my life haven't changed; my responses and my beliefs about myself have.

When I returned to my writing, the challenge then was to write from a new place, one that allowed deeper truths to grind a lens through which I could see and understand the woman whom I made a mother. This essay is the result; it is my truth today.

And this is true, too: While my mother and I seem to have little in common, there is one thing we undeniably share. As women, we both tried to find our way through life, each of us the product of our parents and their culture, the product of the families, communities, and societies we grew up in and those in which we became wives and mothers. Each of us bears the wounds inflicted, either knowingly or unknowingly, by those concentric circles.

This writing journey wasn't simply cathartic for me; it was transformational. Looking for my mother beyond the narrative of our relationship, letting the story be only about her, had a profound effect on me. The compassion I'd previously felt for my mother returned and was soon replaced by something richer; for the first time in my life, I felt empathy for her. Before I came to this writing project, hurt and righteous anger kept me firmly planted in my own shoes, unwilling to step into hers to see or experience another perspective.

And the gifts kept coming: the roots and strong stem of compassion and empathy produced an elegant blossom of forgiveness. I didn't have to work at it or make up my mind to forgive my mother. I didn't have to cede any real or imagined ground to her; it evolved organically from a willingness to see and allow her to be more than my mother.

I am at peace with my mother. I hope my daughters will be able to say the same.

To any woman who would like to follow a path similar to the one we have taken with *Compassionate Journey*, I would say this: This isn't an ordinary writing project; it's a journey that sometimes felt like an Outward Bound experience. As such, certain preparations are important. Choose the right time to begin; travel lightly; let people know where you're going—you may need their help and support; stop when you're tired; take care of yourself. And, if you can't find your map, don't worry—there is none.

Lastly, choose your traveling companions well. It will be their honest and respectful comments, encouragement, and—when you need it—gentle prodding to stay on track that will sustain you throughout this extraordinary, and sometimes breathtaking, journey.

I have the deepest gratitude to the women in this writing group for allowing me to take the time I needed to heal, without judgment or expectation of when I could begin again. They held the space for me, and waited with patience and care for me to write again.

Sunday's Child *by Martha Rice*

I. The Time and Place for Growing Up

1954. A tiny village in western New York State. One Main Street. Two full-time cops. One police car. A volunteer fire department summoned by the loud, mournful blast of a whistle on the roof of the village hall. Five blasts: an accident. Two short, one long: a fire or home emergency. Margaret, the switchboard operator for the telephone company, operates command central. Pick up the phone, and when she connects with "Number please," she'll tell you all you need to know. From her perch on the third floor of the bank building, she can see Main Street—Teel's Dress Shop, Carlson's Pharmacy, Endicott-Johnson Shoes, The News Room, Ellis Brothers Soda Fountain, Carnahan Shearers Clothiers, Pinter's Restaurant, and The Westfield Department Store. She knows just about

everyone in town by number, name, occupation, and habit—the fifties
version of Google. Small towns don't like secrets.

I grew up in this village, the youngest member of a blended
family of six. There were four of us children, and we kept a lot of little
secrets from each other and from our parents, whom we called the
"folks." The term suggested parental respect far superior to the "old
man" and "old woman" references bandied about by the smart-alecky
townie kids who carried their cigarettes rolled up in the cuffs of their
T-shirts, hung out at the Sunoco on Main Street, and never seemed
to have curfews.

As part of the old guard in the town, my stepfather Hal was
one of those respected Protestants who had earned his place through
hard work, community spirit, and a certain amount of accumulated wealth. Money wasn't his issue, however; respect was, particularly after he was elected mayor of the village. The rule to never
besmirch the family name became such a frequent admonishment
from "the folks" that it might have been set to music or included in
dinner prayers.

My two stepbrothers paid little attention to the admonishment. Jim, the eldest, rumbled around the countryside with his
friends, knocking over the outhouses that still existed on some of
the farms. Al, the youngest, smoked cigarettes in the fort that he and
his friends had built out in a vacant field, and one day they couldn't
resist shouldering the two giant boulders that adorned the front
steps of the town library down the steep terrace just for the pleasure
of seeing them bump and slide down the grass.

My sister and I were more discreet, but I remember getting into
serious trouble with my mother when my friends and I had a bit of
a wild party. About twelve of my friends and I were at a slumber
party when we learned rivals of ours from Mayville had arrived at
the YMCA on Main Street. I think our conflict had something to
do with a boyfriend of one of the girls in our group, and we decided
it would be funny if we drove the Mayville girls out of town. What
followed was as absurd as it was silly and harmless, but the events

entranced the gossip pools of the little village and briefly damaged all of our reputations.

We chose weapons for our attack, but unfortunately, we didn't have much to choose from—two heads of lettuce, a couple of tomatoes, several squash, a couple of cucumbers, and some brownish bananas. Supplies in hand, we headed for Main Street, so deserted at that time of night that we could safely march up the centerline, shouting loudly and brandishing our weapons. The Mayville girls dove into their car, but we had a triumphant moment as we surrounded them before they drove off, laughing and shouting back at us.

Then, Mr. Trippy, the policeman whom we all loved, arrived. Then the state troopers arrived. Having rounded us up, Mr. Trippy sent us back to our party and warned us to stay off Main Street, and one of our group stayed behind at the little police station to explain our bizarre disturbance of the peace and to apologize. We thought that was the end of it.

When Mother came to pick me up early the next morning, however, she had already heard about our adventure, and she was furious.

"What on earth possessed you to do that?" she said. Mother tended to use phrases that brought in the supernatural, particularly if she was angry.

"But, Mom," I said, "it was just a joke."

"Well, I thought I could trust you," she said. "How do you think Hal feels?"

I had forgotten about the family admonishment, and I was embarrassed.

Even worse than my mother's lecture was the sermon delivered in the Episcopal Church later that morning. I was in the choir facing the congregation from the apse of the church. At the eleven o'clock service, Father Bailey, a handsome man with graying hair and a slight stammer, hesitated a moment longer than usual before beginning his sermon. I swear he looked directly at me, and then slowly he began.

"Last night," he said, "something happened on Main Street that each and every one of us should pay attention to. A group of young people—not boys who get into skirmishes with each other and quickly resolve their problems and go along their way—no, these were girls. Teenage girls from our town attacked girls from Mayville. On Main Street. And they carried weapons. Homemade weapons, and they threatened the girls from Mayville who had come in all innocence to watch a basketball game at the YMCA. Innocent girls with no weapons attacked on our Main Street by an unruly, weapon-bearing gang. The police and the state troopers were called and dispersed the crowd. This is a serious matter all of us need to concern ourselves with. Matters of this sort get worse unless they are stopped. I pray you will all go home and speak to your children and to your neighbors' children. We need to stop this infiltration of violence in our community before it progresses. And now, in the name of the Father, the Son, and the Holy Ghost, let us pray."

During the quiet muttering of prayers, I kept my head down, hoping the congregation would remember the number of times I had played the Virgin Mary at Christmas pageants and not connect me with the Mayville food riot of the night before. I stared fiercely at the red carpet in front of the choir pew and prayed that no one would take seriously the fiery sermon—so out of character for Father Bailey and the entire tradition of the Episcopal Church. But the words *infiltration, unruly, weapon-bearing,* and *gangs* couldn't be dismissed from my mind or from the minds of the other members of the church congregation.

Yet, I had been there; Father Bailey had not. The weapons he mentioned weren't named, so people in the congregation probably imagined that our rotten bananas and tomatoes had actually been knives and sticks. They couldn't have heard the laughter amidst the shouts as the Mayville girls escaped from town. They wouldn't know that Mr. Trippy had laughed too as he told us to go back to our party. I walked down the aisle of the church that day feeling that Father Bailey had no sense of justice and, worse yet, no sense of humor. I felt even more righteous indignation when I got home and discovered that church members of every denomination in town—even the Catholics—had received the same message. My friends and I were shaken, humiliated, and confused that adults couldn't see a bit of the humor in the escapade—especially in our choice of weapons.

The next morning, the folks took off for Florida, leaving me with Lena, our housekeeper. Mother hugged me and kissed me good-bye, but she never mentioned the teenage gang activity; in fact, she never brought the topic up ever again. If I hadn't been ashamed enough when Father Bailey delivered his sermon, my mother's dismissal of the incident really did the trick. I decided it might be best not to let her get too close to what I was doing or thinking in the future, since she seemed more likely to criticize than to understand.

Our family, like many middle-class households in the fifties and sixties, was governed by rules reminiscent of the Victorian age. The adults were the "big people" who made the rules and the decisions. The children were the "little people," and they were expected to follow the rules and abide by the decisions. Although my family was defined as a "blended" family because we were two families joined together, the larger definition of *blended* didn't apply. An imaginary line, like the yellow police tape at the scene of a crime, separated us and kept us apart.

There were not-to-be broken rules and clear expectations. Mother made it clear to me that I was expected to get good grades in high school so I would be accepted at a good college where I would meet respectable and intelligent young men from good families. If all went well, I might fall in love with one and marry him. One of Mother's favorite aphorisms was "It's just as easy to fall in love with a rich man as it is with a poor man." I heard the saying so often that I deliberately went out of my way to hang around with guys who didn't have any social status. This was the period just prior to the early sixties, so most of the people my age were beginning to question our parents' beliefs and ideals. We didn't need money! We needed the freedom to exercise our individuality. Even if we didn't want to live in communes where we'd have to share everything and not bathe daily, we didn't want to be shallow and materialistic like our parents. But we did like to break the rules by sneaking out at night or making out down by the lake with older boys from school. That was our pleasure and revolt. Our way of asserting ourselves.

Mother continued to nag me about learning skills I'd need to be a teacher, a secretary, or, if I wasn't too tall, an airline stewardess. "You need to have something to fall back on," she said, "in case your husband should die or you should get divorced." She didn't mention my father's early death, but it was clearly an underlying issue. Worst of all, Mother didn't ask me what I wanted to do in the future.

Fortunately, I quickly wiped the idea of becoming a secretary off the list the summer I spent working in my stepfather's office when I was sixteen. "Gee, Christmas," he said. "I think she'd better take up teaching instead. She can't even do payroll for the ten people I've got working down at the factory." My ineptness at doing any of the secretarial tasks was a kind of triumph at a time when women were only meant to handle the intricacies of secretarial work.

Most of my high-school friends suffered from the same frustrations that I did about their mothers. We wanted our mothers to be positive characters in our lives. In this prepill, prefeminist era, we felt something was missing in our relationships with our mothers, but like Winnie the Pooh bumping downstairs on his head behind Christopher Robin, we couldn't stop bumping long enough to think what it was. We longed for more from our mothers, but we weren't quite sure what more was, so we imagined how wonderful it would be if our mothers, instead of being the people who tried to control our lives, were our best friends.

The mothers of our imaginations bore little resemblance to the ladies who cooked for us, cleaned for us, and took us clothes-shopping. The women we conjured up had tiny waists, wore fashionable clothes, and if they smoked, used long cigarette holders. Not only were the mothers of our imaginations sophisticated and beautiful, they treated us as equals. They would listen and nod as we railed against our teachers and our peers. They would never offer unasked-for advice. They would never be shocked or chagrined by our comments, and they would never try to weasel information out of us, particularly when it came to the boys we liked or the places we went. No lectures about drinking, smoking, or sex. No criticism of our hairstyles or the skimpy pedal pushers we liked to wear because we knew they made us sleek and sexy.

The topic about which we knew the least was sex. I think most of our mothers steered away from discussing sex because their mothers hadn't discussed it with them. Perhaps they also felt if they didn't talk to us about sex, we wouldn't experiment in dark cars at the lake at night. My mother never mentioned sex to me, and even on the day that I married at age twenty-seven, she turned to my sister and whispered, "Does she know everything that she should?"

Sex education wasn't taught in most high schools in the fifties, so my friends and I gleaned our imperfect information from forbidden magazines like *True Confessions* and, in my case, the sexually explicit illustrations from a volume of Boccaccio, which my parents kept on the bottom shelf of the bookcase in the living room. Mother didn't mind Boccaccio because his work was considered to be literature, but she thought *True Confessions* was trashy, so I couldn't read it at home.

Smoking cigarettes spelled glamour to us. Our parents disapproved, even though they themselves smoked. My mother looked so sophisticated gesturing with a cigarette in one hand and a drink in the other that I wanted desperately to look just like her, so I learned to smoke, but I couldn't do it in public because someone my parents knew might see me and tell.

Drinking in our household took place in private. Each night at five thirty, my mother and stepfather settled in their bedroom upstairs, a small room papered with delicate blue flowers that looked out over the trees in the front and across at Colonel Rider's mansion. We could hear the folks laugh and talk as they had cocktails, but the cocktail hour was reserved for them alone, no children and no Lena. Our housekeeper was a staunch Methodist teetotaler who lived in a room in our attic my stepfather had sectioned off when he and my mother had married. It's doubtful that their cocktail hour was a secret from Lena, but she never referred to it, and she lived with our family until I was sixteen and ready to go off to college.

As children, we didn't recognize the hypocrisy of the "do as I say, not as I do" world in which we lived; we just knew we'd better not get caught puffing on a Pall Mall or stealing a sip of sherry. No discussion was needed. The "big people-little people" dynamic was well oiled, and it drew the boundary lines around my early relationship with my mother by setting limits; it also curtailed emotional involvement that I really needed and wanted. I didn't get to know my mother until I was much older.

II. To a Manner Born:
My Mother's Development, 1901–1920

The Essential Handbook of Victorian Etiquette (1873 and 1890) *was written by Thomas E. Hill and republished in 1994 by Bluewood Books. William P. Yenne, editor of the 1994 edition says in the introduction that Hill "categorized the etiquette that governed an entire epoch." Today we may view Professor Hill's rules of etiquette as amusing, but my grandmother Bondi, having grown up in the late 19th century, would have taken at least some of his rules seriously.*

Despite the negative feelings about my mother that emerged in adolescence, when I was five years old, my mother was the most beautiful woman in the world. She had black curly hair, deep blue eyes, a crooked smile, and though only five foot six, she was thin and elegant, and in my eyes appeared to be much taller. Her deep voice always fooled telephone operators into thinking she was a man. Actually, she had the perfect vocal control of someone who had been trained for the theater, and her theater training carried over into her movements as well. Her conversations were punctuated with a smile here, a frown there, eyebrows raised in question or disagreement, nods in agreement, a slight tilt of the head. People loved to watch her and listen to her.

The Victorian age was a strong factor in Mother's upbringing, and the influence carried over to us children although we didn't know it at the time. The last of five children, Mother was born on the cusp of the twentieth century in Waterloo, Iowa, "the last leaf on the tree" her mother always said. Bondi, my grandmother, was over forty when she discovered her pregnancy, and Mother arrived a month after her nephew, her oldest sister's son, was born. My grandfather, considerably older than Bondi, had actually fought in the Civil War. He died when Mother was twelve. With all of her siblings so much older than she was, Mother was raised pretty much an only child, free to do as she wished.

Bondi was considered "modern" in her time. She indulged her interests in language, art, and literature by attending classes regularly given by ladies' cultural societies of the time, and ironically, she belonged to the local suffragette movement as well as to the conservative Daughters of the American Revolution.

Although she was freethinking, Bondi clung to the gentle Victorian manners that governed the actions of well-bred ladies and gentlemen of that time. "Young ladies should sit up straight; young ladies should wear gloves and hats; young ladies should speak in quiet voices." She thought that women should absolutely have equal rights with men, but they should keep the reserved demeanor of ladies, a kind of refreshing image of purity. Independence, elegance, and style were qualities Bondi believed in, and she fostered these qualities in my mother.

Mother was not to be held down in some ways, however. She had been named Effie after her mother's sister. The kids at school teased her and made up rhymes about her name, so almost immediately after Aunt Effie died, Mother became Donna, a name she had practiced over and over again in front of the large mirror in the parlor. She'd adopted the name from the label on a popular and expensive brand of Dutch cigars—La Donna. The La Donna lady, whose image enhanced the wooden cigar box, was tantalizing: raven-haired with dark almond-shaped eyes, a come-hither look, and a voluptuous neckline hidden behind a thin lace mantilla. When Mother became Donna, no one laughed at her in school again. As she grew to maturity, she collected and kept many friends.

In the list of songs she wanted played at her funeral, Donna included "Auld Lang Syne." Good friends were primary to her enjoyment of life. She was part of a group of nine ladies—Les Girls, my stepfather called them—who walked together, went ice-skating, planned elaborate parties for themselves and for us children, went to the theater, and worked for Union Relief, an organization that provided food and services for the poor. Occasionally, they played bridge, but only if nothing more exciting cropped up. Female friendship was essential to my mother's well-being.

Mother was the center of many Les Girls activities, but her personal appeal was not limited to those who knew her. Perfect strangers were attracted to her as well. If I met her at the airport when she came to visit, she would inevitably be accompanied by the man who had sat next to her on the plane and had insisted on carrying her bag and making sure that she was safely delivered. The age of her protector was irrelevant. In fact, most often the person who helped her was years younger than she was. But that made no difference to him.

"It was so interesting to talk to you," she'd say to John or Tom or Matt as they put down her bag. "This is my daughter, Martha."

At that moment, I'd shake hands with the new man she'd befriended and thank him so kindly for taking care of my old mother, but I don't think that Mother actually ever thought of herself as old. I'm sure that the young man in question didn't think of her in terms of age. She was just a charming woman in a stylish hat with whom he'd enjoyed a few hours from Chicago to San Francisco. And Donna? Well, even if she didn't seek an audience, she always found one.

Although Mother, like Blanche DuBois, never rejected the "kindness of strangers," any helplessness she might have displayed was a bit of a fake. Although she'd skinned a snake on a dare when she was a kid, ridden a horse across large territories of the Midwest when she acted as the advance person for a theater company, and applied for and gotten a job as a house mother in a girls' school at sixty-seven after my stepfather died, minor tasks that seemed simple to many people were difficult for her: using a can opener, filling her car with gas, or remembering to turn off the iron when she had finished pressing. I share some of these lapses with Mother. I have gotten better about opening cans and filling my car with gas, but I never leave the house without worrying about having left some appliance plugged in. I remember the day that Mother got distracted and left the iron on the wooden ironing board until it burned straight through. Had my brother not noticed the odor of wood burning, the house might have gone up in smoke.

Instead of attending a traditional college as her siblings had done, Donna studied acting at the Lyceum Arts Conservatory in Chicago. Even before she had completed her courses at the conservatory, she was offered a job with Ellison and White's Chautauqua Circuit, a traveling troupe of lecturers, classical musicians, and actors whose goal it was to bring culture to the hinterlands. In her early twenties, she traveled around the western United States, Australia, New Zealand, and Tahiti playing the ingénue in various plays and working as an advance person for the group.

In the late 1920s, after she had tried her luck as an actress on the New York stage, she moved back to Ohio and opened an acting and dance studio with her sister. She gave up the studio when she married my father in 1928.

Most of the memories of my father have been handed down to me by my sister and my mother. I know from pictures that he was tall and striking looking—not handsome exactly, but imposing because he was so tall. When I see a picture of T.S. Eliot, I see my father—dark and intelligent. He graduated from Kenyon College and, according to my mother, would have liked most of all to own a bookstore, as literature was his love. But life didn't work out quite that way because he had his mother to support as well as a wife and, later, two children. And the Depression came about in 1929. Dad took a job with General Motors, first as repo man who recovered cars from those families who couldn't keep up with the payments. Later, he became a manager for the company, but he had been born with a hole in his heart, a condition that had no remedy in the 1940s.

After two heart attacks, he died at age 46, leaving my mother with two small children and a mother-in-law to care for.

Although her family supported her emotionally and my father had life insurance, Mother decided to return to college to receive a degree in speech so she could teach. The plan of returning to school was postponed when just six months after my father died, his sister passed away, leaving my uncle with two young boys. It wasn't uncommon for families to help each other in stressful times, so soon after my aunt died, Mother stepped in to help my uncle and his two young boys. My mother, sister, and I moved from Ohio to New York State in what was supposed to be a temporary mission, but it turned into a permanent arrangement.

III. The Merging of Families, 1946

I am sitting in the second row of the empty Methodist Church in Mayville, New York. My two boy cousins and my sister are sitting beside me, and my mother and uncle are standing in front of the minister at the altar. He is saying something to them, but I can't hear what it is. I swing my legs back and forth and hit the back of the pew in front of me; my sister hits me hard in the arm to make me stop bumping the pew. Finally, the minister stops talking, and my uncle kisses my mother. My cousin Al yawns. My cousin Jim laughs. The minister says that my mother and my uncle are "man and wife." That means that my cousins are my stepbrothers and my uncle is my stepfather. I glance at my sister; she looks like she's going to cry. I am bewildered.

I was too young to have my mother's marriage mean much to me at all. For my older sister, it was a different story, particularly since she had heard about the impending marriage from a neighbor.

It seems odd now to think that my mother and uncle married without consulting us children, but it wouldn't have been unusual at the time for the adults to make decisions without consulting the children—not exactly like the old Victorian adage, "Children should be seen and not heard," but close. I'm sure they thought what they were doing was best for all of us. In our family, things were seldom discussed. It was the old "big people-little people" dynamic played over again.

Did my mother and uncle truly love each other enough to marry within a year and a half of the deaths of their spouses? They may actually have been attracted to each other while my father and aunt were still alive, but there is also the possibility that love was not on either one of their minds initially. In the late forties and early fifties, men were acknowledged to be the breadwinners, and women were left with the child-rearing. There were surely practical reasons for them to marry: for my mother, companionship and financial security; for my stepfather, companionship and a stable household. The union of the two families must have made a lot of sense to them both.

My stepfather, Hal, was kind and generous at heart, but he was high-maintenance and had a short temper, particularly with children. Because I was the youngest child, I didn't incite his anger as much as his own sons and my sister did. Although he was proud of his sons, it's possible he would have been better off without children because they annoyed him so much. And then, he drank—and as he grew older, he relied more and more on liquor each day. The basement in our big Victorian house was divided into two sections. One half of the basement had an earth floor and a cistern. That part of the cellar was moist and moldy—a place to stay away from. A place to store canned fruit and vegetables. The rest of the basement had a cement floor and housed the furnace, a coal chute, and a couple of other little rooms for storage. In a wooden box in one of these rooms, my stepfather hid his whiskey. Each afternoon, he went directly down to the basement when he came home from work. He'd have a nip or two alone, and then he'd join my mother in their second-floor bedroom for cocktails at five thirty.

Alcohol was the enemy that destroyed my stepfather's personality. While another person with a few drinks might have been cheerful, Hal became despondent and negative. Only when he was on vacation and out of the town in which he had grown up did he become charming and funny after a drink or two. At home, he seemed beset by some strange and unknown demons of his childhood.

My mother did what she thought she should to support him, but she was an enabler. He was supersensitive and felt inferior. He needed boosting up a lot of the time. Outside of our family, no one knew about the drinking, and to be fair to him, it didn't become an obvious problem until later in his life. Nonetheless, I remember the disparaging comments he'd make about people in the town when he'd had a drink or two, and I've never forgotten the night when I was sixteen and he caught my dog licking the butter off the dish on the kitchen table. In a rage, he threw the poor dog down the steep basement stairs. That was, in a way, the beginning and the end for me. It was definitely the first time I realized that he was an alcoholic. I ran upstairs in tears and anger and kicked the end of my Victorian bed so hard that one of the ornaments crashed to the floor. My mother eventually came up to comfort me, but it did little good.

"Now, Mary Martha," she said, "don't take him too seriously. He's upset with something at work."

"The dog didn't do anything so bad," I said.

"It's all right. We'll get a new dog."

"I don't want a new dog," I said. "I want a new uncle."

The next day, the dog, Bucky, was taken to the vet and put to sleep.

After that incident, I was ready to go to college, first in Ohio and then in Vermont. Although I was the only family member who sat in the hospital beside my uncle when he died of a cerebral hemorrhage in 1962, our distance had been established by then.

The effect of the merger between our two families on my nine-year-old sister was tremendous. She had worshipped my mother and thought of her as a friend, particularly after my father died, so she felt betrayed, and for years, she and my uncle/stepfather had an uneasy relationship.

As a five-year-old, I cared for my uncle even though he wasn't my father; my memories of my dad were vague. When he died, I was four. Almost five. My remembrances are as fragmented and fragile as aspen leaves—flutters and whispers. I can see him holding me in the big red chair in the living room as he reads me stories at night. I am with him when he pushes me in the wooden swing in the side yard and carries me around the block on his shoulders. I can remember sitting on the floor in my parents' bedroom on the morning the men came to take him away to the hospital. And I was there with him at the funeral home as my grandmother took me by the hand and lifted me up to kiss him. Despite his presence in my memory, it was his absence from my life that affected me most. His death created a hole in my family tree, the impact of which was so strong that even as a young adult, I looked closely at tall, heavyset men on the street, imagining that by some mistake, my father hadn't really died. He had simply escaped and started a new life without my mother and me.

By dying, he had, in effect, abandoned me, and for many years, I feared abandonment more than anything else. The fear affected the way I related to all of the men in my life. I feared that each man who professed his love for me would abandon me as my father had done.

When I was five, it was much easier for me to accept a step-father than it was for my sister. And my mother, concerned that I might forget my father entirely, set up a ritual that we went through each night to make his image indelible in my mind.

IV. Remembering My Father When I Was a Young Child

"Our Father, who art in heaven," Mother says, and I join in with the fervor of a five year old. I grow particularly dramatic as we reach the "forever and ever. Amen," at the end of the prayer; then, after a short pause, I add, "Good night, dear Daddy."

My eyes are closed, and I see my father sitting on the edge of a cloud with his legs crossed. He looks like a real person, not an angel, and he's smiling.

Besides keeping the memory of my father alive through those nightly prayers, Donna called on my father to help her in child-rearing. He became part of the familiar chants she used to modify my behavior as I was growing up.

"Daddy wouldn't approve of that," she would say when I didn't clean up my room.

"Don't be such a Sarah Bernhardt," she would say when I cried or pouted over some real or imagined slight. "What would Daddy say?" Or "Can't you smile? No one likes a sulker." I knew that the "no one" she referred to was my father, even though she didn't say his name. Stored somewhere in my subconscious was the as-yet unexpressed thought that my father had abandoned me by dying. Hidden deeper in my subconscious was the belief that I could displease him even in absentia.

In the forties and fifties, there were no centers for grieving children, and there was a stigma attached to seeing a psychiatrist, so no one focused attention on helping me understand my father's death. I was stuck with a recurring Technicolor nightmare in which I was chased through thick green fog by an unseen monster. A heavy, sweet smell of carnations suffocated me, and I would wake up crying. Until I was ten years old, I couldn't go to sleep without having a light on in the closet, and I frequently woke up terrified in the middle of the night. All the way through high school, I prayed I wouldn't get a bouquet of carnations from a prom date. Even today, I have total recall of the Technicolor nightmare that frightened me so terribly when I was little. For many years, I would awaken my mother in the middle of the night because I was afraid. Although my mother never tried to get me to talk about my anxiety, she never failed to crawl out of her warm bed and snuggle down with me in my room until I could go back to sleep.

Not having my fears about my father's death sorted out had a definite effect on me. I remember how scared and lonely I was, but I was shy and afraid of being laughed at if I told anyone how I felt. As the youngest child, I was out of step with the rest of the blended family. My stepbrothers teased me incessantly, and my sister, four years older than I, ignored me most of the time. Since

I was convinced that anything I said or did would get ridiculed, I defended myself by withdrawing.

My mother's insistence on keeping the memory of my father alive led me to daydream about him, particularly if I was feeling lonely. Since I spoke to him each night in my prayers, it was easy for me to imagine he hadn't died at all, a common fantasy for any child who loses a parent. I would play "search for my father," a mind game in which I imagined myself walking down a crowded street and catching sight of a tall, heavyset man who looked like my father. I'd run ahead to catch up with him, but I was always just a little too late. He disappeared into the crowd. Although I had very few real memories of my dad, whenever I felt misunderstood or neglected, I imagined that if my father were alive, he would listen to me and, of course, always take my side.

V. Blending a Family, Early 1950s

It is six o'clock, and Lena, the housekeeper, has put dinner on the table. My mother has hit the gong in the front hall, summoning the family to the table. My stepfather stands at one end of the table ready to serve the chicken. We children stagger in. My sister, wrapped in a woolen blanket as a protest against the thermostat that never rises above sixty-eight degrees in the winter, slouches down in her chair next to my stepbrother Jim. My stepfather responds to her silent protest by removing his corduroy jacket and draping it over the back of his chair. My mother, always alert to possible dissension, tries to divert attention away from my sister and my stepfather by asking Jim about his plans for the weekend. Her innocuous question elicits an innocuous answer, but she has averted a disagreement about the temperature in the room.

I am sitting next to my stepbrother Al, who is five years older than I am and twice my size. He is particularly fond of knuckle-hitting me in the leg throughout most dinners. My parents don't notice because the table-cloth hides the attacks. And I'm not going to tell on him! On this partic-ular evening, I wait until he has reached for the salt with his knuckle-

hitting hand. When he draws back his hand, I reach out and stab it with my fork. Al screams and holds his barely bleeding hand in the air for all to see. My mother leaps up from the table, then sits back down. My brother Jim and my sister laugh.

"It's not funny," my mother says. "He could get blood poisoning."

My stepfather looks at the hand; then he looks at me.

"I think you deserved it, Al," he says. "You may be excused from the table."

Everyone is silent for a moment. Then Jim, as if called upon to create levity, brings up one of his favorite topics: the impossibility of the Virgin Birth. Jim's topics are always meant to stir things up, and they usually continue until my stepfather throws up his hands in disgust and calls the discussion over.

When controversy threatens the dinnertime peace, my mother often leaves the table quietly and returns with a volume of the Encyclopedia Britannica. *Like a good peacekeeper, she is prepared to turn the conversation to something that she has found in the encyclopedia—fact, not opinion—and dinner is saved.*

Producing the encyclopedia was a very positive move on my mother's part. My stepfather could enjoy his meal in peace, and we all learned things such as the depth of the Amazon River, the flora and fauna of Alaska, and the native costumes of France.

Donna's encyclopedia trick was just one example of her ongoing quest to create harmony in her marriage with my uncle. Her attempts didn't always work, particularly in the later years when he was sliding slowly into alcoholism and she became his adversary rather than his companion, but she nonetheless clung to the code that defined her role as wife in a sometimes very difficult position. Paraphrased, the code might have been written like this:

Marriage According to My Mother

It is important for the woman to take the "back seat." She should be loving, caring, giving, trusting, sharing, honest, forbearing, brave, and forthright, and she should, above all, never burden the marriage with her troubles. If she has all of the aforementioned virtues, she will be protected and revered, and life will be harmonious. Harmony is what one seeks in a marriage, and it is the woman's job to bring about harmony.

Later in her life, I think that Donna realized the limitations of her thinking, but by then her ideas had been ingrained in my mind, and I wrestled with them throughout the feminist era that followed.

VI. Sunday's Child—Images of My Mother

Monday's child is fair of face,
Tuesday's child is full of grace,
Wednesday's child is full of woe,
Thursday's child has far to go,
Friday's child is loving and giving,
Saturday's child works hard for a living,
But the child that's born on the Sabbath day
        is bonny and blithe and good and gay.

—Old English Rhyme

My mother was always a little uncertain as to the exact year of her birth because the records had been destroyed in a fire, and at the turn of the twentieth century, records weren't as meticulously kept. She seemed very certain she had been born on a Sunday, and if one believes the old nursery rhyme predicting a child's qualities according to the day of the week on which she was born, the prophecy would fit my mother to a tee, for "the child that's born on the Sabbath day is bonny and blithe and good and gay."

Believing there was no point in dwelling on the negative because the positive was so much more appealing, Donna went out of her way to view people and incidents in the lightest, brightest way she could. She never gossiped, and people she hardly knew often confided in her and depended on her to listen, so she knew a lot of things that might be gossip-worthy. She knew which women focused on tomorrow's grocery lists while their husbands made love to them; she knew which husbands visited the Tap Room and which went to Buffalo or even to Silver Creek to visit the clubs. She knew which young girls were sent away for a few months to live with relatives until they delivered the babies that would be put up for adoption.

"I could write a fascinating book about life in a small town," she often said, but she never did, and she never would have done it, for that would have meant betraying an unspoken trust. If she commented on anyone at all, it was more likely she would mutter "poor soul" and let it go at that. I remember coming home from my summer job as a waitress at one of the few restaurants in the village and telling my mother a prominent lawyer in town and his secretary had spent the evening in one of the remote dark corners of the restaurant. The rumor of their liaison was already common knowledge in the neighborhood, as was the fact that his wife was an alcoholic, so I thought I was just bringing home a juicy tidbit for us to enjoy together. My attempt at establishing camaraderie through gossip failed miserably. Donna made it very clear that not only did she not want to hear any more of my story, she didn't want me to repeat it to anyone else, either. An expression she frequently used has stuck with me through the years. As soon as she heard even the hint of gossip, she would look the bearer of rumor in the eye and in her deep voice, utter an old vaudeville line: "Vas you dere, Chollie?" She meant that if a person didn't witness the incident in question, he or she shouldn't conjecture about what happened or didn't happen. The conversation would stop.

Mother's positive approach to people extended to situations as well. She could cast light onto any dingy situation. In the theater, a common gel used to light the stage for a comedy was called "bastard amber" because it bathed the stage in a bright pinkish light.

Mother approached most situations as if she saw them lit with "bastard amber." She had been a city person before she married my stepfather and moved to western New York State. As soon as she drove past the sign that declared the area to be the Grape Juice Capital of the World, my mother declared our new home to be the "dear little village" that she wanted it to be. Had she been a painter, she would have loaded up her palette with delicate beiges and warm yellows. Each house would have been Victorian and each yard would have been enclosed by a picket fence. No weeds would have grown on lawns that glowed green in the sunshine, and each house would have had a welcoming light shining from a lamp in the front-room window.

The first year she was in town during the fall grape harvest, she was clearly disappointed that there was no festival at which grapes were stomped to make the juice. Going to the factory to see them pressed through heavy grape blankets was too mechanical and boring for her romantic mind. Had my mother had her way, we would all have been dancing in the streets singing songs from Lerner and Loewe.

My mother's ability to create romantic images out of the ordinary made the world a happier, kinder place for us all, but she could also be strong-willed. She was an intelligent woman who had been brought up to be independent. Mother might have idealized our little village, but she wasn't exactly the type of woman who voluntarily stayed home and baked bread or made pies. For several years when they were first married, Mother had my stepfather convinced she did know how to bake pies, and she produced one a week. Actually, she ordered them from a woman in town, but it was quite some time before my stepfather caught on.

When Mother arrived in town, she must have immediately recognized the fact that without a car, she couldn't go shopping in nearby large cities like Buffalo; she couldn't get out to go to the theater; she couldn't even get around the tiny village unless she walked. I don't know if she and my stepfather discussed the issue of transportation, but Donna took the problem on by herself. Once a week, she'd get on the train and go the sixty miles to Buffalo to take driving lessons. It wasn't until she received her certificate and her driver's license that she made any family announcement. The next week, a bright-red Plymouth convertible was parked under the elm tree in the yard. A present from my stepfather. My mother had won her freedom. From then on, she could travel anywhere her little "red number," as she called it, would take her.

When Donna talked, she often made graceful gestures with her hands. As a trained actress, she knew the power of a gesture as an accessory to a comment. Because her hands were an integral part of her persona, she was devastated one day to have an accidental encounter with an electric mixer. It wasn't that Donna didn't know how to cook, but I'd have to say that it wasn't her most developed skill. On the day of the accident, she was making a cake as a surprise for my stepbrother's birthday, and for some reason, she thought she could scrape the bowl while the electric mixer paddle was mixing the batter. The blades caught on her ring and drew her hand into the bowl, severing the tip of her index finger and half of her little finger. There was little to be done for the index finger, but the small-town surgeon was able to reattach the little finger, although it would never be straight again. In later life, she told me that she was sure no one would love her again because of her disfigured hand. Indeed, for many years after the accident, she tended to keep her right hand in her lap when in public.

Although Mother wasn't vain, she knew what her attributes were, and she hated losing them to age. In New York, she had worked as a photographer's model for shoes and gloves. She had long, narrow feet and enviable legs. I still remember on one of her last visits to our home in California, she came out of her room one day and in a dejected voice announced, "My legs have gone."

What she meant was she could see in the mirror the changes that aging had brought to the appearance of her beautiful legs. At the time, I thought she was being silly, but as I have reached a certain age, I understand the sadness that she must have been feeling. When I was forty-five or so, there came a day when I realized I was becoming invisible to men. Fewer and fewer heads turned when I walked into a room. Locking eyes with strangers became a thing of the past.

And just the other day, I looked in the mirror and saw those very distinct wrinkles that mysteriously develop overnight as one ages, and I remembered and could identify with my mother's horror and sadness when she recognized her beautiful legs had finally aged.

VII. Meeting My Mother Halfway— Growing Up Together, 1965

As much as I loved her, I didn't really get to know what Donna felt and thought while I was growing up. I won't take complete responsibility for not knowing her very well; part of the distance between us was her fault. My mother didn't seem able to talk to me directly about any fears that she had, and I didn't seem to be able to talk to her either, so we played a kind of cat-and-mouse game where she lectured and I dismissed what she was saying. She continued chanting to me when I was in high school just as she had when I was a little girl, but we never really had a good conversation. It seemed to me that she was too busy worrying about what I might be doing to really talk to me.

"Don't look at yourself in the mirror so much. It's vain."
"Pretty is as pretty does."
"Can't you do something with your hair?"
When I arrived home from a party or a date, she would invariably be sitting by the fireplace in the living room with a cup of tea in hand. I couldn't really confide in her because I always anticipated that her response would be a lecture. So the confidences that we might have shared became cover-ups of the truth.
Mother: "Who was at the party?"
Me: "No one special."
Mother: "What did you do?"
Me: "Nothing much."
Mother: "I hope there wasn't any drinking."
Me: "NO."
Mother: "Did you have a good time?"
Me: "I'm tired. Night, Mom."

When it came time for me to go to college, we did sit down and have a little chat. The gist of it came down to two points: "You don't need to finish college if you don't want to. You can get married anytime now," and "It's just as easy to fall in love with rich man as it is with a poor man." The last message was repeated like a refrain at significant times until I actually did get married.

I finished college. It never occurred to me to drop out and get married. I thought that girls who got married right out of college were stupid and weak. After graduating, I went to New York, studied acting, did some summer stock theater and some off-off-Broadway work, and then fell in love with an artist from California. I was engaged to marry him, and we went home for Christmas to meet Mother.

"Well," she said after he left, "he certainly won't set the world on fire."

For a moment, I felt as if I were five years old again and had left myself open to ridicule and criticism. My mother had judged the person I was in love with, and she didn't even see that she had hurt me deeply.

I didn't marry the artist from California that my mother said would "certainly" not "set the world on fire," but I don't know that my mother's words affected me as much as the fact I was unable to decide what I wanted to do. At the time, I felt she was telling me that I had made a bad choice, and I guess she was, in a way, but not just to be critical. Now, I understand that her comment was probably an attempt at protecting me by suggesting I consider the possible pitfalls of marrying someone who might not be able to provide for me financially. She had to make choices when my father died, and she was passing her fears along to me. It was still hard for her to step out of her role as mother. It was also hard for me to accept her words as kindly. I felt defensive and withdrew.

After I married and had children of my own, I understood my mother's motives a lot better. What I saw as her need to control me was really a need to protect me and guide me on the path she thought would offer me the best advantages. Her chants, those words that had influenced me so much throughout my life at home, diminished in power as I went off to college and then to New York, but the fact that I can remember them now is a testimony to their strength. I made it a point not to chant to my own children, but I don't think my decision made them any happier or closer to me.

My mother's own experiences, of course, served as the basis for the kinds of information she passed on to my sister and me. Being widowed at forty-four was emotionally devastating to her because she had loved my dad, but love didn't erase the demands of the situation. She hadn't gotten a college degree—that degree that would have allowed her something to fall back on. She had two young children, and despite the fact that her siblings loved her and supported her, she was a proud woman and had always been independent. Remarriage was the logical step to take. The marriage to my uncle was often problematic, but not during the time when we were growing up.

Our blended family was not unhappy: we had vacations in Canada, square dances in the barn, parties, family canasta in front of the fireplace, ice-skating in the winter, fishing in the summer. We watched television and ate popcorn in the music room. Together. Not only were our basic needs met, but our blended parents supported us through a number of embarrassing scrapes, and Donna interceded on our behalf when it was necessary.

Mother was always a worrier of the first order, and my sister and I both inherited her trait. Was the stove/iron/toaster/hair dryer turned off? Was there enough money? Were my brothers and wives happy in their marriages? Was there anything she could do if they weren't? Would I ever get married? Would my sister ever get married? Would my mother's car make it through her lifetime? Would my sister make it back from Vietnam where she was a reporter? Would I be safe in New York? We got used to her early-morning phone calls telling us what she had worried about the night before. After giving us her ideas and suggestions for whatever problem she had worried about, she would hang up. Having done the worrying, she put aside the problem and let us worry about it.

Shortly before she turned eighty, in the middle of my sister's MBA graduation ceremony, Mother had a heart attack and was shipped off by ambulance to St. John's Hospital in Santa Monica. There her doctor, after stabilizing her, urged her to consider having surgery to correct heart problems caused by age and a full life of smoking. She refused.

"I hope my daughters won't be hurt, but I'm not willing to go through an operation," she said to the doctor. "I know people who've had that surgery, and they slowed down to nothing. They might have been alive, but not really alive. That's not what I want."

To my sister and me, she apologized.

"I've had a good life," she said. "I'm not ready to pass out of the picture yet, but I don't mind going when I do. Now that I've had a heart attack, I don't have to worry about having a stroke. That's a relief."

While her heart attack/stroke reasoning may have been a bit off, she was back to normal within six months except for using an electric chair to go up to her bedroom on the second floor. She still smoked because, to her, there didn't seem to be any reason to stop doing things that gave her pleasure. She still drove her car as well, having justified in her own mind that if she had another heart attack while driving, she would have time to pull over to the shoulder and not hurt anyone.

When Mother was eighty-one, my sister asked her to go along with her to Egypt on a press trip. Mother was very worried she might have a heart attack on foreign shores, and she agonized over whether or not she should go. Finally, she called my cousin, who was a physician, and asked him what he thought.

"Well, Donna," he said, "what are you worried about? If you have a heart attack and live, they'll get you to a hospital and arrange to fly you home. If you have a heart attack and don't live, you won't know the difference, but they'll still fly you home. You might as well go."

My stepfather had died in 1962 when he was sixty-five, leaving my mother, who lived for another twenty years, short of long-term money. He had suffered a stroke and lived only two weeks, despite the lobbying that my mother did with God. I happened to be home when he died, and I stayed for several months. During that time, the things that had kept us from communicating with each other disappeared. I think what actually occurred was a power switch. My mother, who had always been the strong one, was now the one who needed support. I, who had always resisted her strength, was now able to assert myself. I helped her deal not only with the shock of my stepfather's death—bad as that was—but also with the worst shock of all, the realization that my stepfather had divided his money equally between his two sons and my mother. She was to live in the house as long as she wanted to, but the house itself and the apartment behind it had been willed to my stepbrothers. Donna was overcome. It was hard to tell which was the most overwhelming aspect—the death of my stepfather or the fact that he had not left her enough money to live in the manner she had become accustomed to in the twenty years that they had been married. She was shocked, hurt, and furious. Over and over again, Donna replayed the scene.

"He asked me to go through the finances with him," she said, "but I just relied on his judgment. I trusted him with the money, like I always had. I thought he'd take care of me like he always had."

I listened to the dirge as she sang it and felt sorry, but there was nothing that I could do except provide comfort by listening and vow forever and ever that I would never allow myself to let someone else control my finances and future.

"I will share what I have, but I won't let anyone else control it," I said to myself.

In the meantime, I found my brief return to western New York State a lot of fun. No longer a teenager, I reunited with people I'd grown up with, including my stepbrothers and their wives. I caught up on all of the town gossip, dated a few guys, picked up a couple of classes at the local college, and confidently drove my stepfather's Cadillac through New York snowstorms to attend classes as well as rehearsals for a play in which I had been cast. I had no responsibilities, except for my mother, and I had a wonderful time. I fell in love briefly with my English professor, was propositioned by the director of the show I was in, and got taken to dinner and drinks by a variety of new men. I didn't remember ever being so popular when I was growing up in the town, so I figured my time had come.

While I was busy fending off suitors, Mother gathered up all of the books that belonged to my stepfather's family and put them out on the dining room table for perusal by the sisters-in-law who didn't know that my stepfather's family was very pious and didn't read much in the way of classical literature. Donna dutifully unloaded the china that had belonged to my stepfather's family and piled it neatly beside the books. Then she went through the rest of the house and took anything that she could identify as having belonged to my stepfather's family and placed it on the dining-room table. The family literary treasures amounted to a lot of religious treatises from the early twentieth century. Most of the books went to the Salvation Army, but Donna was vehement about giving everything that had belonged to my stepfather back to his children. She wanted none of it cluttering up her life, and giving it up was also an act of puri-fication. In that delicate moment of mourning and anger, she was purging herself of the evil thoughts that threatened her otherwise temperate personality. However angry her thoughts of my stepfather might have become, she chose to get rid of them—along with the books and the china and anything else she found.

Mother and I developed a kind of routine while I was there. At night, we'd have drinks in front of the fireplace, and that was the time when we usually shared things. We talked and laughed a lot. About death and the past. About my future. About her future. She went through the house with me and explained the importance of her own possessions. And I listened, not because I really cared about the possessions themselves, but because I knew that they meant some-thing to her, and she needed to tell someone about them. When she died, my sister and I discovered that she had written our names on things that she was leaving us, and many times, we discovered that she had made sure that each of us had an equal share. Mother and I went to the theater and had people in for dinner while I was there. By the time I was ready to leave, we were closer than we'd ever been before. In essence, Donna had loosened her mantle of motherhood, and I had let down my guard of defensiveness. We became best friends.

VIII. The Magic of Christmas, 1984

Grandma Donna, as my children call her, arrives a week before Christmas, and as soon as she walks in the door, we all rush to her side. My fourteen-year-old son picks up one of her bags and pushes it out to her room at the end of the hall. My eleven-year-old daughter takes her coat and hat and hangs them up in the closet. My five-year-old grabs her hand and seats her comfortably in the overstuffed chair by the fireplace. Mother has arrived and has brought the spirit of Christmas with her.

The entire week before Christmas, Donna, the mistress of make-believe, devoted herself to telling stories and singing songs in a voice deepened by years of smoking and chronic bronchitis. Each afternoon, she prepared tea, and she and my daughter would dress up and have tea-party conversations about the proper way to hold a teacup and to arrange a napkin on one's lap while holding a plate in one hand. They also discussed the proper treats to leave for Santa Claus and his reindeer, and by the time Christmas Eve arrived, we all were imbued with the spirit and had no doubt that Santa Claus would arrive on a sleigh with his reindeer and slide down the chimney—despite the fact that our fireplace had an insert. He would eat all of the cookies and leave us everything we desired for Christmas.

On Christmas Eve, we sat around the tree while Donna read *The Littlest Angel* aloud. Then we sang Christmas carols accompanied by my husband on the guitar. It felt a little like Norman Rockwell had been channeled into our family, and we were happy to have him there. After the children had been tucked into bed, and the adults had filled the stockings and checked the snacks for Santa and his reindeer, we all went to bed. I slept soundly until around three in the morning, when I heard a strange sound coming from somewhere in the house. It was a high-pitched whimper, and thinking that it was one of the children, I leapt up. As soon as I got to the hall, it became clear that the sound was coming from my mother's room. When I knocked and then opened the door, there she was in a little heap on the bed, clutching her sides and rocking back and forth, clearly in pain.

"Pills," she said, "in my bag." It took me a minute or two to locate the pills and place one under her tongue. By this time, my husband, who had sensed my mother might be having a heart attack, appeared at the door to tell us he had called emergency and an ambulance was on its way. Instead of feeling comforted, my mother looked even more distressed than she had when I went into the room

"My nightgown," she said. "Get a fresh nightgown out of the dresser."

"Mom. They're going to take you to the hospital. They'll have a nightgown there."

"Get it, please." Her voice was quiet but determined. I had heard the tone many times when growing up; she meant business.

I shook out the fresh nightgown and helped her struggle into it. Then she lay down and was quiet for a minute as the nitroglycerin took hold.

"Oh, dear. I hope I won't ruin the children's Christmas," she said.

When the ambulance arrived, the men found that they couldn't get the gurney to make a forty-five-degree turn at the end of the hallway, so two of them carried her camp-style down the hall. As they placed her on the gurney, my mother smiled up at them and thanked them graciously as she might have done had they all been at a party. Then she took my hand. She was smiling as if to tell me that everything would be all right which, of course, it wasn't, because even oxygen couldn't keep her from dying. Before the ambulance had reached the end of our street, my mother was gone.

Reflection: "Sunday's Child"

Writing about my mother was troublesome to me; in fact, at times I would stash the manuscript under a huge pile of papers labeled "Sort and File" and pray that it would morph itself into a piece of writing and remembrance that I felt proud of and wanted to share. All of my conjuring didn't do a bit of good, and I was finally forced to acknowledge that writing about a real person in memory time wasn't as easy a job as I had imagined it to be. First of all, it's hard to find the memories sometimes; then when one does find them, it's hard to pinpoint their significance. While the memories recalled may produce sharp emotions for the writer, it's hard to judge the emotional impact on the reader. Finally, one wants to be fair to the person being written about; whining has never been an effective persuasive tone, and I don't know of anyone who doesn't have at least one thing to whine about in the relationship that exists between child and parent.

Having stated the truths above, I have to say that I think by investigating her life, I have been forced to look at a key incident in my own life—my father's death. I had always placed the experience in the "ordinary" file, yet the more I thought about it and wrote about it, the more I realized how great an impact his death had on my life. The loss of my father in some way impacted my ability to establish caring and trusting relationships with others for fear that they might abandon me as he had done. I also realized early on that families operated in much different ways than they do today, and any understanding of my mother's experiences and mine, for that matter, had to be tied into the mores and standards of mid-twentieth-century America.

My parents lived through two world wars and the Great Depression. They knew from experience that the opportunities that America provided were not to be taken for granted; life choices should be well thought-out and the risks might be dangerous. In short, our parents knew some things that we children didn't, and it was their responsibility to teach us what they knew.

In attempting to understand the decisions that my mother made, I had to try to understand the causes behind them. Although I may have made some wrong conjectures, I made the best effort that I could in understanding the challenges that life presented to her.

Conclusion

Throughout this project, the power of writing as an avenue into memory was clear. We found, over time, that writing loosened and ultimately released memories, images, and feelings that we could bring to the page. New insights and understanding bloomed from familiar memories as well as from those that, until our writing was underway, were left unexplored. Other memories gained significance only when they found their places in the narratives of our mothers' lives. Concurrent to writing our essays, all of us continued to take classes and workshops as part of our personal, ongoing commitment to improve our writing skills and hone our craft.

Through our individual writing practices, we opened our minds to memory and our hearts to the experience of the women who mothered us. And somehow during this mysterious process, we developed empathy—not only for our mothers, but for the generations of women who came before them. Putting into words the struggles of these women was challenging, moving, and a powerful exercise.

In writing our way to a compassionate acceptance of our mothers, we also came to a more compassionate acceptance of our own, flawed selves; from their stories, we now understand ourselves differently. More understanding and less judgmental than when we started, we have been changed by the writing, too. Our experience attests to the alchemy and treasure of this process.

While the motives that prompted us to write about our mothers' lives are unique to each author, there was a common desire that everyone shared: each of us wanted to acknowledge and honor our mother's life. We wanted the world to know she had lived, and that her life mattered.

It is our deepest hope is that you will find yourself and your mother in our writing, and that you might come to see your mother more fully—independent of her relationship to you. If you're a writer, you may find deeper truths or understandings about yourself and your mother by putting pen to paper, as we did. Finally, we hope that by finding moments of grace, you can heal the wounds and celebrate the affection.

The Nuts and Bolts of a Compassionate Journey Writing Group

(Where we give you our secrets to success)

Step one...Are you ready?

A certain degree of healing, understanding, and prior reflection is important to this work, allowing us the distance needed to begin to see our mothers as women beyond the mother/daughter relationship. Some of us have, in the past, worked with a number of issues in therapy; others have spent much time in deep reflection talking and sharing with friends and other family members about their memories and relationships with their mothers. So, in one way, this project was another step on a journey that began years before.

As you begin this work, you may very well come to new understandings about your father, your siblings, and other family members. So, with that in mind, be prepared for the possibility of new insights.

Perhaps the most important way to know if you're ready is to ask yourself—am I willing to let go of my own story about who my mother is and allow her to have her own? When you can answer yes, you'll be "cleared for takeoff."

How to Structure a Meeting

We chose to work collaboratively and nonhierarchically. This meant some decision-making processes took longer, but it also ensured that everyone's voice was valued, heard, and part of the end result.

During the first eighteen months, we met every other month for three hours. If someone couldn't be physically present, we used Skype or Zoom so that person could still participate in the meeting. We usually met between 10:00 a.m. and 1:00 p.m., so lunch was always part of the meeting.

Our meetings opened with a check-in, when each woman shared what was going on in her life since we last met and talked about the writing she was currently working on. If a group member talked about a difficulty she was having with her writing or because of her writing, this sometimes led to a conversation in which everyone contributed their thoughts and experiences. This is one way we supported one another. We always made sure everyone had a chance to share.

Once we completed our check-in and any discussion, we moved on to reading our work to the group. We came to each meeting having already shared our writing via email. Sometimes, though not always, we had time to read and respond electronically before we met. During the last year of our project, our meetings were shorter because only those making substantive revisions or completing unfinished portions of their essays read aloud.

At the end of each meeting, we set our agenda for the next one and established what, if any, tasks would need to be done between then and the next meeting, and who would do them.

Our meetings were facilitated by the person who hosted the others in her home. You may choose to have one facilitator or rotate facilitation.

Why We Critique

The purpose of seeking critique for our writing is to make it stronger. We believe that sharing and receiving feedback in a safe, supportive environment is essential for the process to be meaningful and truly helpful. In all cases, critiquing one another's work requires honesty. In our situation, we applied the Amherst Writers & Artists (AWA) workshop guidelines to ensure respect and care for the writer, particularly because underlying emotional experiences often arose.

Responding to a Member's Writing

As mentioned, we used the AWA workshop guidelines for manuscript review. This meant that individually, we each commented first on what we thought was strong about the writing—what was working well, what was memorable, and if something particularly resonated with us. There were times, however, when the power of someone's words called us to simply hold the silence for a few minutes before offering any verbal response. Our initial remarks were then followed by what we thought might need greater emphasis or clarification, or where the writing could be strengthened or sharpened.

Sometimes what one person liked or thought was working well prompted another person to feel differently, and we would discuss these differing views to tease out what would be most helpful to the writer or the story. Unlike the brutal, harsh honesty some of us experienced in other workshops we'd attended, our critiques were accompanied by kindness, concern, occasionally tears, and very often shared, wholehearted laughter. Through this process, we became better writers.

Reading work aloud is an invaluable tool to reinforce each story, and it also allows the writer to hear any rough spots in the organization and flow of the writing that would otherwise be missed.

Some Last Words of Wisdom

We're going to end here with two pearls of wisdom from one of our writers:

At first you will be meeting or corresponding with people whom you don't know intimately, so you may have to make a leap of faith and believe everyone in your group is on your side.

Support each other just as you would assist a member of your own family.

And from all of us, it's unanimous: If there's a secret ingredient for supporting the success of both an individual writer and the group, it's respect.

A Compassionate Journey Travel Guide

This is where we share with you, dear reader, what we've learned from our extraordinary experience of writing together over four years. We can't offer any shortcuts—you'll have to forge your own way through—but we can offer some guidance to help you get started and find your footing.

Choosing Your Travel Destination:
The Path of Personal Journey or the Route to Publication?

No matter which road you take, deciding on a time frame for your adventure is a good idea. Having a specific beginning and end date will allow you to set benchmarks and experience a sense of progress along the way. Closer to finishing, a time frame will direct your focus toward completion.

In case you're wondering, no, we did not choose four years as our time frame to produce a manuscript for publication, which brings us to an important note: The journey may take longer than you expect it will. You might get lost. You might decide to explore the road less traveled. Someone might need to rest. The group might need to rest. You might need extra time to research and learn. Someone might become ill. Bottom line—life happens, and as a caring, supportive group, you respond and deadlines are adjusted.

If your group exists to provide a safe community where women can find and tell their mothers' stories with no intention of publication, this is less likely to happen. You can decide to meet for six months or a year, and once you reach your end point, renegotiate another if you want to continue to journey together.

Practical Information Before You Go

Whether your group chooses the Path of Personal Journey or the Route to Publication, there are certain practicalities and preparations common to both endeavors. After you decide on which direction you'll go—but before you take those momentous first steps—it is important to create the structure or container that will hold the group together as you advance further along on your quest. We are convinced our taking the time to do so was the key to our success as a group that not only stayed together, but flourished over four years.

Here are what we consider to be the most important components of the structure that contained us.

Be clear on the intention of your group and write it down. Be as specific as you can; by doing so, you'll clarify your vision and discover the motivation that, when you need it, will help you press forward. This intention will become your North Star. When the going gets tough, or when you feel you've lost your way months into the journey, your intention will bring you back to center. Our intention was to write and publish our mothers' stories along with a guide that would support and encourage others who might want to make the same journey. Having that North Star to guide us when our next step or direction wasn't clear, or when our path was muddled with exciting possibilities, allowed us to explore off-trail without losing sight of our vision and what we set out to do.

Have a mutual commitment to one another. Our mutual commitment was to help each writer's work be the best it could be. As a group, you will decide what that will look like in practice. For us, it meant we offered each other respect, attention, kindness, time, honest feedback, and a willingness to share the group tasks that came up from time to time (more about that later).

Another critical component of mutual commitment is holding to schedules. The fact is that life will continue to throw curveballs, and if, as a group, you avoid keeping to a schedule, you won't fulfill your intention. There were times our group could easily have dissolved. Loss, illness, moves from one home to another, and business changes are just some of the life events that could have derailed our process, but none of us let that happen. If one person needs to pause, it is important that the group continues moving forward, meeting its objectives within the agreed time frame. This provides the safety of a structure that everyone needs for the success of the project. For the person on pause, they have the comfort of knowing the group is there and will continue to be there, vital and working, while they take time out. By staying on track and holding the place of the absent member, the group maintains its integrity and commitment to all members.

Once you have defined your intention and commitment to each other, there are a few more things to decide before you're ready to rock and roll.

1. Will you make your decisions by consensus or majority? We always tried to find consensus. There were times when it was by majority, but that was usually when someone didn't feel strongly about an issue and conceded to what others wanted. Please note, consensus often means compromise. You're a group of diverse individuals, bubbling with ideas and opinions; when decisions are unanimous, treat it like the astronomical phenomenon of a blue moon—marvel at this uncommon event and give out a cheer.

2. Where will you meet? We found it easiest, not to mention more comfortable, to meet in one of our member's homes. This arrangement is especially convenient when one or more members attend the meeting by Skype or Zoom.

3. How often will you meet? Generally we met every other month, and the length of our meetings varied, based on the number of items on the agenda and the number of essays to be read and responded to.

4. Who will create and send out the meeting agendas?

5. Who will lead meetings and be responsible for reminding and ensuring members meet deadlines?

6. Who will take notes at meetings and send them out?

Sharing responsibility by rotating tasks four through six ensures no one gets burned-out in their role and allows each of you the opportunity to try your hand at herding cats.

Travel Information

As you head into any foreign territory together, respecting the norms of a culture will help you fit in with ease. Here are some that we discovered.

Customs: Punctuality, participation in the community, sharing resources and goodwill, and celebrating are enjoyed all over the world. The citizens of your group will respond well to them, too.

Language: We might think we understand what group members mean when they use the terms like *home, mother,* or *generous,* but our understanding is most likely based on our own experience. The effort of deep listening to the writing takes us into the writer's world, where we will learn what *mother* or *home* or *generous* means to that individual. Take time to learn each person's language.

Etiquette: Good manners, respect, and sharing—all the things your mother taught you will serve you and your traveling companions well, wherever you are.

Tips For a Safe and Enjoyable Trip

Be patient. Almost certainly your group members all have different cognitive processes. Some articulate more quickly, some think more quickly. Some memories are sharper than others. While some people run on various speeds like a high-end Vitamix, others have three: slow, slower, and stop. Respect your differences by rewarding them with patience.

Watch for signs. When the group's energy, and maybe enthusiasm, is flagging, take a break. Find your North Star, remember where you're going, and take a break. The group battery will be recharged when its members replenish theirs. Plan for holidays and holy days of all group participants. Take time for your life outside of your writing.

Honesty, with kindness, is always the best policy. Whether it's responding to someone's work, weighing in with your opinion on a matter of group process, or struggling with the need for a personal break, we believe that honesty delivered with kindness is always the best policy. It's healthy for you, and it's healthy for your group.

Hold an attitude of reverence. Appreciate others' risks. This is a journey of the heart, and as such it is imperative for the group to remain vigilant about how participants receive and comment on another's writing. In the safety of the group, you are trusting one another not just with your stories, but with your mothers' stories, too. In our group, some long-forgotten memories or things we hadn't disclosed before made their way into the writing. Hold and maintain a safe space for what is shared.

Confidentiality. This is pretty much "What happens in Vegas, stays in Vegas." Confidentiality is the cornerstone of trust, and trust is what your group members need in order to do the work. As stated earlier, this work is not just about you and your stories, it's about your mothers and their stories. Honor and respect each other and your mothers by upholding this principle.

Take advantage of rest stops and scenic views. That's what they're there for. This is where you lighten up, review where you've been, and stop to smell some flowers. Because everyone needs that, right?

Personal Security and Health

Take care of yourself, body, mind, and spirit—this is deep, sacred work.

Unresolved issues may arise during this writing process. If you find you can't resolve them on your own, an empathic therapist can help you. Several of us have been in therapy before. But because we were approaching familiar territory from a different perspective, we were revisiting situations at a deeper level, and some of us found engaging the expertise of a skilled therapist helped us do that.

Banking

Several things may come up that require monetary decisions and contributions. Here are some suggestions based on our experience.

Decide early how you will handle expenses. We divided each expense by the number of group members for an equal distribution of cost.

Some expenses you might incur include photocopies and services from professionals such as editors, graphic designers (for covers or other artwork), and attorneys. (For those of you who choose publication, having a legal agreement is an excellent idea.)

Communication Services

By phone:

All group members should have an accurate and updated list of everyone's home and cell phone numbers. If it's possible, when someone goes away for a considerable length of time (a month or more), make sure that person can still be contacted by phone or text in case Internet services are unavailable.

Internet access:

Today email is the best way to stay in touch for things like sharing essays, sending meeting reminders, asking questions, and having immediate group discussions instead waiting for the next meeting. And, while we're on the subject of email, for most communication it's a good idea to hit "reply to all" and copy everyone when responding. This keeps everyone in the loop, and by maintaining a thread, allows members to track all discussion on a topic.

Internet access is also necessary for nonlocal group members to participate in meetings via Skype or Zoom. We have used both and find Zoom preferable because all participants can be seen at the same time.

Emergency Numbers

A list of emergency numbers will come in handy for several reasons. If you're concerned because you haven't heard from a group member in a while, is there a family member or friend you can contact? This might be the logical place to put an editor's phone number, too!

Checklist of Other Essentials for Your Backpack or Portmanteau, As the Case May Be

- Sense of humor
- Willingness to be vulnerable
- Respect
- Good manners
- Writer's eye and ear
- Kindness
- Tissues
- Tea—pots and pots of it
- Writing prompts (which can be found on page page 263)

If you have more questions, you can go to FAQs on our website, www.CompassionateJourneyHonoringOurMothersStories.com, where you'll also find our contact information if you don't find the help you are looking for.

Go gently, and safe journey.

Writing Prompts for a Compassionate Journey

As writers, we know it can sometimes be hard to find a way into a story, or to begin your writing, so we wanted to offer some writing prompts to help you get started. Prompts are a means of spurring memory and leading writers down paths we might not otherwise pursue. Pat Schneider, in her book *Writing Alone and with Others*, describes the importance of prompts in her writing method, AWA. In Pat Taub's workshop "Discovering Our Mothers' Stories," Pat offered prompts to spur our memories of our mothers. In the same spirit, we offer these prompts to spur your writing.

1. Gather together some photographs of your mother. If you can, find photos of your mother at these ages, during these important events, or involved in these activities. She doesn't have to be alone in the photograph.

   - infancy
   - toddler
   - little girl/schoolgirl
   - teenager
   - young adult
   - midlife
   - later years
   - engagement
   - marriage

- with her mother, at any age
- as a mother
- as a grandmother
- celebrating a special anniversary—twenty-fifth, fiftieth, or sixtieth
- working at her job/career
- at her hobby
- any time she doesn't realize the camera is on her

Choose one of these photos of your mother; take in the details, and allow your eyes to rest on whatever they are drawn to. After looking at the image for a few minutes, begin your writing with "In this one, you are…" Write as though you are writing to her. Allow your pen to flow with whatever thoughts come. You can use this prompt for all of the photos you've gathered.

2. Using a photo or an image of your mother that comes to mind, begin your writing with "I always wanted to know…"

3. Write about your earliest memory of your mother.

4. Write ten words that describe your mother. Ask your siblings, your father (if he's still alive), an aunt, a cousin, a close family friend, or a friend of your mother's what ten words they would choose to describe her. Write about the differences/similarities. What comes up for you?

5. Again, using a photograph or an image you have of your mother and holding that image in mind, begin your writing with the question "What did you really want?" This prompt can be used with all of the photographs you've collected.

6. While thinking of your mother, hold an image of her in mind as you respond to these prompts:

- "My favorite memory of you is…"
- "My most disturbing memory of you is…"
- "My most surprising memory of you is…"
- If your mother has passed, write in response to: "If I could have you back for one more hour…"
- If your mother is still alive, write in response to: "If we could spend an hour together, I…"

7. Take some time to research what was going on in the world during your mother's teenage years, her twenties, and the years when she was newly married. What were the role expectations of women? How did the culture value what she did? Once you have that information, begin your writing with "My mother was _____ in a culture/family that _____." Allow your pen to flow with whatever comes to mind.

8. Begin your writing with "I never understood…"

9. Begin your writing with "Being my mother's daughter…"

10. Bring to mind an image or memory of your mother as a daughter to her mother, your grandmother. Write in response to "I imagine…"

11. Write about what was most important to your mother, and then write about where you think that came from.

12. Often our mothers gave or left us unexpected gifts. Think of your greatest strength, something people have admired or commented on. Explore how your mother influenced this by writing in response to "Because of my mother…"

Questions for Discussion

1. Were there situations in the essays that you could easily relate to?

2. How did the ethnic or cultural backgrounds of some families create challenges for the authors? How did socioeconomic status affect the authors?

3. What specific women's issues were common to all the mothers and daughters in these essays, despite the various ethnic, cultural, and socioeconomic groups represented?

4. How did societal expectations influence family life?

5. How did economic factors affect the mothers' lives? What choices in particular were impacted by the lack of financial resources?

6. How were the authors' initial choices of professions reflective of the time in which they lived, and how were those choices different from those offered to their mothers? What created the expanded range of choices available to the writers of these essays?

7. What societal changes affected the writers of all five essays, and how did those changes make the writers' lives different from their mothers' lives?

8. How did alcohol and/or the overuse of prescription drugs affect some of the families in these essays?

9. What coping mechanisms are exhibited by the mothers in these essays?

10. Wordsworth said, "Fill your paper with the breathings of your own heart." How does this quotation resonate with this collection of mothers' stories?

Questions Specific to Each Essay

1. In Jane's essay, what effect does Jane's father's death have on her family dynamics? How did her father's death affect Jane?

2. How did Jane's mother's acquisition of a profession later in her life change her relationship with Jane?

3. What symbolic force did food or food preparation have in Jane's family?

4. In Cheryl's essay, she talks about becoming estranged from her family as a means of coping with its problems. How common do you think this reaction is? Have you seen examples of this?

5. Why do you think Cheryl's siblings reacted differently to the dysfunctional effect of their mother's illness on the family? Might birth order, personality, or gender have an effect?

6. In Cheryl's essay, she speaks about the secrecy surrounding her mother's illness. Is stigma still attached to mental illness today?

7. What sacrifices does Jenny's mother make for her family? How might her choices be different today?

8. What role did religion play in Jenny's family?

9. How does Jenny's mother's departure from life reflect her personality? How did her mother's death affect Jenny?

10. Can you identify the factors that influenced the mismatch between Maggie and her adoptive mother? In what ways did the relationship not seem to meet their needs?

11. Maggie tells her readers, "Frank was the tender underbelly of my mother's heart." What effect did Uncle Frank have on Maggie's mother and her life, and indirectly on Maggie?

12. Maggie writes about her experience of trauma. Have you experienced trauma in your life?

13. What are your thoughts and feelings in regard to the way in which Martha's memory of her father was kept alive in the bedtime story she was told? What were the effects on Martha as a child?

14. Martha writes, "We longed for more from our mothers, but we weren't quite sure what more was." Do you believe this to be a common theme in mother-daughter relationships? Did you feel this way about your mother? If you are the mother of a daughter, do you think your daughter feels this way about you?

15. Martha's grandmother Bondi was a suffragette. Is it important for young women today to learn about the work of these women? Why?

Acknowledgments

While we have many people to thank, we must start with offering our profound and immeasurable gratitude to our mothers: those who gave birth to us and those who raised us.

We also wish to thank all the other women who have mothered or mentored us—our aunts, cousins, teachers, friends—and all the women who have offered us their love, guidance, and wisdom. We thank you for showing us that mothering can come in different and unexpected ways.

We offer our appreciation to the fathers, uncles, brothers, husbands, friends, and other men in our lives.

Many thanks to Pat Taub, whose book, *The Mother of my Invention,* and whose workshop, "Discovering Our Mothers' Stories," opened the door to our journey. We also appreciate her help in assisting with the formation of our collaboration and her presence at our first two meetings.

A deep bow of gratitude to Pat Schneider, creator of the Amherst Writers & Artists Method and author of *Writing Alone and with Others,* and *How the Light Gets In: Writing as a Spiritual Practice,* for the spacious doorway she opened to a nonjudgmental, rich, and rewarding writing life.

Our thanks to Mary Carroll Moore, author of *Your Book Starts Here,* whose editorial consultation helped shape our anthology in the early days of our collaboration.

Our thanks to Meredith Hall, author of *Without A Map,* for her inspirational classes and workshops where two of us refined our essays.

Boundless thanks to Susan Conley, author of *The Foremost Good Fortune* and *Paris was the Place*, whose classes helped a number of us hone our essays. Her skilled consultation and editorial eye also helped all of us to sharpen our focus and clarify the manuscript. Susan's encouragement and belief in our project, as well as her generous spirit, deeply enriched this anthology.

We are lucky in Maine to have the benefit of the Maine Writers & Publishers Alliance, an organization that offers classes and workshops, many of which have helped to sharpen our writing skills. We offer our thanks to Josh Bodwell, MWPA's director, who offered information and encouragement as we moved forward with this endeavor.

We deeply appreciate The University of New England's Maine Women Writers Collection, which offered classes led by David Kutcha, who introduced some of us to each other and set us on a writing path.

We send our gratitude to the authors of *Still Here Thinking of You* for sharing their publishing journey with us, and offering advice and encouragement.

Very special thanks to our many friends, family members, and readers who took time to read our essays and offer suggestions. Your time and honesty helped us immensely.

And our deepest thanks go to each other, for the support, encouragement, wisdom, patience, and the time we have spent together on this journey, working collaboratively over the course of five years to bring this anthology to completion. We were blessed to have met each other in that MWPA workshop, to have undertaken this exploration, to have made this commitment, and to have taken such a deep dive with trustworthy and skilled companions.

Author Biographies

Maggie Butler is a writer and retired psychotherapist who lives on the coast of Maine and in Dublin, Ireland. As a certified Amherst Writers & Artists workshop facilitator, she leads creative writing workshops and retreats in the US and Ireland. In 2011, Maggie was named a finalist for the Maine Literary Award for Drama and won the Maine Literary Award for Short Fiction. Her screenplay, *Pilgrimage of Grace*, won a Best Screenplay award at the 2004 Moondance Film Festival. Her poetry has appeared in the *Aurorean*, *Crannóg Literary Magazine*, the *Naugatuck River Review*, and the *Mom Egg Review*, among others. She is currently working on a novel and collaborating on a screenplay.

Cheryl Gillespie, a retired English teacher, has published in professional journals during her forty-year tenure. She has also been published in *Write to Woof*, a 2015 anthology by Grey Wolfe Publishing, LLC, and has received recognitions from Ocean Park Writers for works of fiction and nonfiction. She contributes articles to the magazine *Bethel Living*. Cheryl is working on a fictionalized biographical sketch of her parents' struggle in their younger lives.

Jenny Radsma moved south from northwestern Alberta to live in northern Maine, where she is employed by the University of Maine at Fort Kent. A nursing professor by day, she writes on weekends. She continues to take writing workshops, and her work has been published in *Goose River Anthology*, *Echoes*, the *Sun*, and the *Canadian Journal of Netherlandic Studies*. When Jenny is not teaching, reading, or writing, she can be found biking, hiking, or snowshoeing, depending on the season. She still has hopes of learning to speak Dutch, Frisian, and French.

Martha Rice has been an actress and a teacher as well as a writer. Her short fiction has appeared in a number of literary magazines, and she coauthored a writing textbook for ESL students. She taught college-level English and speech for twenty-some years, and, in addition to teaching, she developed curriculum for critical thinking classes. In 2015, she was named a finalist in the Maine Writers and Publishers Literary Award for Drama.

Jane Sloven is a psychotherapist and retired attorney who lives in Portland, Maine, with her husband, Joe, and dog, Benji. Her mystery, *Termination of Benefits*, was published in 2018, and she is working on a sequel. In addition to clinical articles, Jane's short stories, essays, and poetry have been published in *River Poets Journal: 2016 Special Edition, Signature Poems*; Grey Wolfe Publishing, LLC's literary journal *Legends: Paranormal Pursuits 2016*; *River Poets Journal: 2013 Special Edition, Tales from the Matriarchal Zone*; and *Chicago Now* (2013).